DISPLACED

D0168010

THE KATRINA BOOKSHELF

Kai Erikson, Series Editor

DISPLACED

LIFE IN THE KATRINA DIASPORA

EDITED BY LYNN WEBER AND LORI PEEK

with

SOCIAL SCIENCE RESEARCH COUNCIL RESEARCH NETWORK
ON PERSONS DISPLACED BY HURRICANE KATRINA

University of Texas Press

AUSTIN

Copyright © 2012 by the University of Texas Press
All rights reserved
Printed in the United States of America
First edition, 2012

Requests for permission to reproduce material from this work should be sent to:
Permissions
University of Texas Press
P.O. Box 7819
Austin, TX 78713–7819
www.utexas.edu/utpress/about/bpermission.html

∞ The paper used in this book meets the minimum requirements of
ANSI/NISO Z39.48–1992 (R1997) (Permanence of Paper).

LIBRARY OF CONGRESS CATALOGING-IN-PUBLICATION DATA

Displaced : life in the Katrina diaspora / edited by Lynn Weber and Lori Peek ;
with Social Science Research Council Research Network on
Persons Displaced by Hurricane Katrina. — 1st ed.
p.   cm. — (The Katrina Bookshelf)
Includes index.
ISBN 978-0-292-73577-4 (cloth : alk. paper) — ISBN 978-0-292-73764-8
(pbk. : alk. paper) — ISBN 978-0-292-73578-1 (lib ebk)
1. Hurricane Katrina, 2005—Social aspects.   2. Refugees—Louisiana—New
Orleans—Social conditions.   3. Internally displaced persons—United States—
Social conditions.   4. Disaster victims—United States—Social conditions.
5. Disaster relief—Social aspects—United States.   I. Weber, Lynn.
II. Peek, Lori A.   III. Social Science Research Council (U.S.).
Research Network on Persons Displaced by Hurricane Katrina.
HV636 2005. N4 D57   2012
305.9'069140973—dc23   2011048526

For the survivors of Katrina

CONTENTS

FOREWORD ix
Bonnie Thornton Dill

ACKNOWLEDGMENTS xiii

1. Documenting Displacement: An Introduction 1
Lynn Weber and Lori Peek

2. The Research Network 21
Lynn Weber

SECTION I
RECEIVING COMMUNITIES 25
Introduction by Lee M. Miller

3. They Call It "Katrina Fatigue":
Displaced Families and Discrimination in Colorado 31
Lori Peek

4. The Basement of Extreme Poverty:
Katrina Survivors and Poverty Programs 47
Laura Lein, Ronald Angel, Julie Beausoleil, and Holly Bell

5. Living through Displacement:
Housing Insecurity among Low-Income Evacuees 63
Jessica W. Pardee

6. When Demand Exceeds Supply:
Disaster Response and the Southern Political Economy 79
Lynn Weber

7. Katrina Evacuee Reception in Rural East Texas:
Rethinking Disaster "Recovery" 104
Lee M. Miller

8. Permanent Temporariness:
Displaced Children in Louisiana   119
Alice Fothergill and Lori Peek

SECTION II
SOCIAL NETWORKS   145
Introduction by Jacquelyn Litt

9. Help from Family, Friends, and Strangers during Hurricane Katrina:
Finding the Limits of Social Networks   150
Elizabeth Fussell

10. "We need to get together with each other":
Women's Narratives of Help in Katrina's Displacement   167
Jacquelyn Litt

11. The Women of Renaissance Village:
From Homes in New Orleans to a Trailer Park in Baker, Louisiana   183
Beverly J. Mason

12. Twice Removed:
New Orleans Garifuna in the Wake of Hurricane Katrina   198
Cynthia M. Garza

13. After the Flood: Faith in the Diaspora   218
Pamela Jenkins

SECTION III
CHARTING A PATH FORWARD   231
Introduction by Lynn Weber

14. Community Organizing in the Katrina Diaspora:
Race, Gender, and the Case of the People's Hurricane Relief Fund   233
Rachel E. Luft

AUTHOR BIOS   257

INDEX   261

FOREWORD

In October 2006, I joined members of the Social Science Research Council Research Network on Persons Displaced by Hurricane Katrina on a site visit to New Orleans and the Gulf Coast to view the impact of the storm and floods. As someone who had first become acquainted with the project through an initial meeting convened by Jacquelyn Litt and Kai Erikson in August 2006, I was eager to do whatever I could to encourage and support systematic and principled explorations into the lives and experiences of people who had been directly affected by this disaster, as well as to learn as much as I could about what was being and had been done up to that point.

That trip was a deeply moving one for all of us. For those who had begun to work with displaced families now living in new and unfamiliar communities, it provided context and a better understanding both of what people had lost and what remained. One year later the extent of the devastation was still vast, and the desolation in many areas was eerie. Among the many memorable experiences was a visit to a Federal Emergency Management Agency (FEMA) trailer camp in which one member of the group, Rachel E. Luft, a faculty member at the University of New Orleans, was living. As Rachel showed us the small and cramped living quarters, she asked us to notice the smell. She told us that all of the trailers reeked of formaldehyde and that she kept her windows open so that she was always getting fresh air—even in the heat. She made a wry remark about how it felt like a double assault; first they were displaced, then they returned only to be buried alive in toxic FEMA trailers. About six months later, the issue of formaldehyde in FEMA trailers made national news and created quite a controversy. But Rachel, like so many others who were living the experience of the hurricane, flood, displacement, and relocation, knew the truths of this story long before state and federal officials acknowledged it. This book is about those kinds of truths: truths that arise as people recount and share their lived experiences of having their home and family moorings blown away, flooded out, and scattered across the country; truths that are revealed as people are trying to resettle in new communities or return to the old ones.

The organization of this edited collection reflects the assertion made in Lynn Weber and Lori Peek's introduction: Most of the contributors, when asked how they came to do this work, said, "It came to me." The chapters in the first section grew out of the researchers' engagement with Katrina survivors who relocated to new communities. This set of essays examines the community context and the interactions and encounters of displaced Gulf Coast residents in Colorado, Louisiana, Missouri, South Carolina, and Texas, where a number of the authors lived and worked. Their analyses show the difference that location makes in a community's ability to welcome, accommodate, and provide resources that facilitate the adjustment of newcomers, many of whom become long-term residents.

The chapters in the second section of the book reflect the authors' engagement in and observation of relationships and interactions among Katrina survivors. It focuses on the ways in which social networks, both within and far from hometowns, simultaneously served as a lifeline for survival and recovery, yet also fractured under the stress and duration of these events. Through their explorations of personal networks, community organizations, and religious institutions, the authors illustrate how race, class, gender, and citizenship intersected to create differing sets of constraints and opportunities regardless of whether people ended up near or far from their former homes. The book ends with a brief final section, "Charting a Path Forward." It describes one post-Katrina social movement's effort to organize displaced New Orleanians, and identifies the possibilities and challenges of movement building in the context of disaster.

This book makes contributions to the scholarship on Katrina that are important and unique for a number of reasons. First, it not only documents the existence of a Katrina diaspora resulting from the dispersion of tens of thousands of people across the United States, but also provides "thick description" and astute analyses of the experience. It tells the insiders' stories. Second, the book is a collaborative product, the result of a series of meetings, conversations, site visits, and shared manuscripts among the authors. Extended intellectual dialogue and collaborative feedback among so many authors, themselves spread across the country, are unusual, yet they are apparent in the intellectual cohesiveness of the collection. Third, an intersectional analytical framework informs all of these essays and reflects the authors' efforts to grapple together with how to best understand and explain what they learned.

Finally, this book is unique in the Katrina scholarship because it is written by and focuses primarily on women. All of the authors, with the exception of one coauthor, are women, and many are noted Women's Studies scholars. Like Weber, they are people who have written extensively on the concept of intersectionality, illustrating how different dimensions of difference and inequality shape and inform each other: Litt a scholar of gender, family, and carework, and Lein, who has published noted books and articles on women, families, and poverty, among others. Far too little of the writing on Katrina has paid serious attention to gender and especially to the intersections of gender with race and class. This book, then, fills a space that has been almost empty for too long.

Also noteworthy in the case of this particular volume is that the racial and class dynamics being studied are reflected in the very conduct of the research itself. For not only are the authors predominantly women, they are overwhelmingly White and middle-class women, with one African American and two Latinos in the group, while the vast majority of the displaced women they write about are Black, with only a small number of Whites and Latinas. At the same time, however, half of the twelve-member collective were displaced themselves and had their own stories of survival and relocation as a lens and source of engagement with their respondents. What makes the complexities of this particular set of researcher-subject differences worth mentioning here is the reflexive manner in which they are revealed and discussed in the book. In the introduction, Weber and Peek openly share how the research network wrestled with these inequalities and carefully considered how they affected their methodologies and the stories they were told. This self-awareness suggests the possibilities for a level of authenticity in the relationship between researchers and respondents that gives the reader an increased level of confidence in the ethnographic findings reported here.

As someone who, like the authors and so many others, was shocked and angered by the discrimination and inequities that shaped the response to Katrina, I found these studies to be particularly meaningful in revealing the lived experiences that displaced Katrina survivors shared about their hardships and victories, as well as their sources of strength and hardiness. The book, however, is more than a chronicle of human suffering and resilience. As skilled social scientists, the authors deftly analyze structures of power that were at play as people were forced to relocate and disperse and as they sought to return and rebuild. They reveal long-term and intransigent patterns of discrimination and inequality that either resulted in a rejection of evacuees or shaped changing attitudes toward evacuees.

In sharing the "truths" of people who are part of the Katrina diaspora, the authors give us greater appreciation of the ways race, class, gender, age, and citizenship intersect to create the response to, and shape the long-term effects of, the events that began in August 2005. As readers of this volume, we are left with the challenge to use this knowledge to create social changes that result in enhanced social justice for Katrina survivors and survivors of future social disasters.

Bonnie Thornton Dill
Professor and Dean, College of Arts and Humanities
University of Maryland
January 2011

ACKNOWLEDGMENTS

This edited volume and the collaboration of our research network would not have been possible without the assistance and generosity of many people and organizations.

As Chair of the Social Science Research Council's (SSRC) Task Force on Katrina, Kai Erikson organized the first meetings, which spawned the research network, sought funding to support future meetings, and later provided thoughtful feedback on the manuscript. Bonnie Thornton Dill, Nancy Foner, Heidi Hartman, and Rubén Rumbaut served as our project advisors. The American Sociological Association funded the first meeting of the network in 2006, and the Rockefeller Foundation and the SSRC supported subsequent meetings over the following three years.

During our meetings in New Orleans, we benefited from the insights of many local experts. We offer our special thanks to Kali Akuno, formerly of the People's Hurricane Relief Fund, and Allison Plyer of the Greater New Orleans Community Data Center.

We appreciate the thorough review of the manuscript by Nancy Foner. Jean Astolfi Bohner carefully read and edited the entire manuscript. Jennifer Tobin-Gurley assisted with the formatting of the chapters and cross-checked all references in the book. Kelly Renner offered a thorough review of the page proofs.

Theresa May, Victoria Davis, Nancy Bryan, Colleen Devine and the editorial and production staff at the University of Texas Press have been exceptionally supportive of this project. We are grateful for their expertise.

The royalties from this volume will be contributed to the Royal Castle Child Development Center in New Orleans. Although its building was badly damaged in Katrina, Royal Castle rebuilt and achieved a five-star rating from the Louisiana rating system. Dedicated Royal Castle staff are committed to providing the highest quality of care to more than a hundred children from diverse socioeconomic and racial backgrounds.

This volume is dedicated to the survivors of Katrina—those who have made their way home, as well as those still searching for home. Thank you for sharing your stories with us.

DISPLACED

DOCUMENTING DISPLACEMENT
AN INTRODUCTION

I don't know where my family is. . . . I done lost everything.
The place where I grew up at, that's gone. My high school—gone.
My elementary school—gone. I can't never bring my kids and show
them where I come from.

AFRICAN AMERICAN WOMAN, TWENTY-EIGHT YEARS OLD

I was kind of a little shaken up because this was all new to me.
We were on a bus and tears just began to run out of my eyes because
I was going to an unfamiliar place that I have never been. I've been
in New Orleans all my life. All my children were born and raised
in New Orleans. My entire family, that is where we are from. New
Orleans . . . Then we had to go into a shelter with tons of people
that I didn't even know. We are all sharing a bathroom and we are
sleeping together. You had to get accustomed to living like this.

AFRICAN AMERICAN WOMAN, TWENTY-THREE YEARS OLD

On Monday, August 29, 2005, Hurricane Katrina devastated more than 90,000 square miles of the US Gulf Coast and, when the levee system gave way, drowned the city of New Orleans. Katrina:

- Forced the evacuation of about 1.5 million people from across the Gulf Coast.
- Destroyed or made unlivable approximately 300,000 homes.
- Severely damaged 150,000 businesses.
- Caused between $80 and $200 billion in economic losses—the costliest disaster in US history.
- Killed 1,720 initially and hundreds more in the months following from suicide, drug overdoses, and other "indirect" causes.[1]

LYNN WEBER AND LORI PEEK

According to one study, nearly half of the estimated 110,000 people who remained in New Orleans did so because they did not believe the storm would be as bad as forecast.[2] And, although some media outlets disparaged them for their decision, they were right: The full force of Katrina bypassed the city. But the miles of weak levees could not withstand the storm surge.[3]

The vast majority of those who either chose or were forced to stay behind were African American, poor, elderly, and/or living with a disability.[4] As the levees collapsed and the city began to fill with water, children and adults sought refuge in attics, on rooftops, and on highway overpasses and other patches of dry ground. As many as 60,000 eventually made their way to the Superdome and the New Orleans Convention Center, often with the help of other stranded survivors.

After awaiting relief and rescue, people were forced, sometimes at gunpoint, to evacuate.[5] They were loaded into buses and airplanes and taken away, almost always with no idea of where they would end up. Although at first most of Katrina's evacuees sought and received shelter close to home,[6] in the weeks following the hurricane, evacuees were scattered across all fifty states (see Figure 1.1). More than five years after the storm, tens of thousands of former Gulf Coast residents remain displaced.[7] Some are desperate to return to the region but do not have the means. Others have chosen to make their homes elsewhere. Still others found a way to return home but could not find a way to remain.

This volume describes the experiences of people who were displaced as a consequence of Katrina. They have been variously labeled as refugees, victims, survivors, evacuees, exiles, and environmental migrants—and the authors in this collection use many of these terms. The most appropriate term, however, might be "internally displaced persons," which refers to people forcibly dispersed from their homes within a country by a disaster.[8]

The chapters in this volume feature the work of a group of scholars who conducted research with displaced persons in thirteen different communities in seven states across the nation. Each chapter draws on ethnographic accounts to examine the full range of evacuee experiences—from the substantial obstacles the evacuees faced to their often remarkable resourcefulness in overcoming them. This resourcefulness is especially apparent among the women who led households and were responsible for the health and well-being of the very old and the very young. The chapters also consider the short- and long-term impact that evacuees have had on receiving communities and how this impact has revealed many opportunities for social change that would improve the lives of our most vulnerable populations and blunt the impact of future disasters.

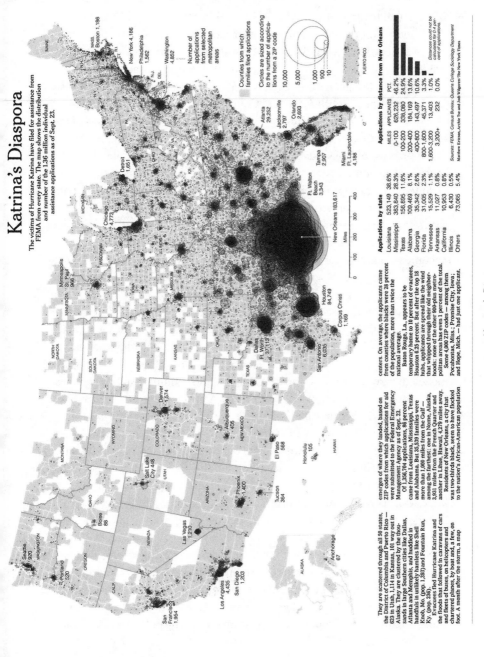

Katrina's Diaspora

The victims of Hurricane Katrina have filed for assistance from FEMA from every state. The map shows the distribution and number of the 1.36 million individual assistance applications as of Sept. 23.

Counties from which families filed applications

Circles are sized according to the number of applications from a ZIP code

10,000
5,000
1,000
100
10

Number of applications from selected metropolitan areas

They are scattered through all 50 states, the District of Columbia and Puerto Rico — 623 in Utah, 1,114 in Kansas, 101 way out in Alaska. They are clustered by the thousands in large Southern cities like Dallas, Atlanta and Memphis, and huddled in handfuls in unlikely hamlets like Shell Knob, Mo. (pop. 1,383) and Fountain Run, Ky. (pop. 236).

The evacuees fled Hurricane Katrina and the floods that followed in caravans of cars and fleets of buses, by boat and, a few, on foot. A month after the storm, a map emerges of where they landed, based on ZIP codes from which applications for aid were submitted to the Federal Emergency Management Agency as of Sept. 23.

Of 1,356,704 applications, 86 percent came from Louisiana, Mississippi, Texas and Alabama. But 35,539 families were more than 1,000 miles from the Gulf — among the farthest: one in Nome, Alaska, 3,931 miles from the French Quarter, and another in Lihue, Hawaii, 4,279 miles away.

Residents of New Orleans, a city that was two-thirds black, seem to have flocked to the nation's African-American population centers. On average, the applicants came from counties where blacks were 28 percent of the population, more than twice the national average.

Baton Rouge, La., appears to be temporary home to 10 percent of evacuees, Houston 6.25 percent. But after the top 15 hubs, applicants are spread like the wind that whipped through their old neighborhoods: one in each of the other 80-plus metropolitan areas has even 1 percent of the total.

Some 4,000 ZIP codes — among them Pocahontas, Miss.; Promise City, Iowa; and Hope, Mich. — had just one applicant.

Applications by state

	Applicants	Pct.
Louisiana	523,149	38.6%
Mississippi	383,840	28.3%
Texas	156,695	11.6%
Alabama	109,469	8.1%
Georgia	35,342	2.6%
Florida	31,005	2.3%
Tennessee	15,529	1.1%
Arkansas	11,027	0.8%
California	10,953	0.8%
Illinois	6,430	0.5%
Others	73,065	5.4%

Applications by distance from New Orleans

Miles	Applicants	Pct.
0-100	626,232	46.2%
100-200	338,080	24.9%
200-400	184,169	13.6%
400-800	143,497	10.6%
800-1,600	45,371	3.3%
1,600-3,200	13,403	1.0%
3,200+	232	0.0%

Distances could not be calculated for 0.4 percent of applications.

Sources: FEMA, Census Bureau; Queens College Sociology Department
Matthew Ericson, Archie Tse and Jodi Wilgoren/The New York Times

FIGURE 1.1. Katrina's Diaspora

Map labels:
Seattle 920, Portland 530, San Francisco 1,954, San Diego 1,203, Los Angeles 4,435, Las Vegas 1,210, Boise 88, Salt Lake City 448, Phoenix 1,400, Tucson 364, El Paso 568, Denver 1,574, Albuquerque 405, Honolulu 105, Anchorage 67, Corpus Christi 1,169, San Antonio 6,035, Dallas/Ft. Worth 37,113, Houston 84,749, New Orleans 183,617, Ft. Walton Beach 3,343, Chicago 4,771, Minneapolis/St. Paul 909, Detroit 1,651, Atlanta 29,252, Orlando 2,693, Jacksonville 2,797, Tampa 2,907, Miami/Ft. Lauderdale 4,188, Washington 4,852, Philadelphia 1,562, New York 4,186, Boston 1,186

When taken together, the studies in this volume represent the most extensive research on the experiences of Katrina's displaced to date. Interviews with evacuees, first responders, service providers, and receiving community residents took place in: Colorado (Denver), Georgia (Atlanta), Louisiana (Baker, Baton Rouge, Lafayette, New Orleans), Mississippi (Jackson), Missouri (Columbia), South Carolina (Columbia/West Columbia), and Texas (Austin, Dallas, Houston, Huntsville). Figure 1.2 shows the locations of the researchers' study sites.

All but two of the studies began in the fall of 2005, and data gathering continued in some instances through 2011. Taken together, these studies included 767 in-depth interviews—562 with displaced persons; 104 with first responders, service providers, and community organizers; and 101 with other residents in the receiving communities. Many of the studies employed multiple methods, including open- and close-ended interviews, document analysis, participant observation, and focus groups. To capture the flow of respondents' unfolding lives, seven of the studies followed respondents over time.

Almost all of the evacuees you will meet on these pages lived in the city of New Orleans before the storm. And in their extended quest for stability and home after Katrina, displacement from their former neighborhoods was just the beginning. While some evacuees moved only once or twice, most moved three or four times, and others had to move more than twelve times.

The people we interviewed were mostly African American: Five studies included only African Americans; five others were over one-half African American. This representation reflects both the composition of New Orleans, which was about two-thirds Black before the storm, and the high concentration of African Americans among the poor and most vulnerable, the focus of many of these studies. Fothergill and Peek's research draws on interviews with children and youth. Fussell's, Mason's, and Pardee's studies included only women, and the remainder included both men and women or boys and girls.

Studies also covered a wide range of household living arrangements—single individuals, single parents, partners with and without children, and multigenerational families. Similarly, respondents' employment statuses before Katrina were quite diverse—employed in blue- and white-collar work, unemployed, disabled, retired—some receiving public assistance and many others not.

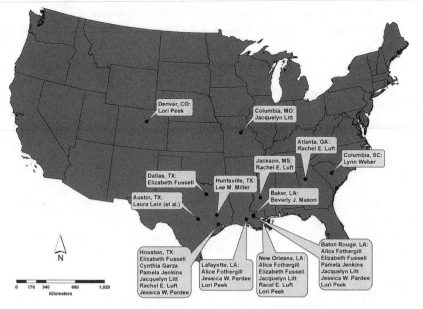

FIGURE 1.2. Research Sites of the Network Members

NEW ORLEANS AND THE RECEIVING COMMUNITIES

Table 1.1 presents selected characteristics of the pre-Katrina city of New Orleans and the receiving communities and their surrounding population areas where we conducted research.[9]

Compared to the receiving communities, New Orleans was midsized, with relatively large Black and small Latino, foreign-born, and White populations. Compared to the Metropolitan Statistical Areas (MSAs) represented here, New Orleans had higher rates of poverty, unemployment, and female-headed households; had lower median family incomes; and ranked in the mid range on educational attainment. A high percentage (42.4 percent) of renters were paying rents that were 35 percent or more of their household incomes, and New Orleans had a comparatively high rental vacancy rate—9.1 percent of all available rental units. The descriptive statistics that follow illustrate how different New Orleans was from the destinations of many evacuees represented here and suggest how they may have felt out of place in their new communities.

TABLE 1.1. Selected Characteristics of the City of New Orleans, LA, and the Metropolitan Statistical Areas of Twelve Receiving Communities

	*New Orleans, LA	Denver, CO	Atlanta, GA	**Baker, LA	Baton Rouge, LA	Lafayette, LA
Total Population	437,186	2,413,844	5,122,275	13,793	753,299	252,877
% Black	66.90%	5.30%	30.50%	52.90%	35.00%	26.60%
% Latino	3.10%	21.70%	8.90%	0.90%	2.30%	2.10%
% White	26.20%	67.30%	54.90%	45.60%	59.80%	68.80%
% Asian	2.40%	3.30%	4.00%	0.40%	1.60%	1.30%
% Other	1.40%	2.40%	1.70%	0.20%	1.30%	1.20%
% Foreign-Born	3.70%	12.50%	12.60%	0.60%	3.10%	2.70%
All Families Below Poverty Level in Past Year	21.80%	8.00%	8.50%	13.40%	13.10%	12.40%
Unemployed***	13.20%	5.90%	7.20%	3.10%	7.20%	5.60%
Female Householder w/Children	12.60%	6.40%	8.50%	13.40%	9.40%	10.00%
Median Family Income ($)	39,428	71,531	67,568	38,621	56,360	54,882
Post–High School Education	55.40%	64.30%	59.10%	42.10%	49.60%	48.70%
Rent 35% or more of Household Income	42.40%	38.50%	38.10%	30.40%	38.40%	33.60%
% Vacant Housing Units	23.40%	8.30%	11.10%		10.30%	8.20%
Rental Vacancy Rate Estimate (%)****	9.10%	8.60%	12.50%		7.10%	5.20%
% No Vehicles Available	26.00%	6.30%	5.90%	4.70%	7.00%	7.50%

Source: U.S. Census Bureau, 2005–2007 American Community Survey, Data Profile, available from http://factfinder.census.gov/servlet/ADPGeoSearchByListServlet?ds_name=ACS_2007_3YR_G00_&_lan=en&_ts=275224857065, accessed November 20, 2009.

*Source for New Orleans, LA, data: U.S. Census Bureau, 2005 American Community Survey, available from http://factfinder.census.gov/servlet/ADPGeoSearchByListServlet?ds_name=ACS_2005_EST_G00_&_lang=en&_ts=277996775685, accessed December 1, 2009.

**Source for Baker, LA, data: U.S. Census Bureau, Census 2000 Summary File 1, available from http://factfinder.census.gov/servlet/QTTable?_bm=y&-geo_id=16000US2203985&-qr_name=DEC_2000_SF1_U_DP1&-ds_name=DEC_2000_SF1_U&-_lang=en&-redoLog=false&-_sse=on, accessed November 20, 2009.

	Jackson, MS	Columbia, MO	Columbia, SC	Austin, TX	Dallas, TX	Houston, TX	Hunts-ville, TX
	529,030	159,467	703,807	1,533,263	5,979,240	5,485,720	64,111
	46.40%	8.00%	32.90%	7.30%	13.80%	16.70%	22.80%
	1.40%	2.40%	3.50%	29.40%	26.30%	32.80%	15.30%
	50.40%	83.80%	60.30%	57.10%	53.50%	43.60%	59.30%
	0.90%	3.30%	1.50%	4.30%	4.60%	5.50%	1.00%
	0.90%	2.50%	1.80%	1.90%	1.80%	1.40%	1.60%
	1.50%	5.20%	4.40%	14.10%	17.70%	21.30%	10.30%
	12.40%	9.80%	9.90%	8.60%	10.00%	12.10%	16.60%
	7.00%	5.60%	6.10%	6.10%	6.60%	7.10%	11.10%
	11.10%	7.20%	9.20%	6.70%	8.00%	8.30%	7.60%
	53,852	59,239	58,734	69,012	63,719	60,188	38,584
	58.60%	67.90%	56.60%	64.50%	57.00%	53.10%	40.80%
	38.00%	40.20%	32.90%	37.10%	36.00%	37.50%	44.80%
	10.60%	7.50%	10.70%	8.70%	10.00%	11.60%	14.90%
	9.80%	6.70%	9.40%	8.50%	11.50%	12.60%	7.20%
	6.30%	5.90%	6.70%	5.10%	5.10%	6.40%	7.90%

***Population over 16 in labor force unemployed.

****"Rental Vacancy Rate—The rental vacancy rate is the proportion of the rental inventory that is vacant "for rent." It is computed by dividing the number of vacant units "for rent" by the sum of the renter-occupied units, vacant units that are "for rent," and vacant units that have been rented but not yet occupied, and then multiplying by 100. This measure is rounded to the nearest tenth (source: U.S. Census Bureau, American FactFinder, Glossary, available from http://factfinder.census.gov/home/en/epss/glossary_r.html, accessed June 13, 2011).

The communities we studied are quite diverse. Some were relatively close to the disaster zone (Baker, Baton Rouge, Houston); others, considerably farther away (Denver; Columbia, South Carolina). Some were large cities (Atlanta, Denver, Dallas, Houston); some, midsized cities (Baton Rouge; Jackson; Columbia, South Carolina); some, smaller towns and rural areas (Huntsville; Columbia, Missouri).

The racial and ethnic composition, as well as the prevalence of female-headed families, varied among these locales and between them and New Orleans. New Orleans was 66.8 percent Black and only 3.1 percent Latino, making it more like the Deep South destinations (Atlanta; Baker; Baton Rouge; Jackson; and Columbia, South Carolina), each of which had an MSA over 30 percent African American and less than 10 percent Latino. In contrast, all of the Texas destinations, as well as Denver and Columbia, Missouri, were less than 20 percent African American. Denver and the Texas communities ranged from 15 percent to 32.8 percent Latino and, with Atlanta, had more than double New Orleans's foreign-born population. Strikingly, while New Orleans was only 26.1 percent White, all of the other cities, with the exception of Baker (45.6 percent) and Houston (43.6 percent), had majority White populations.

EDUCATION, INCOME, UNEMPLOYMENT, POVERTY, AND HOUSEHOLD COMPOSITION

The proportion of New Orleans's population with some education beyond high school (55.4 percent) was smaller than that of most receiving communities, which had more high school graduates and larger college-educated populations. The largest cities (Denver, Atlanta, Austin, Dallas, and Houston) had significantly higher median incomes than New Orleans, reflecting the heavier concentrations of highly paid professional and managerial occupations, more lucrative industries (e.g., high tech, transportation), and higher government employment than New Orleans, whose economy is heavily reliant on low-wage service and tourism industries.

New Orleans had higher unemployment (13.2 percent) and poverty rates (21.8 percent) than any of the receiving MSAs. Compared to New Orleans, the relatively low unemployment rate of some of the cities in Louisiana (Baker, Baton Rouge, Lafayette) may reflect the unevenness of the recovery across Louisiana, the mismatch between the kinds of jobs available in New Orleans after the storm (e.g., construction) and the work people performed before the storm (e.g., service work), and the hiring preference of outside private contractors for low-wage migrant workers over local workers. In terms of household composition, only Baker had a higher concentration of female-headed families than New Orleans, while Denver, Austin, Huntsville, and Columbia, Missouri, had significantly lower ones.

HOUSING AND TRANSPORTATION

We had one client one night who was staying in a hotel out by the airport. He was a computer programmer. He got a job with Blue Cross/Blue Shield. . . . Of course, that's twenty-five miles or twenty miles or whatever, which required two different bus transfers. . . . So evidently, he got off on Two Notch Road at the wrong bus stop and had no idea where he was—had nobody he knew he could even call. . . . It was like in October or November and it was cold and a policeman finally stopped and said, "Where are you?" He had that nervous breakdown kind of . . . all of a sudden it just came crashing in on him.

WHITE WOMAN SERVICE PROVIDER,
COLUMBIA, SOUTH CAROLINA

To give some idea of the housing markets the displaced entered, we also include in Table 1.1 housing unit availability, rental vacancy rates, and the proportion of renters paying 35 percent or more of their household incomes for rent, an amount generally considered to burden families. Some of the cities with the lowest number of available housing units were those least like New Orleans on other indicators (poverty levels, household composition, and educational attainment—Austin; Denver; Columbia, Missouri), suggesting the additional difficulties that landing in those communities posed for long-term resettlement. Further, although Dallas, Atlanta, and Houston had relatively high rental vacancy rates (11.5 to 12.6 percent), Baton Rouge, Lafayette, and Columbia, Missouri, had lower rates (7.1 percent or less). The statistics confirm reports from New Orleans's evacuees that finding affordable housing was challenging and, given the high poverty rate in New Orleans, that many would be paying more than 35 percent of their household incomes on rent.

New Orleans had an unusually high number of households (26 percent) with no access to an automobile—a rate three to four times as high as any of the receiving MSAs. For evacuees adjusting to a new city, acquiring a car or learning the public transportation routes introduced additional challenges.

We recognize that these data in no way capture the full landscape of the hundreds of places across the nation where more than one million evacuees landed. Although most receiving communities shared some characteristics with New Orleans, none came close to resembling its major socioeconomic and demographic contours. The estimates we offer here represent only an abstract picture, somewhat like an aerial view, of the exact nature of what evacuees experienced in their individual receiving communities. But the statistics reveal the sizable gap between New Orleans and these places where evacuees made their new homes. As the subsequent chapters reveal, numerous other complex and meaningful social divisions, relationships, and cultural characteristics shaped what the evacuees actually saw and experienced.

COMMON THEMES

This volume is organized into three sections, each beginning with a brief overview. The first section looks at the communities that received Katrina's displaced. The second section describes the role of informal and formal social networks in the evacuation, relocation, and resettlement of individuals and families displaced by Katrina. The third section offers a case study of the People's Hurricane Relief Fund and illustrates the challenges grassroots groups face in providing relief and advocating for social change in the aftermath of disaster.

Each of the twelve research projects described in this volume reflects a different perspective on people displaced by Hurricane Katrina. Although the settings and samples are distinct, the methods varied, and the conclusions unique, as we see below, common themes appearing throughout the volume offer important lessons for the future.

THE FORCED RELOCATION OF EVACUEES AMPLIFIED TRAUMA AND IMPEDED RECOVERY

I thought we was really going to die because me and my girls slept on the streets for five days. I didn't know where I was going. I just got on a plane. I was scared because I had never been on a plane before. Everybody thought they were going to San Antonio, but then they wind up here.

AFRICAN AMERICAN MAN AND KATRINA SURVIVOR LIVING IN DENVER, FORTY-ONE YEARS OLD

Many of the people who evacuated before Katrina struck New Orleans exercised some choice in where they ultimately sought shelter. They shared rides or drove out of the city in the days and hours before the hurricane made landfall. Once out of harm's way, many had few resources—financial or otherwise—to help them survive.

Tens of thousands of other evacuees had little or no choice in where they ended up after the storm. After seeking refuge at the Superdome or the Convention Center or being plucked from rooftops or dry highway overpasses, mostly low-income African American men, women, and children were transported out of New Orleans and taken, according to the prerogatives of federal government agencies, to unfamiliar destinations.

The ad hoc evacuation, combined with the lack of a central database for identifying and tracking evacuees' whereabouts, resulted in government-induced separation of family members.[10] These separations not only were emotionally traumatic,[11] but also caused severe material and financial stress among families already living at the margins of poverty. Indeed, more often than not, the families separated by government relocation efforts had previously survived by pooling resources generated through extensive kin networks. Breaking up these networks left these evacuees with few alternatives for reuniting with their families or returning to the Gulf Coast.

> *A lot of people were on the loose. A lot of people asking about their*
> *families. A lot of people were running loose . . . babies, fathers . . .*
> *I have friends and family in Atlanta, too. They weren't with us*
> *in the house. They couldn't get out at the same time. They didn't*
> *have nowhere to go and they were shipped to a different place. So*
> *many people shipped so far. It's hard, because sometimes you were*
> *shipped to places and you didn't want to be that far. You didn't know*
> *anybody. You don't know where you are. It's hard.*

AFRICAN AMERICAN WOMAN AND KATRINA SURVIVOR
LIVING IN BATON ROUGE, THIRTY YEARS OLD

EVACUEES EXPERIENCED CUMULATIVE BARRIERS IN THE RESETTLEMENT PROCESS

> *Because they didn't have lights. And they didn't have food. So . . . a*
> *lot of people was not mentally capable, and I'm [not] saying they had*
> *a mental illness, but after a natural disaster, they just had to shut*

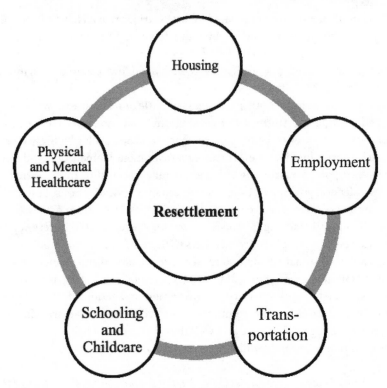

FIGURE 1.3. Basic Needs in Post-Disaster Resettlement

down. You know I was to that point. But that is a lot of it because they didn't have their basic needs, so they couldn't focus on nothing else.

AFRICAN AMERICAN COMMUNITY ORGANIZER

AND KATRINA EVACUEE

As the resettlement and recovery process began in communities across the United States, evacuees had to find shelter, employment, transportation, schools, childcare, and healthcare (see Figure 1.3). But conditions predating Katrina and issues caused by the disaster and displacement hindered the ability of many people to meet these basic needs.

Hurricane Katrina revealed America's long-standing structural inequalities based on race, class, and gender and laid bare the consequences of ignoring these underlying inequalities.[12] Indeed, even before Katrina devastated the region, people of the Gulf Coast—especially women and people of color—were far more likely to be poor and to lack health insurance and were far less likely to earn good wages than people living elsewhere in the United States.[13] The long-standing and complex disadvantages that these residents faced before the storm posed formidable barriers to achieving recovery afterward. Katrina's effects pushed those with limited education, no professional work experience, no savings, and no healthcare into what Lein and colleagues refer to in this volume as the "basement of poverty."

The disaster itself also generated a number of new, interconnected challenges that evacuees struggled fiercely to overcome. Many displaced persons, for example, were left without documentation—birth certificates; Social Security cards; driver's licenses; proof of vehicle registration; and educational, medical, and other vital records—making it difficult if not impossible to apply for jobs, to drive legally, and to enroll their children in school. Social service providers often saw emergency aid as different from regular public assistance. Consequently, evacuees who had relied on public assistance for housing, food stamps, or Temporary Assistance for Needy Families in New Orleans often faced obstacles to obtaining regular welfare payments in receiving communities. In addition, several studies report that when evacuees did qualify for welfare in receiving communities, payments were either less than people had received in New Orleans or were similar in amount but worth less in the receiving community because the cost of housing or food was higher or transportation less available.

> *The government support, the local government and city support, they say they have it, but really it is little or none. Whereas back home, if you fell behind, you had agencies that would help you. I do not find that here. I find it really hard to get back on your feet here.*
>
> AFRICAN AMERICAN WOMAN EVACUEE IN DENVER, COLORADO

Emotional trauma and unavailable or unattainable mental health care further impeded the evacuees' achieving a sense of normalcy and stability, both of which are defining characteristics of recovery.[14] Untreated mental and physical health problems, in conjunction with the lack of reliable transportation, insufficient childcare, and unstable housing situations, made employment, a critical element in recovery, impossible for many. While these issues could easily be seen as "private troubles" for each individual or evacuee family, the research in this volume reveals how bureaucratic barriers and structural conditions gave rise to so much personal and collective suffering and made them into "public issues."[15]

The word "evacuation" suggests the movement of persons from a threatened location to a temporary safe haven. That was the experience of many residents who had to leave New Orleans but were able to return relatively quickly. But for many others, it was a continuing journey. They made several moves before even leaving the city—to and from the Superdome or Convention Center or other places of temporary shelter—and then they endured repeated moves from place to place. Some, for example, moved in with family and friends. But as days extended to weeks, months, and even years, people were forced to move because friends' and families' personal and material resources were often strained beyond their capacity to continue to support evacuees. Further, as federal government and local community programs and housing support changed over time, evacuees had to shift back and forth from shelters to hotels, to apartments, to public housing.

For displaced children, most of those moves meant new schools, new classrooms, new neighborhoods, and struggles to develop new friendships. For adults, the challenges associated with finding employment, housing, and transportation were often overwhelming. And these challenges were further aggravated by an unwieldy, baffling, and all too often unfriendly bureaucratic aid structure. Repeated displacement and adjustment to new locations meant prolonged uncertainty, precluding a return to "normalcy."

RECEPTION OF THE DISPLACED SHIFTED OVER TIME

Here is how I've seen people reacting more recently.
"You aren't my neighbor. You aren't family. You weren't even
in my state, and you're coming in here." Okay? At first it was
"Oh, poor you!" But then after a while it became "You're not
going away, and I've got to pick up the cost."

WHITE WOMAN SOCIAL WORKER IN DENVER

Immediately after Katrina, aid flowed to New Orleans and the Gulf Coast. The federal government contributed billions of dollars to the provision of emergency aid to evacuees.[16] As they attempted to meet the immediate needs of evacuees, communities across the United States drew on federal, state, local, and private resources. Individual volunteers gave generously of their time. Nonprofit and faith-based organizations gathered unprecedented amounts of money and material goods meant to support those displaced by Katrina.

But while evacuees received a warm and compassionate reception in most local contexts, tensions also marked the early stages of the post-disaster relocation. Media depictions of African American New Orleanians as marauding gangs of violent, out-of-control thugs and looters cast a cloud of suspicion over the entire population of Katrina survivors.[17] As the displacement extended over time, community leaders, politicians, and others expressed concern that evacuees were "moving ahead" of local needy individuals on wait lists to receive public assistance. Services and resources were quickly exhausted, even though many evacuees had substantial and enduring needs that were still unmet. Frustration and resentment arose in host communities when displaced people were still present and in need long after local residents and resource providers had expected them to return home or to become entirely self-sufficient.

KATRINA REVEALED STRENGTHS AND LIMITATIONS OF SOCIAL NETWORKS

*I would hate to leave anyone back that I could have saved. . . . I said,
"Tell anybody, whoever it is, get whoever you can get. Tell them I
got money. I'll pay them on this side." And tell the people, whoever's
bringing you, that whoever they got and whoever they got behind
them, bring everybody over. I'll take as much people as I can . . .
if I even got to put y'all outside on my patio. . . . I said,
"Well, bring them because it's real bad."*

AFRICAN AMERICAN WOMAN RESIDENT
OF BATON ROUGE, LOUISIANA

New Orleanians and other Gulf Coast residents were in many ways more rooted in place than the average American. In fact, before Hurricane Katrina, over 75 percent of New Orleans residents were born in Louisiana and had lived most of their lives there.[18] This attachment to place translated into strong and spatially concentrated social networks among many of the displaced.[19] And as much of the research in this volume illustrates, women more often than not were at the center of these social networks.[20]

During the evacuation and in the aftermath of the storm, women mobilized their preexisting networks to provide various forms of support for people in the network. They also organized "non-network support," support that came from either strangers or more formal aid organizations. Both informal networks (family and friends) and formal networks (church and grassroots organizations) helped provide financial assistance, housing, and, perhaps most important, a frame of reference for making meaning out of such a traumatic event.

Just as Katrina revealed the strength and flexibility of these social networks, it also revealed their weaknesses. Because the social networks of so many New Orleanians were exceptionally localized, evacuees often had little experience outside the city or on the road. Many evacuees reported that they did not leave before the storm because they did not know anyone outside of New Orleans or because they had nowhere to go. And because of the concentration of the networks, in some cases every member of the network had experienced some form of loss in the storm. When so many had lost so much, networks became increasingly fragile as people—overwhelmed and stressed to the limit by the storm—attempted to provide material and emotional support for one another.

I just think that everybody was going through it in a different manner. Because all of our family lived in New Orleans, so everybody lost everything. . . . And most of my family lived in the Ninth Ward, where the worst damage was. So they were still traumatized deeply about the loss of everything.

AFRICAN AMERICAN WOMAN AND KATRINA
SURVIVOR, THIRTY YEARS OLD

EVACUEES FACED MANY CHALLENGES IN
RETURNING TO THE "NEW" NEW ORLEANS

At this point I still don't believe home is anywhere. . . . I consider wherever I am with my kids as home. . . . It's like Katrina just stripped me of roots. I don't have any roots [in New Orleans] anymore because it's not the same. And I don't have any roots [in Houston].

AFRICAN AMERICAN WOMAN AND KATRINA
SURVIVOR, TWENTY-EIGHT YEARS OLD

Five years after Hurricane Katrina, New Orleans had returned to about 71 percent of its pre-Katrina size.[21] Both returning residents and new migrants to New Orleans after Katrina were more likely to be White and homeowners and have higher incomes and were less likely to be parents of children under the age of eighteen. Blacks, poor or lower-income residents, parents with young children, and renters were clearly less able—or less willing—to return to the new New Orleans.[22] The chapters in this volume attest to the many challenges that individuals and families faced in deciding whether to return to New Orleans and, later, in actually making their way back to the city.

First, those whose homes suffered the most catastrophic structural damage were those living in predominantly Black neighborhoods.[23] And this population was most likely to have been forcibly relocated, making the possibility of return more costly and difficult.[24]

Second, within days of the levee failures, several public housing projects, which had been almost entirely occupied by African American residents, were closed and barred from reopening. In 2008, the four largest projects in the city were demolished, leaving thousands of Black New Orleanians with significantly diminished prospects for affordable housing. As a group, African Americans also encountered widespread covert and overt discrimination in the post-Katrina rental and housing market.[25]

Third, with the demographic and cultural shifts in the city, many residents felt out of place in their former neighborhoods. And the contentious and highly politicized rebuilding process further amplified the sense of being unwanted—particularly among Black and poor New Orleanians, who were conspicuously absent from key post-disaster planning events.[26, 27] As one African American former resident explained, "I felt I was being encouraged to not return. . . . They didn't want us to come back so they could do what they want to do."

Fourth, many former residents were deterred from returning to the city because of the destroyed infrastructure and limited availability of social services, educational opportunities, healthcare options, and public transportation. The rebuilding process in New Orleans has been so slow and so uneven that many former residents described themselves as incapable of "making a life" in their old city. A dilapidated levee system, potential toxic environmental risks, distrust of the government, and the fear of future hurricanes made residents more hesitant to return.

There are many individual success stories in the lives of Katrina's displaced people, stories of people who have built healthier, more productive lives— stories we clearly heard and report here. Yet we cannot ignore the devastating reality of the lived experiences of most of the evacuees. Years after the disaster, tens of thousands of Katrina's displaced are still strewn about the country, struggling to meet their basic needs. Most will never return home. Hearing their voices and critically examining their experiences highlight what remains to be done to address the ongoing legacy of Katrina and to mitigate the next disaster.

ACKNOWLEDGMENTS

We thank the members of the research network for their feedback on earlier drafts of this chapter. We are especially grateful to Jean Astolfi Bohner, Kai Erikson, and Elizabeth Fussell, each of whom provided many thoughtful suggestions for revision. Jennifer Tobin-Gurley, a graduate student at Colorado State University, helped compile information about the research samples. Christopher Burton and Jennifer Castellow, both graduate students at the University of South Carolina, deserve special recognition for the roles they played in generating the maps and assembling the data for this chapter.

NOTES

1. Lori Peek and Kai Erikson, "Hurricane Katrina," in *Blackwell Encyclopedia of Sociology*, ed. G. Ritzer (Oxford: Blackwell, 2008).

2. Timothy J. Haney, James R. Elliott, and Elizabeth Fussell, "Families and Hurricane Response: Evacuation, Separation, and the Emotional Toll of Hurricane Katrina," in *The Sociology of Katrina: Perspectives on a Modern Catastrophe*, ed. D. L. Brunsma, D. Overfelt, and J. S. Picou (New York: Rowman & Littlefield, 2007), pp. 71–90.

3. William R. Freudenburg, Robert Gramling, Shirley Laska, and Kai T. Erikson, *Catastrophe in the Making: The Engineering of Katrina and the Disasters of Tomorrow* (Washington, DC: Island Press, 2009).

4. Mollyann Brodie, Erin Weltzien, Drew Altman, Robert J. Blendon, and John M. Benson, "Experiences of Hurricane Katrina Evacuees in Houston Shelters: Implications for Future Planning," *American Journal of Public Health* 96, no. 8 (2006): 1402–1408.

5. Contrary to widespread belief, martial law was not imposed following Hurricane Katrina. However, the Katrina relief effort—the largest in US history—did include military assistance. Because a state of emergency was declared in Louisiana, Mississippi, Alabama, and Florida, armed National Guard units were deployed to the affected region. See Keelin McDonell, "What Is Martial Law? And Is New Orleans Under It?" *Slate*, September 2, 2005.

6. Appleseed, "A Continuing Storm: The On-Going Struggles of Hurricane Katrina Evacuees" (Washington, DC: Appleseed, 2006).

7. Campbell Robertson, "A Much Smaller New Orleans after Katrina, Census Confirms," *New York Times*, February 4, 2011.

8. Mtangulizi Sanyika, "Katrina and the Condition of Black New Orleans: The Struggle for Justice, Equity, and Democracy," in *Race, Place, and Environmental Justice after Hurricane Katrina: Struggles to Reclaim, Rebuild, and Revitalize New Orleans and the Gulf Coast*, ed. R. D. Bullard and B. Wright (Boulder, CO: Westview Press, 2009), pp. 87–111.

9. The focus of this research is on the experiences of evacuees in these thirteen locations in the years after the storm. Therefore, we present data from the American Community Survey on the receiving communities that are three-year averages for the years 2005–2007. And since the evacuees were widely dispersed throughout the receiving cities and towns, the data we use are for the Metropolitan Statistical Area (MSA) of each community. Because almost all of the evacuees studied here lived in the city of New Orleans before Katrina, however, New Orleans data are for the city, not the MSA. These data are for 2005, to represent the character of New Orleans at the time of the storm, when people evacuated. The data we present in this table may vary from data presented in some of the chapters because individual researchers made different decisions about which data were most relevant for their specific case.

10. Anne Westbrook Lauten and Kimberly Lietz, "A Look at the Standards Gap: Comparing Child Protection Responses in the Aftermath of Hurricane Katrina and the Indian Ocean Tsunami," *Children, Youth and Environments* 18, no. 1 (2008): 158–201.

11. Also see Haney et al., "Families and Hurricane Response."

12. Erica Williams, Olga Sorokina, Avis Jones-DeWeever, and Heidi Hartmann, "The Women of New Orleans and the Gulf Coast: Multiple Disadvantages and Key Assets for Recovery. Part II. Gender, Race, and Class in the Labor Market" (Washington, DC: Institute for Women's Policy Research, 2006).

13. Barbara Gault, Heidi Hartmann, Avis Jones-DeWeever, Misha Werschkul, and Erica Williams, "The Women of New Orleans and the Gulf Coast: Multiple Disadvantages and Key Assets for Recovery. Part I. Poverty, Race, Gender, and Class" (Washington, DC: Institute for Women's Policy Research, 2005).

14. David Abramson and Richard Garfield, "On the Edge: Children and Families Displaced by Hurricanes Katrina and Rita Face a Looming Medical and Mental Health Crisis," a report of the Louisiana Child and Family Health Study (New York: National Center for Disaster Preparedness and Operation Assist, Columbia University Mailman School of Public Health, 2006).

15. C. Wright Mills, *The Sociological Imagination* (New York: Oxford University Press, 1959).

16. The White House, "The Federal Response to Hurricane Katrina: Lessons Learned" (Washington, DC: White House, 2006).

17. Kathleen Tierney, Christine Bevc, and Erica Kuligowski, "Metaphors Matter:

Disaster Myths, Media Frames, and Their Consequences in Hurricane Katrina," *Annals of the American Academy of Political and Social Science* 604, no. 1 (2006): 57–81.

18. Elizabeth Fussell, "Leaving New Orleans: Social Stratification, Networks, and Hurricane Evacuation" (New York: Social Science Research Council, 2006).

19. John Barnshaw and Joseph Trainor, "Race, Class, and Capital amidst the Hurricane Katrina Diaspora," in *The Sociology of Katrina: Perspectives on a Modern Catastrophe*, ed. D. L. Brunsma, D. Overfelt, and J. S. Picou (New York: Rowman & Littlefield, 2007), pp. 91–105.

20. Elaine Enarson and Joseph Scanlon, "Gender Patterns in Flood Evacuation: A Case Study in Canada's Red River Valley," *Applied Behavioral Science Review* 7, no. 2 (1999): 103–124.

21. Census data revealed that in 2010, the city had roughly 24,000 fewer White residents and 118,000 fewer Black residents. See Robertson, "A Much Smaller New Orleans."

22. D. Alfred, "Progress for Some, Hope and Hardship for Many" (New Orleans: Louisiana Family Recovery Corps, 2008).

23. John R. Logan, "The Impact of Katrina: Race and Class in Storm Damaged Neighborhoods," report by the American Communities Project, Brown University, 2006, http://www.s4.brown.edu/katrina/report.pdf (accessed February 18, 2011).

24. Elizabeth Fussell, Narayan Sastry, and Mark VanLandingham, "Race, Socio-economic Status, and Return Migration to New Orleans after Hurricane Katrina," *Population and Environment* 31 (2010): 20–42.

25. Tracie L. Washington, Brian D. Smedley, Beatrice Alvarez, and Jason Reese, "Housing in New Orleans: One Year after Katrina. Policy Recommendations for Equitable Rebuilding" (Washington, DC: National Association for the Advancement of Colored People, 2006).

26. Robert D. Bullard and Beverly Wright, "Race, Place, and the Environment in Post-Katrina New Orleans," in *Race, Place, and Environmental Justice after Hurricane Katrina: Struggles to Reclaim, Rebuild, and Revitalize New Orleans and the Gulf Coast*, ed. R. D. Bullard and B. Wright (Boulder, CO: Westview Press, 2009), pp. 19–47.

27. For example, according to Mafruza Khan, 75 percent of the participants at an October 2006 Unified New Orleans Plan (UNOP) meeting were White, and 40 percent had an annual household income of more than $75,000. Before Hurricane Katrina, 67 percent of the city was African American and only 2 percent of households had incomes over $75,000. See Mafruza Khan, "The Color of Opportunity and the Future of New Orleans: Planning, Rebuilding, and Social Inclusion after Hurricane Katrina," in *Race, Place, and Environmental Justice after Hurricane Katrina: Struggles to Reclaim, Rebuild, and Revitalize New Orleans and the Gulf Coast*, ed. R. D. Bullard and B. Wright (Boulder, CO: Westview Press, 2009), pp. 205–228; cited data from p. 216.

2

THE RESEARCH NETWORK

The research presented in this volume is the result of a collaboration among twelve feminist social scientists. From our initial meeting we realized that the process of engaging with this group would shape how we conducted our individual studies. And our collaboration changed not only what we were able to see in our own research, but also how we would interpret and present what we saw. Our process turned out to be a unique and rewarding experience for each of us no matter how long we had been practicing our professions. We each felt that the product of our work together enriched our individual projects and this volume, making them better, truer, clearer, and more useful in the project of social change. So we conclude this introductory section with a brief description of our network's process.

At the time Katrina hit, six of the twelve of us who eventually formed the Katrina Research Network[1] were living in New Orleans and teaching at universities there (Fussell, Garza, Jenkins, Luft, Mason, and Pardee). As both survivors and trained observers, they felt they had no choice but to become emotionally and intellectually involved in action-oriented research on the disaster. And as Katrina's evacuees arrived in our communities in Colorado, Missouri, South Carolina, and Texas, the rest of us became involved, wanting to help, as well as to understand.

When asked to describe how they came to this work, the members of the network almost to a person said, "It came to me."[2] Rachel E. Luft, a scholar whose work before Katrina had focused on grassroots political movements, describes the interconnection between her life and her work after the storm:

> How did I come to this work? Really, this work came to me. I had been living in New Orleans for twelve months. . . . I evacuated in the middle of the night on Saturday, August 27, 2005. In the months that followed,

LYNN WEBER

there would be no distinction between maintaining connections with my dispersed friends, participating in relief work, and tracking grassroots organizational responses.

Scholars in communities around the country that received Katrina's displaced were also moved to action. Lori Peek describes her entry into this work:

I was in my first week as a new assistant professor at Colorado State University when Katrina made landfall. To be quite honest, for the first few days after Katrina, I kept thinking to myself, "I can't get involved with this." But I also couldn't help but think, "How can I *not* get involved with this?"

When Katrina came to us, we were not a working group. Nor, given the diversity of our scholarly domains and institutional locations, were we ever likely to have become one. But in 2006, Jacquelyn Litt, who was interested in communicating with other researchers focusing on women in the disaster, joined with Kai Erikson, Chair of the Social Science Research Council Task Force on Katrina, to provide a venue for scholars to communicate and collaborate as they studied the Katrina Diaspora in their communities. The group they assembled included people already engaged in research on the displaced, people planning new projects, and people who would serve as consultants.

From the beginning, our group was diverse. Two of us, Peek and Fothergill, were disaster researchers before the storm and were interested in writing about the children of Katrina. The rest of us brought other interests and expertise to the task, including work on social movements and social change (Jenkins, Luft, and Miller), domestic violence (Jenkins), health disparities and intersectionality (Weber), environmental injustice and aging (Mason), motherhood and carework (Litt), migration and transitions to adulthood (Fussell), urban poverty and housing (Pardee), women and social welfare policy (Lein), and urban social change and multiculturalism (Garza). We studied the disaster from widely dispersed vantage points throughout the country and distinct academic settings: the Northeast, South, Midwest, Southwest, and West; urban and rural; research universities and teaching institutions; private and state schools. We ranged from full professor to graduate student.

This diversity has deepened our understanding, challenged our assumptions, and energized our work. Although we employ multiple research methodologies, they are largely qualitative. Feminist and other activist scholars often prefer qualitative methods in part because of the goals of activist research: to uncover power relations in the everyday lives of women, people of color, and other subordinated groups and to give voice to those groups, including a voice in determining the direction and focus of the research.

The research network provided a rare opportunity both to engage in highly specific locally engaged research and to share our emerging challenges, insights, and interpretations with colleagues who were doing similar research but in other settings and who were often in different stages in the research process. This collaboration informed our research and understanding in ways that would not have been possible in more traditional, isolated research processes. Perhaps most significantly, we routinely discussed and debated the ethical and methodological dilemmas that inevitably arose as inequalities played out in our research—both in our individual projects and in the research network itself.

Negotiating the conflict between conducting research and providing resources to the displaced, for example, was one of the tensions that was particularly acute for researchers whose studies involved continuing relationships with the displaced. The greater intimacy—and often longer-term engagement—between many of us as researchers and the people whose lives we were studying forced us to face the question of whether our efforts would be better spent helping people meet immediate needs than taking their time in the research process. Some of the members of the network did indeed help displaced families find housing, childcare, schools, and other resources while ultimately having to confront the reality that they could not begin to address all of the obstacles these families faced. Some of the people we interviewed were clearly in the midst of an ongoing crisis—often depressed and alienated in their new surroundings. We hoped that the interviews would provide evacuees an opportunity to tell their stories and in so doing to gain some measure of temporary relief or healing from their traumatic experiences.

Since most of the members of this network are middle-class White women and many of the displaced we interviewed are African American, we also considered how racial dynamics may have shaped the stories we heard. Jacquelyn Litt, for example, surmised that one African American woman in her study had been battered, because the woman talked about the domestic violence laws being different in her new community and the possibility of her partner going to jail if he were to follow her. But the woman never addressed the nature of her relationship with her partner. Had Litt been African American might the woman have been more explicit?

Different resources available to researchers themselves also shaped our ethical and methodological discussions. Some of us had access to funding to pay interviewees while others did not. We debated whether we had gotten access to different populations as a consequence and how different access might affect our findings. Because we found people in very different ways, we asked each other, which people and experiences of displacement are *not* represented here? Whom did we miss? In the end, we were encouraged by the commonality in the themes that emerged across the studies despite the variety of ways we found people and the diverse locations we found them in.

One of the greatest advantages of the network has been the knowledge and empathy those of us who were not directly affected by the storm have gained from our extended relationships with our colleagues from New Orleans (three of whom still live there and three of whom now live elsewhere). The insider's views from social scientists who lived, worked, and studied in the community before the storm have helped us all to better understand the contexts of the disaster and its human meaning.

NOTES

1. Formally, our network is known as the Social Science Research Council (SSRC) Research Network on Persons Displaced by Hurricane Katrina.

2. In 2007, the twelve members of the research network each wrote a one-page statement describing how they came to this work on Katrina. The statements were then shared and discussed among all members of the network.

RECEIVING COMMUNITIES
SECTION INTRODUCTION

People displaced by Hurricane Katrina landed in communities across the United States, and the six chapters in this section refer to nearly a dozen such locations. Some of the receiving communities described in this volume were similar to New Orleans in terms of racial, ethnic, and socioeconomic composition, while others were significantly different. But in none was the particular combination of city size, race, ethnicity, socioeconomic composition, poverty levels, regional dialect, and cultural heritage the same as that of the home these displaced New Orleanians left behind.

Many communities across the nation welcomed Katrina's displaced with open arms—even hailing them, as Weber points out in this volume, as their "guests." The welcome was not without tensions, however. For example, many long-term residents of receiving communities who relied on social services were disadvantaged by the influx of displaced people and in some cases expressed resentment toward the newcomers who moved ahead of them in social service queues.

The extraordinary destruction caused by Hurricane Katrina and the failure of the levee system surrounding New Orleans prompted a massive internal migration. Yet many people displaced by Katrina, and especially the most vulnerable groups who had no place to go, had little or no choice in where they were taken. They were airlifted or bussed out of the drowned city—often not even informed of their destination until well into the trip or after arrival. Although grateful to be out of the "flooded hell" that was post-Katrina New Orleans, evacuees quickly realized that the places to which they had been, in their words, "shipped" all too often did not have the necessary resources or the social or cultural environment that displaced people wanted or desperately needed.

The destinations described in the chapters in this section shared many, if not all, of the following characteristics. First, many places did not have

LEE M. MILLER

jobs for newcomers to fill (and if they did have jobs, the displaced often did not have the necessary documentation or credentials for the positions available). Second, the services available to people with limited income were already strained by preexisting local demand. Third, housing was unaffordable and hence unsustainable in the long term, once government assistance for evacuees ran out. And fourth, public transportation was often unreliable or unavailable, further limiting access to scarce yet necessary resources.

Each of the receiving communities differed from pre-Katrina New Orleans in some ways. Some of these differences were viewed by evacuees as positive, easing the process of resettlement. For example, the existence of better schools offering extracurricular activities was cited in Fothergill and Peek's chapter in this volume. Other differences judged as helpful were initial offers of free lodging and job opportunities. New homes or better accommodations than evacuees' previous residences in New Orleans were also seen as beneficial aspects of their new surroundings.

However, receiving community characteristics were not all positive. Evacuees emphasized many differences that made resettlement challenging. Unfamiliar, more complicated, and more restrictive social service programs, severe shortages of affordable housing, and a lack of public transportation were among the most frequently mentioned obstacles.

Two losses universally experienced by the displaced were less tangible and harder to measure and yet made rebuilding their lives difficult: the loss of culture and the loss of support networks (see the second section of the volume for a more detailed discussion of social networks). New Orleans was home to a unique culture, and the comfort of its traditions, cultural events, familiar accents, and favorite foods was impossible to find in new locations. Also missing were the social ties to family, friends, and neighbors who helped each other meet the demands of everyday life—from providing information and advice to sharing transportation and taking turns with childcare. As evacuees were scattered across the United States, many lost these networks, making their lives increasingly difficult.

As the following chapters reveal, some of the communities receiving displaced people, then, lacked some, or all, of the factors that usually draw immigrants or mobile Americans in search of a better life. Some of the displaced were able to choose locations and move near family and/or job relocation opportunities, but the most disenfranchised—our subject here—did not have these options. With the possible exception of Denver, Colorado (see Peek in this volume), had evacuees been able to evaluate these destinations before relocating, it is unlikely that they would have chosen them.

The chapters that follow present several different angles of vision on how the receiving community shaped the reception of Katrina's displaced. Several chapters present the perspectives of people—both children and adults—displaced by Katrina. Other chapters offer the voices of host community service providers as well as the voices of the displaced. Miller's chapter focuses exclusively on the reactions of a host community.

Lori Peek's research on families displaced to Denver, Colorado, explores the concept of "Katrina fatigue." Through extensive field observations and in-depth interviews with children and their parents, Peek describes the varied paths people took to Denver and the reception they faced. Despite an initial warm and generous welcome, adjustment to a very different geographic, physical, climatic, economic, and social environment in the receiving community posed a challenge for many. As time went on and the displaced did not, or could not, return home, evacuee case managers claimed that "Katrina fatigue" had set in. Members of the receiving community began to wonder why the displaced were still there and still needy. The displaced found themselves faced with indifference, suspicion, and even overt hostility as they searched for work, housing, and schools for their children.

Laura Lein, Ronald Angel, Julie Beausoleil, and Holly Bell describe what happened when people living at or near the poverty level in New Orleans experienced the disaster and then were displaced to Austin, Texas. The two representative families whose experiences Lein and colleagues chronicle were simply shoved down into the "basement of poverty" from which it is exceedingly difficult to escape. Through these detailed stories, Lein and her co-researchers elucidate the combined impact of labor markets, housing, healthcare availability, poverty programs, and negative public perceptions on the lives and recovery prospects for America's poor. While other chapters in this volume note that resources available to survivors of the storm in all the places they landed were exhausted long before needs were met, this chapter points out how fragile financial survival can be even in "normal" times and how dire the consequences can be when the working poor are torn from their geographically rooted support networks. This research illustrates the impact of a piecemeal welfare system—unable to substantively help people in normal times and even more unable to respond effectively in the aftermath of a disaster.

Jessica Pardee describes low-income African American women's experiences in locating affordable housing and in accessing social services in their new communities. Expanding her research on residents of government-subsidized housing in New Orleans before the storm, Pardee examines the fundamental problem of a shortage of low-income housing and how this affects displacement. Persons who had lived in subsidized housing before have faced unique obstacles to returning to New Orleans since. For many of them, there was literally no place to go home to. Housing demolition projects were rapidly pushed through the New Orleans City Council after the storm, effectively destroying four large low-income housing projects. This loss of affordable housing was accompanied by huge increases in rent, creating yet another barrier that prevented working poor and low-income families from finding housing in post-Katrina New Orleans. Pardee notes that many people faced multiple moves—what we refer to as *repetitive displacement* in this volume. Not only does Pardee's research contribute to a wider discussion of flawed national housing policies, it also points to how New Orleans functioned as a receiving community to its own displaced: it was, in short, inhospitable and unrecognizable to many of its former residents, for whom the "new New Orleans" is no longer home.

By combining the perspectives of the displaced with those of the communities receiving them, Lynn Weber's research reveals how the macro economic policies of the last thirty years—privatization of government functions, deregulation of business, and disinvestment in social spending—shape the reception of the displaced in local communities today. Through a detailed consideration of the social, economic, and political context of Columbia, South Carolina, Weber's research highlights how long-term disinvestment in social reproduction—including low-income housing, public transportation, and social welfare—impacts everyday life for the most disadvantaged in America's cities and renders those cities unable to successfully absorb disadvantaged newcomers for any length of time. Further, recent migration of new populations to Columbia and West Columbia (including African Americans, Latinos from Mexico and Central America, Russians, and Somali refugees) spurred by global economic trends forms the backdrop to how newcomers from Louisiana were viewed. In sum, Weber's research indicates how the conditions of our cities and towns, especially regarding their abilities to meet the needs of poor, low-income, and migrant communities, pose significant problems for both the receiving communities and people displaced by disaster.

Lee Miller's research, like Weber's, explores the role of the receiving community's character in shaping the reception of Katrina's displaced. Given her vantage point in East Texas, however, Miller offers a picture of how a rural community experienced the arrival of people fleeing New Orleans.

Focusing on the perspectives of the local community leaders responsible for managing the temporary sheltering, housing, and assistance efforts for the newcomers, Miller documents the challenges that scarce resources posed for a receiving community and the displaced who landed in it. Miller notes that community leaders' attitudes toward the displaced shifted over time from welcome to suspicion and finally to overt hostility. Community leaders expected that after a brief time of unsettledness, people would be self-sufficient—no matter what their pre- or post-disaster circumstances—suggesting that empathy is a time-limited resource. The deep devastation caused by Hurricane Katrina and the lengthy period it has required for up-rooted and dispossessed people to resettle underscore the need to rethink what we mean by "recovery" and to recognize that traditional time frames may not apply to severe catastrophes.

In the final chapter in this section, Alice Fothergill and Lori Peek examine the worlds of children who were displaced to a handful of different communities in Louisiana after Hurricane Katrina. They draw on the voices of children to describe the challenges and opportunities that the youngest survivors of Katrina faced in their new neighborhoods and schools. Those voices offer poignant accounts of the evacuation and displacement experiences. While many children were supported by family, friends, or helpful advocates during the displacement, they often faced unsupportive, discriminatory, and hostile reactions in their new surroundings. In addition, many children were living apart from family members and friends, often for the first time, and they struggled with this painful separation. Throughout the chapter, we also witness the children's resilience as they discuss their experiences of change and adaptation. The children in the study landed in unfamiliar communities, but they often emphasized the positive aspects of seeing new places and meeting new friends. By comparing the experiences of children who remained displaced years after the storm with those who eventually returned to New Orleans with their family members, Fothergill and Peek shed light on the varied and complex challenges and opportunities inherent in the options of staying displaced versus returning to a changed New Orleans.

The research presented here suggests that, in future disasters, simply moving the most vulnerable out of harm's way will not be enough. Plans must be in place that provide for coordinated transportation and contain information about the receiving communities, including advance verification that the necessary infrastructure and services—employment and affordable housing—are available. Furthermore, public transportation must be a viable way to move around the host community to access jobs, schools, shopping, and healthcare facilities if the displaced are without private vehicles. Local service agencies, and the paid and unpaid people who staff them, should be supported in the event that the newcomers must stay for an extended period.

In short, place matters. In the future it may matter even more. Careful analysis of potential receiving communities prior to disasters is a necessary step in disaster planning and response.

3

THEY CALL IT "KATRINA FATIGUE"
DISPLACED FAMILIES AND DISCRIMINATION IN COLORADO

In the months following Hurricane Katrina, more than 4,500 Gulf Coast families (approximately 14,000 individuals) relocated to Colorado.[1] Although evacuees could be found in all sixty-four counties in Colorado, most landed in the two largest cities—Denver (6,500 evacuees) and Colorado Springs (4,000 evacuees)—with hundreds of others settling in midsize cities like Boulder, Fort Collins, Grand Junction, and Pueblo. In this research, I focused on evacuees in the Denver metropolitan area, home to approximately 2.4 million people.

Denver is about 1,500 miles from New Orleans, and for former residents of the Gulf Coast, the distance only magnified the many differences between the two cities. Denver is nicknamed "the Mile High City" because its official elevation is 5,280 feet above sea level, while much of New Orleans sits well below sea level. Denver is located at the base of the Rocky Mountains, has four distinct seasons, has a semiarid climate, and receives over 55 inches of snow a year. New Orleans, a place where snow never falls, is known for its hot and humid weather and is surrounded by water, marshlands, and bayous. Colorado is not subject to many of the extreme weather events that are commonplace in Louisiana: according to Federal Emergency Management Agency (FEMA) records, Louisiana is near the top (sixth) and Colorado is close to the bottom (forty-fourth) of the fifty states in numbers of federally declared disasters.[2] Denver is one of the fastest-growing metropolitan areas in the United States, with a poverty rate of about 8 percent and a population made up predominantly of Whites (67 percent) and Latinos (22 percent), with much smaller proportions of African Americans (5 percent) and Asians (3 percent). New Orleans has been steadily losing residents for the past several decades and had a pre-storm poverty rate of 22 percent—twice the national average. Before Katrina, New Orleans residents were 67 percent African American, 26 percent White, 3 percent Latino, and about 2 percent Asian.

LORI PEEK

This chapter draws on field observations and in-depth interviews with Katrina evacuees and disaster relief professionals in Colorado. Between October 2005 and August 2008, I collected eighty-five recorded audio interviews with members of twenty-three different families who relocated to Colorado from the most storm-ravaged regions of the Gulf Coast. I interviewed twenty-two mothers, eight fathers, and fifty-five younger people between the ages of five and eighteen years. Most of the people I interviewed were African American, although the sample also includes members of six White and two Latino families. I conducted sixteen interviews with people working closely with evacuees, including church pastors, disaster relief providers, mental health counselors, and community volunteers. I followed up on the formal interviews with dozens of informal interviews and conversations. In addition, I spent over a hundred hours observing in the new homes of evacuees and at community gatherings, informational meetings, memorial events, and a large evacuee aid distribution center.

In this chapter, I use these data to chronicle the experiences of families who arrived in Colorado in the aftermath of Katrina. I draw on the accounts of displaced adults and youth, as well as on the narratives of people who helped with the resettlement process, for two primary purposes: (1) to examine the changing context of reception, which quickly shifted from a welcoming to a hostile environment; (2) to critique the concept of "Katrina fatigue," a term often used by professionals to describe the later phases of displacement, but a term that I will suggest ultimately served to obscure preexisting patterns of discrimination and racism.

WELCOME AND ONSET OF "KATRINA FATIGUE"

A number of factors pushed and pulled thousands of evacuees to Colorado in the aftermath of Katrina. At the most basic level, of course, it was the storm and the subsequent failure of the levee system in New Orleans that prompted the mass evacuation, but many other social and economic factors determined how and why people ended up in Colorado. Some of the poorest and most marginalized survivors were forcibly relocated by the federal government in the aftermath of Katrina. Others came to Colorado because they had lived in the state at some point before the disaster, had friends or family in the area, had received offers of free housing or jobs or other benefits, or simply wanted to start a new life in a different place.

Upon their arrival in Denver, people displaced by Katrina experienced an outpouring of support. Thousands of volunteers offered their services at the temporary shelter established at the former Lowry Air Force Base:

local residents cleaned the buildings, did laundry, and served meals; musicians played jazz tunes on the front lawn; professional chefs prepared New Orleans–style cuisine; and childcare providers set up recreation areas for children. Mental health experts and religious leaders offered counseling and spiritual guidance. A faith-based group ran a twenty-four-hour van service to take evacuees shopping, to appointments, or to look for housing. Donations of food, household items, clothing, shoes, and other goods arrived by the truckload. In fact, so many donations were received that relief workers opened a 10,000-square-foot warehouse, dubbed "Operation Safe Haven," so evacuees could select furniture and get supplies. Students at a local high school made personalized blankets for displaced children as part of their newly established "Warmth of Colorado" program. Various employers advertised jobs designated only for evacuees. Churches and disaster relief agencies organized a picnic in September 2005 and sponsored a Christmas party for evacuees in December 2005, complete with homemade food and gifts for adults and children. A number of Katrina families were "adopted" during the 2005 holiday season by Colorado families, schools, and businesses. Evacuees received presents, cash donations, gift cards, and airline tickets.

For the first three to four months following Katrina, the generous support directed toward evacuees in Colorado continued. However, as several disaster response professionals asserted, somewhere around the beginning of 2006, "Katrina fatigue" started to set in. To sociologists, that ominous-sounding phrase might seem to echo the concept of "compassion fatigue," which refers to a person's diminished capacity for, or reduced interest in, being empathic or "bearing the suffering" of a loved one or a client.[3] "Katrina fatigue," in turn, has been used by the media as a sort of catchall term to describe waning political attention to the disaster, growing national apathy toward the recovery process, declining federal funding allocations, declining private donations from individuals and charities, diminished media coverage of the affected region and its people, and burnout among volunteers and community members who had previously helped evacuees.[4] When professionals in Colorado used the term "Katrina fatigue," however, they were referring much more specifically to the local context in Denver. Although mental health providers, African American churches, and the three major disaster relief organizations working with evacuees in Denver—Catholic Charities, Lutheran Family Services, and Volunteers of America—continued to provide support for evacuees for more than two years after the storm, many Colorado residents, the local media, and employers seemed to lose interest much sooner.

The church pastor who coordinated the donations at Operation Safe

Haven reported that after January 2006, he consistently struggled to find volunteers to help sort clothes or to prepare food boxes for Katrina families. Another pastor was irritated that some of the major aid organizations in the area seemed interested only in helping with events that would be covered by the media. He observed that certain groups "only showed up when the television cameras were around. Once those cameras were gone, they were gone." Newspaper and television stories about Katrina all but disappeared from local media (and only resumed in earnest at the one- and two-year anniversaries of the storm and when cases of disaster aid fraud were discovered), and employers discontinued special programs aimed at hiring evacuees.

A social worker who served as the director of the Katrina long-term recovery program at Catholic Charities in Denver asserted that "Katrina fatigue was a significant issue" that affected the prospects for successful resettlement among evacuees. She attributed the phenomenon, at least in part, to the fact that people in Colorado had not lived through the hurricane and thus could not possibly maintain the same level of empathy as could fellow survivors from the Gulf Coast. She astutely observed:

> In Katrina, what is especially challenging is the disaster started in one place and it's ending in another place. This is a complete anomaly in disasters, because most disasters start and end in one place. In the normal case, the entire community will be affected. Thus their empathy doesn't end, because you were my neighbor beforehand, and my God, this horrible thing happened, so I'm going to help you out until you're back on your feet, because I knew you before and now I'm watching you struggle and I want to help you get back to where you were previously. But with Katrina ending in a new place, it's bizarre, because people aren't connected in that same way. It's not Coloradoans that were affected, it was people from Louisiana and Mississippi. So I think on a community level what we've seen a lot of is: "Isn't that over yet?" "Haven't you moved on?" "Do you have a job?"

A FEMA employee in Denver also believed that Katrina fatigue was a serious issue. He reported having received several phone calls and unsolicited comments from Colorado residents who thought that Katrina evacuees should have long been "over it" and should have already returned to the Gulf Coast. He suggested that Katrina fatigue developed largely as a result of perceptions that evacuees were costing Colorado taxpayers too much money. He described the situation as follows:

Here is how I've seen people reacting more recently. "You aren't my neighbor. You aren't family. You weren't even in my state, and you're coming in here." Okay? At first it was "Oh, poor you!" But then after a while it became "You're not going away, and I've got to pick up the cost." "No wonder Texas wanted to send them over here, but we can't send them back." Things like that.

Other relief workers had encounters with Coloradoans who thought that Katrina evacuees were simply "abusing the system."

I think I've talked to probably four or five people who just randomly called Catholic Charities and said, "Do you have evacuees?" And I'm like, "Yeah, we do." And I describe a little bit about what we do. And they're just like, "You know, I have an issue with that." I'm like, "All right, what exactly is the issue? What's going on?" They're like, "I'm afraid they're just abusing the system." I'm like, "Okay, that happens. It happens everywhere. I don't think because one person abuses the system, it means everyone abuses the system." And they're like, "Oh, well, I think the evacuees that live next door to me are using drugs." And I would say, "Okay, can you tell me a little bit more about that? Why do you think they're using drugs?" "Well, I just think they are." I say, "Is it because they're engaging in bad activities? Do you see bad people?" And they say, "No, I just think they are. I don't think they're very good people." I'm like, "Okay."

Disaster relief providers in Colorado tended to view the hostile remarks, lack of long-term commitment to the well-being of the evacuees, and inability of some Coloradoans to empathize with the evacuees as manifestations of "Katrina fatigue." These people commonly used the term and were able to offer numerous examples of the ways that Katrina fatigue had played out in the period following the storm.

EVACUEE EXPERIENCES IN COLORADO

Interestingly, evacuees rarely if ever used the term "Katrina fatigue." To them, what others referred to as Katrina fatigue was beginning to take on distinct racial overtones. They knew what discrimination looks and feels like, and they began to sense it in public settings, in their search for housing and jobs, and in the schools of Colorado.

Almost all of the African American adults and youth in this study reported encounters with individuals who assumed they were violent, illiterate, poor, engaged in criminal activities, or abusing drugs. These are stereotypes that African Americans regularly face during nondisaster times, of course, but the evacuees believed that their status as victims of Katrina and former residents of New Orleans led to additional resentment and mistrust. A married man and father of three young girls was involved in a physical altercation in December 2005 with a man who wrongly assumed that he was a member of a gang because he was from New Orleans. He and his wife described what happened:

> HUSBAND: There's a lot of people, when they find out [you're from New Orleans], they want to fight. Last Saturday, I wound up getting in a fight.
>
> WIFE: We were at a bar, it's like a bar for older people, a nice place. We was out on the dance floor, me and my husband and my cousin were out on the dance floor, and the DJ gave a shout out, "We got New Orleans in the house!" and we screaming and having fun. And one of the guys, he went to say something about "Killer Colorado," or something—
>
> HUSBAND: He walked up to me like, "Who are you? I'm Killerado."
>
> WIFE: They thought he was part of a gang.
>
> HUSBAND: There's a lot of stuff that's going on that they're watching on the news. So I'm like, "Come on, brother. We ain't come out here for no trouble. We ain't trying to start nothing." I told [my wife], "Come on, let's go."
>
> WIFE: We was about to leave. So when we were pulling off and the guy wanted to come to the truck and was beating on the truck, saying, "Is that on your mind?" That's when they stopped the car and they started fighting. I'm screaming, "You don't know if they have guns. Let's go, let's go."

Those displaced by Katrina also reported that they experienced street harassment and verbal abuse as they traversed their new, overwhelmingly White neighborhoods. A sixteen-year-old African American boy described what happened to him: "I am a young Black male, so I stand out around here. I have had people yell 'nigger' at me as I am walking home [to our apartment] after school. It makes me want to get in a fight, but I know I can't." Later during the interview, I asked him if he wanted to stay in Colorado. He responded emphatically: "Here? No way."

African Americans described various additional encounters with racist individuals in other public places. When a White man refused to move over for an African American Katrina survivor on a bus, she likened the treatment she received to the pre–Civil Rights era in the 1950s and 1960s. She elaborated on the incident:

> You know racism happens everywhere, but to experience it firsthand, is, you know . . . We were on the bus, and the bus was kind of crowded. There was a man, he had a seat towards the window, and I said, "Excuse me," and he didn't move. I had my baby, she was in my arms, and everybody was looking because I said, "Excuse me, can I get by?" So this lady that was sitting two rows over on my opposite side, she got up and she gave me a seat. She said, "You can sit here," and she gave me the seat. So she says something to that man, and they start fussing with each other, and she says, "Did you hear her? She said excuse me. Why didn't you get up and move?" He moved over to let [the woman] sit down and she said, "No, I don't want to sit here. I don't want to sit near you." And so for five minutes, the people on the bus were [messing] with this man because he wouldn't let us sit down. You know, sometimes people don't hear you, but he refused to sit next to us. And see, not that you should excuse it, but you should try and give people the benefit of the doubt. He was an older man and maybe he hasn't caught up with society. He's still back in the sixties, the fifties, where Blacks were not equal. He maybe thought we shouldn't even be on this bus with him.

THE SEARCH FOR HOUSING AND EMPLOYMENT

The stereotyping and consequent negative reactions that Katrina evacuees had to endure jeopardized their physical health and emotional well-being. And, in some cases, this mistreatment led to serious problems with maintaining stable housing and securing employment.

One African American single mother and her two daughters moved to Colorado after their home in New Orleans was destroyed. The family did not accept any aid from FEMA or the American Red Cross because the mother believed that "they treat you like criminals." Proud that she had never been on government assistance, she depleted her minimal savings when she paid for the first and last month's rent on a townhouse in Denver. Soon after she and her daughters moved into their new home, they began having problems with the other residents, who were mostly older and White:

> At first me and the girls moved into some townhouses. And I think we were the youngest family back there, because it was like senior living. They gave me hell. The older people gave me hell. I think we were the youngest family, and we were the only Blacks back there, and they didn't know what we were because of our light complexion. They asked my landlord, "Where is she from?" He was like, "She's a Katrina evacuee." That was a slap right there . . . because of what they've seen on TV and what they've heard. So immediately they didn't want us living there. I was having these old people literally toss trash on my lawn. The lease, you have to maintain the lawn, no trash, or you'll get fined. And after so many violations you would get evicted. And I guess they wanted this to happen to me. There was just a lot of sabotage going on. They sent the police to my house and said I have a lot of traffic in and out. They accused us of selling drugs and prostituting. My seventeen-year-old daughter was home with her best friend when the police came. I called the police station, and I told them, "Don't ever come to my home and disrespect my home, disrespect my daughter, embarrass my daughter in front of her friend." Because her friend was like, "Prostitution and drug trafficking?" Thank God the kid knows us. That was the final straw. I had to get out of there. I was livid. I was livid.

This woman recognized that she and her girls were doubly stigmatized: Not only were they the only Black family in the entire housing complex, they were also labeled as Katrina evacuees, which she knew to be a "bad mark."

A small but vocal minority of the disaster response professionals who worked closely with Katrina evacuees in Colorado perpetuated some of the negative stereotypes. The case manager who helped coordinate post-Katrina housing placements in Colorado frequently alluded to the damage that evacuees had caused in their rental units. He indicated that if a disaster like Katrina happened again, he would try to better prepare landlords for the "culture" of the people that they would encounter:

> I think that's where there could have been some explanation of culture. Tell the landlords, "Don't be surprised if you go into your unit and you find garbage all over the place, because that's how these people live." Tell them, "You should accept whatever is not permanently damaging to your

property, not write them off as worthless folks, and the stuff that's compromising your asset, work with them on stopping that." There could have been some of that. "Here's what you're gonna see. Here's how they're gonna act. You might need to help them figure out how to operate a thermostat." We had stories of people who ran their thermostats at 90 degrees, twenty-four hours a day.

That case manager helped secure rentals for over 950 evacuee households in Colorado. When asked how many he would label as "problem households," he replied: "You know, there were probably less than 50 really ugly events. So for the most part, it worked." "How these people live," then, seems to have been an issue in only about 5 percent of all of the housing cases ending in disputes between evacuees and their landlords. Regardless of the actual number or percentage of housing cases that ended badly, the case manager admitted that he had begun encouraging evacuees to secure housing in low-income areas of Denver.

When they searched for employment in Colorado, former residents of New Orleans also encountered problems related to their place of origin, evacuee status, and race. An African American mental health counselor who ran Katrina support groups said that many of the evacuees were "having a hard time finding jobs because of the stigma that all people from New Orleans are bad." She noted that evacuees felt that they "could not tell people that they were from New Orleans" and that they were removing prehurricane employment information from their résumés. An African American evacuee I interviewed also found that employers had various inaccurate and harmful perceptions about people from New Orleans. For example, she was upset by an employer who would not stop calling her a "refugee," which she felt was insensitive and demeaning:

First, if someone wakes you up at two, three in the morning, you have water up to your neck, you're gonna come out looking like a lot of the people did on the news. I mean, Black women, we wrap our hair at night, so yes, we're gonna have a scarf on our hair. Your skin is gonna be ashy. You're in murky water, and you're in 110-degree weather, nothing to eat, nothing to drink. So you're gonna look like that. And so I guess that was my problem here with jobs. . . . They had this image of us. They thought you would be from the projects, ghetto. And I didn't come off like that or as ignorant. In one interview, the woman was like, "Oh, so you came here with the Katrina refugees?" I was flabbergasted. I said, "We're not refugees, we're considered evacuees or Katrina survivors." So she's walking me around the office, saying to the staff, "Oh, she's one of the Katrina refugees." I walked out. I didn't apologize. I just left.

Both White and African American evacuees had problems finding employment in Colorado. A White evacuee, for example, said employers treated her like she was "stupid" and "uneducated" because of her Southern accent. African American evacuees faced the added layer of racial discrimination as they attempted to secure employment. An African American woman and mother of three who had worked for over a decade at a five-star hotel in New Orleans recounted her experiences:

It might be just me, but I'm having a hard time finding a job. I've been almost promised a job, but when it comes down to you actually getting a job, something would come up or they find somebody more qualified for the job. It's like last night we were in the store, and there was a "for hire" sign in there and I asked the lady, "Are you hiring?" and she says "No. We're giving out applications, we're passing out applications." I said, "Well, may I please have one?" She said, "Oh, okay." She looks in the drawer, just rattles some papers, and I'm watching her, and she's not looking for the application, she rattles some papers and she says, "Oh, we're out of applications." But when you leave out the door, you see the big sign saying, "We're Hiring." There is racism everywhere, but I'm running across more and more of it here. It's more of a hidden, subtle thing. And this is not the first time this actually happened. It's been happening on several occasions.

After Katrina, that same woman suffered a severely broken arm and leg when she fell through the floor of her mother's storm-damaged home in New Orleans. As a result of her injuries, she spent her first several months in Colorado in rehabilitation as she attempted to regain her strength and mobility. After recovering, she was desperate to find work. She was the sole caregiver for her three children and her disabled mother, and her FEMA housing assistance was soon going to end. Thus, the discrimination she faced in the job search process not only left her feeling depressed and demoralized, it threatened the livelihoods of her entire family.

An African American woman from Slidell also faced employment discrimination in Colorado. While she acknowledged that discrimination and racism were more overt in Louisiana, she argued that navigating the social landscape in Colorado was exceedingly difficult because racism tended to be more subtle and hidden:

> One of the things I miss about Louisiana, even though you knew they had prejudice there . . . You knew what you were up against. They was going to let you know their prejudice. But here it is more like a subtle way. It is like—now this is just my experience applying to certain jobs—to have one person shake your hand and then have the person rub their hand on their clothes. To have one man tell you, "Let me show you your way out of here," after being interviewed and passing the test. It really took a toll on me because I experienced that. It was like a subtle way and you had to learn to read between the lines in a different way. In Louisiana you just knew if a person was prejudiced right up front. Here it is more of a subtle way to me.

NEGATIVE ENCOUNTERS IN SCHOOLS

School officials and teachers in Denver were generally supportive of Katrina-evacuated youth, and they worked quickly and efficiently to enroll students who were missing birth certificates, immunization records, grade reports, and other vital documents.[5] Yet both parents and children had negative encounters with school personnel and students that came to overshadow many of their positive experiences. An African American single mother of five children, all of whom were enrolled in the Denver public school system, attempted to register a complaint after her youngest daughter was bullied. When the mother went to the school, she felt mistreated, as if her concerns were dismissed:

> I cannot tell you how many times I have been treated like I can't read, can't write, can't speak because a lot of people try to speak for me and I am just sitting there. So many of us are portrayed as if we don't have an education. We are these poor people that are living hand to mouth. When I am talking to people about my kids, especially in the school system, it is really insulting. My youngest was sworn at by a student, and then I am being told that "No, that doesn't happen here." And I am like, "No, she said it happened and it happens here. I am not saying that it is a part of your policy that students can come in and they have the right to do this and do that, but it happened. And you are telling me that it doesn't happen here?" And it did happen. My daughter was cussed out by a student

and she was spat on. And I had to speak out about it, and then they just treat me like I am a difficult parent.

Youth also faced difficulties as a result of their teachers' assumptions about their literacy and potential for achievement. A thirteen-year-old girl said she had a "real tough time" at her new middle school. She had always earned good grades back in Louisiana, and her mother had high expectations for her. One of the teachers at the school, however, seemed to assume that the teen was incapable of doing well in school. The mother reported:

When I met with her teacher, what I got was this feeling that "she's from Louisiana. Everybody's illiterate in Louisiana." The children are not high achievers. There's no need to waste your time. So when my daughter gets there, she's a different type of student, and she gets there and she's going to class and trying, and one of the teachers made some comments that they weren't looking for her to do well, they didn't think she would excel.

A Denver resident who took in her niece and nephew after Katrina was distressed when she found out that the high school where she enrolled her nephew had placed him in a special class for students with learning disabilities and behavioral problems. She was convinced that they had made this decision because the youth was African American, male, and from New Orleans:

So I went to the school and talked to his teacher and in conversing with them, realized that they had put [him] in a slow learner class. I said, "So tell me something. Why would you put a child in the ninth grade, who's doing eleventh grade work back in Louisiana, in a tenth grade moderately handicapped class?" "Well, because that's the only class that we had available for him." I said, "Really? Is that so?"

Because he was an honor roll student in New Orleans, the woman asked school officials to transfer him from the special education class, but they refused. Much to her dismay, over the course of the 2005–2006 academic year, her nephew began engaging in delinquent behavior, started drinking and smoking cigarettes and marijuana, missed over eighty days of school, and was finally expelled for stealing a cell phone and an IPod. She understood that some of the "acting out" was the result of his separation from his parents and the trauma of the storm. However, she asserted that the most significant contributing factor was that he was now surrounded by negative peer influences. This, she believed, was the direct result of the school's assigning him to a class that was filled with "slow learners" and "delinquent youth."

As with the White adults, some of the White children who were displaced by Katrina were subjected to harassment because of their Southern accents and style of speaking. Holly, a thirteen-year-old middle school student, reported, "I've been made fun of in school. A girl—mom calls her 'the little bully'—created the 'I Hate Holly Club.' She was makin' fun of me because of the way I talk. I guess I have an accent and also maybe that her boyfriend might like me." Similarly, when I arrived at another White family's house for an interview, their son offered only a "Hi" as a greeting, despite his mother's prompting to "say hello to Miss Lori." She later informed me that her son had begun refusing to use "Miss" or "Mr." before saying people's names, which is a common practice throughout the South, because "the kids at school had been making fun of the way he talks."

African American youth were also teased and subjected to racially hostile remarks from students in the predominantly White schools in Colorado that the evacuee children attended after the storm. A displaced African American grandmother from New Orleans who had been caring for her granddaughter since Katrina noted that her granddaughter was the only African American in her third grade class and that her "grandbaby had been being bullied" since starting school in Denver. She said, "They treat her okay in the classroom, but when she goes out on the playground, then those kids really bully her. They are calling her racial slurs, throwing rocks, just doing that kind of stuff." Another African American youth, who was one of only eight Black students in her middle school of several hundred students, initially received a warm welcome. This changed, though, after she was voted by her peers to be a cheerleader. She said that some of the girls started being "really mean" to her. Her mother elaborated:

> They had a club, basically, for "I hate niggers." It was four White students who made this club and they were writing her name [and] "nigger bitch" on the wall, and it said different things were going on. The school she went to back in New Orleans, the school was mixed, but you didn't have the stereotyping as much. You really have stereotyping in schools here, they call each other names. She's doing okay, with all the things she's been through. But I was ready to leave and just pack up the bags and just leave and just go somewhere South where it wasn't so racist.

These African American children had some of the most threatening and damaging encounters with overt racism. Their parents expressed sadness and anger over the mistreatment their children were subjected to in the schools. They were also left feeling uncertain about how to handle the situation: on the one hand, many of the children were now attending academically comprehensive, highly resourced schools that offered their children new opportunities; on the other hand, the bullying and the racism caused much distress among both the children and their parents. Some parents questioned whether they should just "pack up the bags" and leave. Other parents thought it might be better if they tried to find a more racially diverse school in the area. As one mother told me, after recounting a story of the discrimination her daughter faced, "It might be better if she was in a school where there were other children who were the same color as her."

CONCLUSION

In the aftermath of Hurricane Katrina, thousands of persons moved to Colorado. These evacuees initially received a warm welcome from local residents and community leaders. Within a matter of months, however, the welcome had faded, and much of the outreach from the community at large had come to an abrupt end. Disaster response professionals attributed the waning concern from Colorado residents for evacuees to "Katrina fatigue." They reasoned that those living in Colorado could not fully comprehend the magnitude of damage and loss caused by the storm, and consequently were not able to sustain empathy for evacuees for any extended period of time.

Disaster relief providers in Colorado, and the media more generally, used Katrina fatigue as a frame for understanding diminished public support for evacuees as individuals and for the Gulf Coast recovery process as a whole. While professionals and religious leaders clearly witnessed a significant decline in volunteerism and other helping activities among Colorado residents in the months following the storm, the use of the phrase "Katrina fatigue" served to obscure other important social realities and to render evacuees' experiences with discrimination invisible. If the notion of "Katrina fatigue" is turned on its head, it is possible to consider that some of the generosity and goodwill that followed the disaster simply represented a temporary interruption to endemic and pervasive forms of inequality that mark American institutions and culture. Katrina peeled away the thin veneer that serves to suppress public consideration of issues of racism, classism, gender inequality, and ageism. *Forgetting those inequalities in the warmth of the moment, however, is wholly different from changing the structures that perpetuate them.* From this perspective, Katrina fatigue was not simply an indication of exhaustion among political leaders, the press, or the public. It was a return to the familiar.

This lack of long-term commitment to the health and well-being of evacuees had tangible consequences for those who relocated to Colorado after Katrina. Both adults and children, African American and White, encountered many problems as a result of their status as evacuees and as former residents of New Orleans. However, African Americans were the more frequent targets of stereotypical comments and negative assumptions, ranging from perceived illiteracy to criminality. African Americans also experienced additional exclusion as a result of the racial discrimination that they encountered in public settings, in the workplace, in housing situations, and in schools in Colorado. African Americans are regularly confronted with both subtle and overt forms of discrimination during nondisaster times. However, the harmful effects of discrimination were amplified by the displacement, loss of familiar surroundings, separation from usual systems of support, and intense financial insecurity that followed Katrina.

ACKNOWLEDGMENTS

The National Science Foundation, the Midwest Sociological Society, and the Colorado State University College of Liberal Arts provided funding for this research. Ramonda Pitre, a Katrina evacuee and native of the Seventh Ward of New Orleans, contributed significantly to this project. Ramonda introduced me to displaced families, traveled with me to several interviews, and offered support to fellow hurricane survivors. Kate Browne and three of our students at Colorado State University—Krista Richardson, Jennifer Tobin-Gurley, and Megan Underhill—assisted with numerous aspects of this project. The members of the Social Science Research Council Research Network on Persons Displaced by Katrina offered thoughtful feedback on earlier drafts of this chapter. I am especially grateful for the suggestions provided by Kai Erikson, Lynn Weber, Jean Astolfi Bohner, and Rachel Luft. Finally, I would like to thank the people who so generously shared their time and experiences with me.

NOTES

1. David Montero, "Longing for a Taste of Home: Katrina Evacuees Struggle to Adjust to Life in Colorado," *Rocky Mountain News*, March 4, 2006; Susan Sterett, Jennifer Reich, and Martha Wadsworth, "Katrina's Unsettled Aftermath: Colorado Still Host to 14,000," *Denver Post*, August 27, 2006.

2. Federal Emergency Management Agency, "Declared Disasters by Year or State," 2011, http://www.fema.gov/news/disaster_totals_annual.fema (accessed February 1, 2011).

3. Charles R. Figley, "Compassion Fatigue as Secondary Traumatic Stress Disorder: An Overview," in *Compassion Fatigue: Coping with Secondary Traumatic Stress Disorder in Those Who Treat the Traumatized*, ed. C. R. Figley (New York: Brunner-Routledge, 1995), pp. 1–20, quotation from p. 7.

4. See, for example, Donna Brazile, "Don't Give In to Katrina Fatigue," *Time*, November 20, 2005, http://www.time.com/time/magazine/article/0,9171,1132809,00.html (accessed April 13, 2011); Howard Kurtz, "The Media's New Orleans Burnout," *Washington Post*, May 7, 2006.

5. Lori Peek and Krista Richardson, "In Their Own Words: Displaced Children's Educational Recovery Needs after Hurricane Katrina," *Disaster Medicine and Public Health Preparedness* 4, no. 3 (2010): S63–S70.

4

THE BASEMENT OF EXTREME POVERTY
KATRINA SURVIVORS AND POVERTY PROGRAMS

The problems faced by Americans who fall into destitution-level poverty are shared by many Katrina evacuees. Many Gulf Coast residents who had perfected strategies for maintaining and stabilizing households in poverty found themselves demoralized and in dire poverty months after their evacuation. As their stay in host cities extended beyond the availability of emergency services, their experiences highlighted the inability of poverty programs and policies to meet the demands of disaster and displacement. In particular, their experiences highlighted the risks accruing to people who fall into the "basement" of poverty—facing extremes unanticipated by our poverty programs.

Often discounted as unmotivated and irresponsible, people in the "basement" appear intractable to many service agencies. However, the poverty they face, including highly irregular employment, homelessness or virtual homelessness, lack of personal identification, limited access to hygiene products and facilities, poor diets, and detachment from informal support networks, is in itself a barrier both to more regular employment and to the benefits of United States policy programs.

Poverty programs in the United States are increasingly time-limited and based on the expectation that impoverished families and individuals can and should work themselves out of poverty quickly. The implementation of welfare reform during the past thirteen years in the United States follows a decades-long debate over the role the government should play in providing a safety net for those in poverty.[1] There has been increasing interest in devolving responsibility for basic human services from the federal government to states and further to local civil service organizations.[2] While such a complex system allows for considerable variation and rapid response to local pressures and emergencies, it is also fragile and idiosyn-

LAURA LEIN, RONALD ANGEL, JULIE BEAUSOLEIL, AND HOLLY BELL

cratic.[3] Furthermore, the availability and effectiveness of services reflect local expertise and financial resources.

Families on welfare and families in low-income jobs struggle for financial stability.[4] They depend on as many as twenty-five to thirty helping organizations in the course of a year to fill the gap between extremely tight household budgets and the resources provided by welfare, low-paying jobs, or a combination of the two.[5] They also depend on support and resources from informal networks of relatives, neighbors, and others. Furthermore, the fragmented nature of the safety net services and the gaps in them leave families facing multiple problems, periodic crises, and the possibility of destitution.

Core federal poverty programs and the supports provided by nongovernmental organizations are less available to the poorest and least stable households.[6] The most deprived can be served temporarily by emergency services, but are unlikely to receive the same services available to those who already have some resources. Once families fall into the poverty "basement," they may be trapped there, in part by their inability to access services available to others not so impoverished. While there is a population of unattached men who fall into homelessness and extreme poverty,[7] single mothers who are subjected to a traumatic event are particularly vulnerable to such a descent into deep poverty.

This study of Katrina households that evacuated to Austin, Texas, illustrates the problems that emerge for families made destitute by a catastrophe as they struggle toward stability and deal with poverty programs. This chapter focuses on four areas of need that became prominent in the months following their relocation: (1) housing, (2) healthcare, (3) food and nutrition, and (4) access to employment. Families' problems in these areas often coexist with other issues, and several of these, such as involvement with the criminal justice system, are also addressed.

THE STUDY

This chapter draws on two case analyses from a National Science Foundation (NSF)–funded study.[8] Within two months of the hurricane and evacuation, a team of researchers (including the authors) based at the University of Texas at Austin began to identify a panel of households, then tracked them over the following year through a succession of interviews with, when possible, several members of the household. Although interviewing multiple members of a household was often difficult, at the time we wrote this chapter we had completed approximately 120 interviews with representatives of 59 households and were still tracking several households. The most developed cases, including the two on which this chapter is built, illustrate the complexity of the problems faced by dislocated households with children and the ways in which these problems are entwined with poverty policies as they are structured today in the United States. We selected these two households as the foci of this chapter with several criteria in mind. Their experiences reflected those of other households in our study. We were able to speak extensively with more than one member of each household. The evacuees we interviewed were articulate in describing a range of experiences. While these households were by no means well-off in New Orleans before Katrina, earned wages were their primary source of income before they arrived in Austin. To illustrate the similarities and differences in strategies available to each, we selected a single-parent household and a two-parent household.

The interviews covered their life in New Orleans, their household preparations just before the storm, their evacuation experience, their first weeks in Austin, and their experiences settling their families in Austin. However, the interview structure was left flexible so that respondents might concentrate on those issues most salient to them. The parents in the study focused a great deal on their children, on their efforts to maintain family life, and on their demoralization when children did poorly in spite of their efforts to parent well. This combination of effort and discouragement permeated the "basement" of poverty. While the two families described below managed to secure some of the basic elements of family living, they found maintaining ongoing stability virtually impossible.

THE TWO CASES

Henry and Xia, an African American couple in their late forties, had lived in New Orleans all of their lives before Hurricane Katrina. Life there was a "struggle," but they met their expenses, if barely, by working three jobs between the two of them. After years of work and waiting lists, just before the hurricane they had acquired a Section 8 housing certificate and had moved into a house with their new public assistance. They had purchased living room furniture to mark this new start in their lives. With no resources to leave New Orleans and with a deep conviction that they should take care of the new house and furniture they had acquired with so much effort, they stayed through the hurricane. They were forced out by the National Guard as the water continued rising into their house in the aftermath of Katrina.

They packed up a few critical belongings, food, and water and headed with their five children toward the Superdome. At that time they believed they would be returning home in the next few weeks.

Appalled at the conditions just outside the Superdome and fearing what was occurring inside, they stayed on an interstate bridge for five days, foraging for food and water when their meager supplies ran out. Over that time they joined forces with a neighbor family to stay together and keep their children supplied with basic necessities. They were airlifted out on the Saturday after the hurricane and concentrated their efforts on staying together as a family. After being flown to Austin, they were housed in the Convention Center shelter there. From the Austin Convention Center they were placed in a hotel and, when they qualified for eighteen months of emergency rental assistance, moved to a house. Our research team first met them in this house. As a two-parent family, they had drawn on their ability to hold down several jobs when in New Orleans. As their evacuation experience unfolded, Henry and Xia continued to depend on each other for both practical and emotional support.

Louise, a middle-aged African American single mother and grandmother, had also lived in New Orleans all of her life. She had four children and several grandchildren. Not only was she a single parent, but her own mother had died when Louise was a young woman. Louise began high school, but she dropped out in the tenth grade to take on the care of her mother as her mother's health failed. Eventually she acquired her GED and found a job as a deputy in the jail system, although it is unclear whether she still had this job at the time of the hurricane. She remembers this as the best job she ever had. Because she was a single mother with responsibilities to both her children and her mother, her way of life was heavily marked by the job she was able to maintain.

At the time of the hurricane, Louise and her children lived on the second floor of a public housing building and expected to stay in their apartment through the storm. Though faced with the rising water coming well into their home and terrified of drowning, they remained in the apartment for several days. Louise risked one foray out to a local corner store that had been opened by a group of young men to bring home food for herself and her children. Eventually she and a neighbor walked out from the apartment and headed toward the Superdome. Frightened by the disorder she saw and reports of crime in the Superdome, she and her family moved out to one of the paved areas outdoors, living outside the Superdome until they were loaded on a plane to Austin.

Louise's housing, as well as her access to other services, remained unstable throughout our research project. During our interviews, she spoke often of her efforts to parent her own children, as well as to help care for the children of friends and neighbors. With no other adult in her household, no partner or older relative, she bore a heavy responsibility. Like Henry and Xia, she faced difficulties with food, housing, and access to healthcare. The pressures on her were exacerbated by the difficulties she faced as her children encountered both new schools and the criminal justice system. All of this took place in a setting very different from New Orleans, a setting often difficult for evacuees to understand.

AUSTIN: THE RECEIVING COMMUNITY

Texas received hundreds of thousands of evacuees, and approximately twelve thousand of them came to Austin. At its fullest, the public shelter system in Austin housed over four thousand evacuees.[9] Many, if not most, of those in the Convention Center were carried to Austin by the public evacuation effort after the hurricane struck, often not knowing until they arrived where they were headed. At least an equal number of evacuees found housing through friends and relatives, churches, and other informal and formal organizations.

According to the accounts of the evacuees, Austin presented a very different physical, social, and service environment from New Orleans. Austin was a wealthier city (with 14.4 percent of persons below the poverty line, compared to 27.9 percent for New Orleans), with a high level of education (83.4 percent of Austin residents had a high school education and 40.4 percent a bachelor's degree, compared to 74.7 percent and 25.8 percent, respectively, for New Orleans). About 10 percent of the Austin population was African American, while 31 percent was Hispanic (compared to 67.3 percent African American and 3.1 percent Hispanic in New Orleans).[10] The city's economy revolved around higher education, state government, and the high tech industry. State services and the several independent school districts that serve the greater Austin area had new and complex eligibility requirements and regulations. Gaining access to schools, to services, and eventually to potential employers required use of an often inadequate public transportation system. In this context, evacuees struggled to meet their basic needs and to gain some semblance of a normal routine and dependability in their lives.

In the Austin context, many of the evacuated families from New Orleans faced multiple and complex problems in securing their basic needs, let alone family well-being. The two families we focus on here were in poverty or near-poverty in New Orleans, although they had successfully developed strategies there to maintain their families. These strategies included jobs, although often insecure, detailed knowledge of how helping agencies worked in their neighborhoods, and a considerable depth of support and helping networks to turn to in times of need. Evacuees arrived without any of their home resources. They brought little, if anything, with them. The sudden displacement scattered their social support networks. Once in Austin, they faced a different agency, social, and work context. As they considered a long stay in Austin rather than a quick return to New Orleans, they struggled in many arenas.

FOOD AND NUTRITION

Evacuees were offered short-term emergency food stamp assistance; they also had access early on to a variety of emergency food services. However, within a few months evacuees remaining in Austin were expected to apply for the regular food stamp program, a complicated process for evacuees. Henry and Xia spent months without food stamps when their three months' temporary eligibility ran out. While local food pantries and other services could fill part of this gap, the evacuee families knew little about such resources in Austin, what they provided, and how to get to them. Furthermore, these local services also expected families to obtain food stamps as soon as possible. While even the poorest families had some access to soup kitchens if they could travel to them, finding local resources was difficult for families with no community-based knowledge of their own and only a weakened social support system to help with transportation, incidental childcare, and detailed knowledge about eligibility, application procedures, and locations.

And unbeknownst to the evacuees, the recently privatized process for determining food stamp eligibility in Texas ceased functioning for a time (Texas has been aggressive in the past ten years in privatizing previously public services).[11] Henry and Xia, along with thousands of other evacuees and longer-term Texas residents, waited months for recertification. Many others were denied inappropriately. "They gave us a temporary, three months, food stamps. When that ran out, it basically took us two months to get recertified."

Eventually, months later, the state terminated the private contract and returned the eligibility operations to a state agency. Meanwhile, those like Louise who had managed to maintain their food stamps tried to stretch them to cover the food needs of others who were not so fortunate.

> I love her [oldest daughter], I wouldn't do the things I do for her, I'm taking care, I'm taking care of three houses by myself. I take care of mine, my daughter's, and my friend's. The reason I take care of my daughter is because she's still my child. She don't need me to take care of her, but I make sure she has something to eat in her house because she don't get no food stamps, I get the food stamps. Rona don't get no food stamps.

Under such pressures, even the recompense for our research interviews (a twenty-dollar grocery gift card) became part of an elaborate and labor-intensive set of strategies for keeping three households in food and, when there was enough food, for generating resources to meet other needs. While she welcomed the chance provided by research interviews to tell her story, she also needed the research payment—sometimes to use for groceries and sometimes to sell for other purposes. Even the gift cards we provided became currency. As is clear in the comments below, Louise was concerned that a friend of hers might go out to sell the grocery card before determining whether her children needed food. In caring for other households, Louise made sure that mothers in those households used resources appropriately for their children.

> This is why I be doing these interviews, I be loving to see you. I want you to come by. I want an interview. Now you just left me now with a card. She's [her friend] about to sell that card, she was about to sell that card. You heard me when I came from out, when I left, when I came back, I made sure [before she had a chance to sell the card], I asked the children, was they hungry.

Louise's friend had succumbed to drug use, and Louise felt the additional responsibility to check on her friend's children to make sure they were adequately cared for.

Other programs also presented barriers to food access. Children who had difficulties adhering to regular school attendance faced a number of educational problems and lost regular access to school breakfasts and lunches. Further, school registration demanded evidence of up-to-date inoculations. Having arrived in Austin without such documentation, the children were required to redo a number of inoculations. The time spent figuring out how to access inoculation programs and the demand for a series of inoculations kept several of the children out of school for weeks and consequently away from subsidized lunch and breakfast programs. When children were sent home from school for health or behavior problems, they also lost their breakfasts and lunches.

HEALTHCARE

Children faced impediments in gaining access to Medicaid and experienced ongoing difficulties in using it. Families like Henry and Xia's lacked the basic documentation required for almost all program eligibility proceedings. Their lack of birth certificates, documentation of earlier healthcare, and other necessary proofs made it difficult to acquire first Medicaid and then medical care. Xia described her efforts to use short-term emergency coverage after disaster-related coverage had stopped. In fact, this hard-won coverage lapsed within days of her notification that it had started.

> So we've been here seven months, we've only had Medicaid for the kids for basically a month. So it took six months for us to get Medicaid for the kids, they gave it to us, we got the letter saying that we all was approved and had Medicaid. So like, we got the letter Thursday of this week. Monday of next week, we got the letter saying it had ended and it was supposed to be thirty days. Well, once they approved it the thirty days was already rolling. About the time they sent the letter saying we was approved, the letter saying that it was up—the thirty days was up—was right behind it. So it was like I had made all these appointments for all of us for the following week and the letter came that Monday and that Wednesday was the last day.

Transitional emergency services had short time spans and complicated eligibility procedures. Acquiring medical care coverage and then locating medical practitioners who would provide the care was time-consuming and exhausting. Even though they knew they were declining physically, under multiple pressures many mothers reported that they had no remaining resources for seeking out and using healthcare for themselves. Louise described this dilemma:

I feel so tired, I just can't never stop and do nothing myself, I can't never stop and go see the doctor for my [blood] pressure. I can't stop and go see the doctor for my leg, I'm helping everybody.

While mothers struggled to obtain medical care for their children and coped with often untreated conditions of their own, mothers' and children's mental health went unattended. Evacuees' access to mental health care was limited both by demands on the services and by mothers' own limited time and energy. As in Louise's case, they did their best to ignore conditions and dealt in home remedies.

Of course I'm depressed. I drank [vinegar] all day long to keep down my depression because I ain't got no more depression pills.

While mothers recognized that many of their own and their children's mental health problems stemmed from the traumas experienced during the storm and the evacuation, they believed they should be able to manage on their own. In some ways parents echoed the rhetoric among service agency personnel and in the news media indicating that after six months or a year, evacuees should be moving toward recovery. Louise explained her struggles with her son:

I could send my son to Job Corps August first; he failed all of his classes in the tenth grade. [How come?] His mind is on the work but he can't put it on paper, the teachers been told me on the phone, I went to the school, he's very smart, when they ask him questions and he do his homework at home, everything is excellent, but he can't put it on paper, like homework, like class work. . . . [Why not?] I don't know what his mind is on. [Did he have that problem when he was in New Orleans?] No ma'am, I told you I think I told you once before that, it have a lot to do with this little boy that he was close to that drowned in the what ya' call it, but it's time, I think he should have got over that, I really do, I think he could have got over this hill.

When household members or close family connections faced substance abuse problems, families were often even more conflicted about seeking help. They feared the involvement of the criminal justice system and child protective services with their households if drug or alcohol problems became known to service agencies.

The search for stable housing was also difficult, even for families like Henry and Xia's that ended up living together in a single-family home. As the Austin Convention Center closed down its shelter after four weeks of operation, families were first moved into subsidized housing with local agencies, hotels, and apartment complexes. Over time, this support declined or lapsed, and respondents had to either pay their own rent or move into the regular public housing system in Austin. But even though Katrina evacuees were given preference, the public housing system was complex. And since Austin had a long-standing shortage of low-cost housing, families were often entered onto lengthy waiting lists. Programs for which evacuees had been eligible in New Orleans required new certification and proof of eligibility. Some evacuees who had received short-term emergency assistance in Austin were not necessarily eligible in Texas for long-term assistance similar to what they had received in New Orleans.

In particular, families struggled to obtain Section 8 certificates, even though the certificates sometimes created new difficulties. Section 8 housing certificates required families to locate their own housing. Such a search presented daunting obstacles for evacuees in a strange city who had little understanding of Austin's limited public transportation and little access to other transportation. These obstacles were exacerbated because mothers had to provide documentation not just for themselves but for all of their children and any other coresidents as well. Furthermore, families with children and with more than two generations grouped together found the search for housing with enough bedrooms difficult. As Louise and a visitor of hers tried to describe:

LOUISE: I'm on Section 8.

INTERVIEWER: Yeah, but they want to have your identification.

LOUISE: They've been harassing me about the birth certificates of my kids but now . . .

INTERVIEWER: Right now is your housing in jeopardy because of that?

LOUISE: Yes, yes, ma'am, like I said I was in every line because when I was in New Orleans I was in the projects so I was in housing authority, Section 8, whatever. So . . . after we came through everything they gave me this here apartment for Section 8 temporarily but I knew for a fact they gave me this apartment through FEMA first, October, November, December, January, February, March, right? . . . Then I went to the housing projects to a meeting they had all over brochures and everything, and I went and they gave me a voucher I remember showing you.

INTERVIEWER: Yes, I remember.

LOUISE: For, for, Section 8, now the program that they have me in it's eighteen months. I'm thinking it was supposed to start the time that I went in April . . .

INTERVIEWER: Oh, yeah.

VISITOR: No the program started like in February, January, right?

LOUISE: Yeah.

VISITOR: In other words I've got until this May, on the Section 8, they've been sending me—

INTERVIEWER: Now what happens in May?

VISITOR: I've got to move because what they didn't tell me, they didn't tell me during the time, I don't know if you was down here, a month or two ago it was all over the news, where they was taking applications for Section 8. They had people sleeping on the sidewalk at five o'clock in the morning, but I didn't know I had to go there to extend my voucher.

INTERVIEWER: Oh, okay.

VISITOR: I went to the meeting last time she said that's what I'm supposed to do, but no one told me that, so I'm on the list, I'm number thirteen on the list for the housing project. I'm going to get one next month but it's holding me back because I don't have my children's birth certificate; I don't have no up-to-date ID.

Because it was difficult to understand the extent of their original FEMA benefits, families were often plunged unexpectedly into the search for housing. Evacuees discovered that their rent or utility support was more limited than they had understood. Louise describes her belated discovery that FEMA had stopped paying her benefits.

INTERVIEWER: But they're not, when did they [FEMA] stop paying utilities?

LOUISE: In August . . . And I did not know until November.

VISITOR: She didn't know until it all builded up at one time.

LOUISE: The disconnection notice came saying they was going to come and cut the lights off so I called and the lady told me that my bill was a thousand something dollars so she contact FEMA and they only paid up until July, so from August to November I was supposed to be responsible, but they didn't send me no letter saying they were going to stop paying it so now I owe energy like seven hundred dollars and I got to pay it out of my pocket.

The insecure housing arrangements left parents and children feeling unstable and without a home they could depend on. The potential for frequent moves made mothers worry about the consequences for their children's schooling, access to other services, and sense of well-being. Under these circumstances, mothers like Louise saw their children getting into trouble, and they often felt helpless to intervene.

WORK

For many of our respondents, problems finding a job were entangled with other problems they faced. Members of both families struggled with employment issues after the evacuation. Louise found it impossible to begin any job she located because of her need for better identification:

I can't get a good job because I don't have a certain ID. . . . Every time I try to go out and get work, I have my feet in the door, and when it's time for me to get the job, they ask me to present an ID. I have one . . . but it's temporary; it expired, so I can't get no more until they send me my birth certificate. Me and my niece waiting on my birth [certificate], my kids ain't got theirs yet; the only one that got theirs is my oldest daughter. . . . She got hers faster than anybody, we still waiting on ours . . . and it's hard for me to cash checks, it's hard for a lot of things.

Although Henry and Xia had worked hard in New Orleans, as Henry described it, their jobs barely provided the resources they needed:

In New Orleans we really had struggles. We had to work two jobs; well, I worked two jobs, and she worked a job, and we just barely made ends meet in New Orleans.

Their first attempts to secure jobs in Austin were unsuccessful. Unlike many others, they had carried with them references from previous jobs and found employment right away. But they lost their first jobs almost as soon as they started, attributing the loss to their status as "refugees," a status they rejected. As Xia explained:

By me and my husband having a reference . . . , we got a job two days after being here in Austin. You know them people that took that job away from us and told us they couldn't hire us because we were the refugees and contaminated. . . . You feel what I'm saying? I was born in the United States. I've been living here the whole of my life. Now all of a sudden I'm a refugee. I only thought that was what they called people overseas that was trying to get to the States.

After another major effort, both Henry and Xia landed jobs in schools. But this effort failed when Henry went to jail. As they jointly explained:

HENRY: I went to jail because me and my wife was arguing in the parking lot, and somebody took it upon theirself and said me and my wife was fighting. So the police came here to our house.
XIA: They talked to us.
HENRY: And talked to us.
XIA: And we thought it was all over. Three weeks later they came and got my husband out of the bed at five o'clock in the morning.
HENRY: In my drawers and had me outside in the freezing cold bringing me to jail. . . . We had just got jobs, paying nine dollars an hour. She had just got a job. So when that happened that meant I lost my job and she lost her job.
XIA: Because he wasn't here to bring me to work.
HENRY: The people came to see me before I went to court. They say I had a ten-thousand-dollar bond. . . . The judge asked me, "Are you a Katrina victim?" I'm like, "Yeah." He said, "Well, I know you all don't have any money for you to be getting out of jail," he said. "Well, I'm going to take the ten-thousand-dollar bond off so people can release you, and you know you can keep your job." [But in the end] ain't nobody came to get me.
XIA: They said the reason that he didn't qualify [for release] was because he was a flight risk from being from New Orleans.

In fragile families, the arrest and incarceration of a wage earner, even for a short period of time, can mean destitution for the entire household. Unexpected episodes of incarceration made it more difficult for families to keep jobs and keep their children in school.

Some evacuee youth also entered the criminal justice system. Louise was worried about her children. As her housing changed, her children moved from one school to another and started getting into trouble. The children had little connection to any of the schools, and they knew almost no one at them. Louise explained the difficulties with her son:

> I been going backwards and forth with courts with him. It's not nothing pertaining to school, like playing hooky, sassing teachers, or cutting class, no. The first time he went off of campus, went out with some boys and smoked some marijuana. Came back on campus they smelled it. So, that was the second time. The first time, because I told you, in the Convention Center when he broke the boy nose, at [his school] . . . Now we been here just seven months, this the third school my baby been into. . . . He's going to [another school]. [T]hey have a lot of [potential benefits] like a lot of activities and that stuff there. But it's a big school. There's a lot of children there, to where if you walked the hallway you got to touch somebody, like crawdads. They jumped on Nathan twice. They jumped on him last Thursday.

While feeling that there is little left for her in New Orleans, Louise worried aloud about whether she could create any kind of life for herself and her children in Austin. Her children might well get labeled as troublemakers, she feared:

> Alena may have a little smartness by the mouth, but you know my kids cause they from New Orleans. I am thinking about going back home, just to keep my children safe, I would do anything for my children, but I don't see where that is going to work for me, because right now . . . I hate New Orleans because they took a lot from me.

As children dealing with trauma, marginalization, and poverty entered Austin schools, they sometimes experienced difficulties that led to a change in school, entry into school disciplinary programs, or involvement with the criminal justice system. Single mothers often faced the dilemma of seeking employment to support their families or staying unemployed and remaining more available to care for their children who were finding themselves in trouble.

CONCLUSION

The experiences of evacuee families with children illustrate many of the pathways that take families into the "basement" of poverty. The largely minority and previously poor or near-poor families that were evacuated to Austin, particularly those housed in public shelters, were struggling before the hurricane and evacuation to provide their children and households with necessities. They had developed strategies that depended on the local informal and formal resources available to them in New Orleans. The dislocation often shattered these networks and left families without support and without the local knowledge to begin to make their way post-Katrina.

The experiences of Henry, Xia, Louise, and their families illustrate the quagmire created by traumatic dislocation that led to near-destitution poverty for many of New Orleans's poor and near-poor. The temporary safety net offered by short-term disaster services and piecemeal United States poverty policies provides insufficient resources and consistency to be of ongoing assistance to families. Families facing mental and physical health issues, job loss, and the loss of support provided by families, friends, and home communities are not only plunged into deep poverty, but have little sense of the way out.

When faced with dire poverty, parents struggle—often with limited success—to support their families financially while caring for children and other dependents. Their previous strategies, often based on long-term relationships with casual employers and with the knowledge and support provided by informal networks and families, are unavailable at the same time that public supports become less accessible.

NOTES

1. Gøsta Esping-Anderson, Duncan Gallie, Anton Hemerijck, and John Myles, *Why We Need a New Welfare State* (New York: Oxford University Press, 2002); Jacob S. Hacker, *The Divided Welfare State* (Cambridge: Cambridge University Press, 2002); Paul Pierson, *Dismantling the Welfare State? Reagan, Thatcher, and the Politics of Retrenchment* (Cambridge: Cambridge University Press, 1994).

2. Helmut Anheier, Marlies Glasius, and Mary Kaldor, eds., *Global Civil Society 2001* (Oxford: Oxford University Press, 2001); Amitai Etzioni, *The Spirit of Community: Rights, Responsibilities, and the Communitarian Agenda* (New York: Crown Publishers, 1993); Robert D. Putnam, *Bowling Alone: The Collapse and Revival of American Community* (New York: Simon and Schuster, 2000); Lester M. Salamon,

ed., *The State of Non-Profit America* (Washington, DC: Brookings Institution Press, 2002).

3. Ronald Angel and Laura Lein, "Living on a Poverty Income: The Role of Non-Governmental Agencies in the Scramble for Resources," *Journal of Law and Policy* 20, no. 75 (2006): 75–99; Paul Pierson, "The New Politics of the Welfare State," *World Politics* 48, no. 2 (1996): 143–179; Wendy Zimmerman and Karen C. Tumlin, *Patchwork Policies: State Assistance for Immigrants under Welfare Reform* (Washington, DC: Urban Institute, 1999), http://www.urban.org/url.cfm?ID=309007, accessed February 19, 2011.

4. Kathryn Edin and Laura Lein, *Making Ends Meet* (New York: Russell Sage Foundation, 1997); Kathryn Edin and Laura Lein, "The Private Safety Net: The Role of Charitable Organizations in the Lives of the Poor," *Housing Policy Debate* 9 no. 3 (1998): 541–574; Robin Jarrett, "Living Poor: Family Life among Single Parent, African-American Women," *Social Problems* 41, no. 1 (1994): 30–49; Laura Lein and Deanna Schexnayder, *Life after Welfare* (Austin: University of Texas Press, 2007).

5. Edin and Lein, "The Private Safety Net."

6. Elise D. Riley, Andrew R. Moss, Richard A. Clark, Sandra L. Monk, and David R. Bangsberg, "Cash Benefits Are Associated with Lower Risk Behavior among the Homeless and Marginally Housed in San Francisco," *Journal of Urban Health* 82, no. 1 (2005): 142–150; Loïc J. D. Wacquant, "The Rise of Advanced Marginality: Notes on Its Nature and Implications," *Acta Sociologica* 39, no. 2 (1996): 121–139; Loïc J. D. Wacquant, "Negative Social Capital: State Breakdown and Social Destitution in America's Urban Core," *Journal of Housing and the Built Environment* 13, no. 1 (1998): 25–40.

7. Barrett A. Lee and Chad R. Farrell, "Buddy, Can You Spare a Dime? Homelessness, Panhandling, and the Public," *Urban Affairs Review* 38, no. 3 (2003): 299–324.

8. This research was partially supported by the National Science Foundation, grant number 0555113, and by grant 5 R24 HD042849, awarded to the Population Research Center at the University of Texas at Austin by the Eunice Kennedy Shriver National Institute of Health and Child Development. The interview count has changed since the time these data were selected for analysis.

9. City of Austin, "A City within a City: A Model for the Nation," City of Austin Hurricane Katrina Shelter Operations After Action Report (Austin: City of Austin, 2006).

10. United States Census Fact Sheets for Austin and New Orleans. http://quickfacts.census.gov/qfd/states/48/4805000.html (Austin), http://quickfacts.census.gov/qfd/states/22/2255000.html (New Orleans), accessed February 19, 2011.

11. Dave Mann, "What Hawkins Knew," *Texas Observer*, April 6, 2007.

5

LIVING THROUGH DISPLACEMENT
HOUSING INSECURITY AMONG
LOW-INCOME EVACUEES

The destruction of housing was among the most stunning material losses caused by Hurricane Katrina. Roughly 70 percent of the housing supply in New Orleans sustained some level of damage.[1] This was devastating to a city that already had a shortage of affordable housing. Low-income and working-poor families were the people most significantly affected by this shortage, as they faced unprecedented rent increases—35 percent in the first year after Katrina.[2] They also had few to no rights. They were evicted from undamaged units or faced rent hikes for failure to pay while evacuated. Many people lost their homes outright, and those who did not were vulnerable to eviction and displacement even when their apartment or residence suffered no damage.

Included in this vulnerable group were families in public housing. Immediately following the storm, the Housing Authority of New Orleans (HANO) prevented residents from returning to their units by barricading them shut. Soon after, HANO and the City Council publicly announced that only "working residents" could return to their units, damaged or not, lease or not. While this statement was quickly rescinded, the tensions it created between HANO and residents remained strong.

In this chapter, I reveal the challenges faced by low-income women in housing programs as they attempted to reestablish housing stability in new, often hostile, environments. I examine the conflicting demands these women had to negotiate, in order to expose the contradictions posed by post-disaster housing policies, which were created and maintained in a context of limited and rapidly diminishing housing availability. Finally, I consider the lingering barriers these women will face for years to come.

argument

JESSICA W. PARDEE

Public housing residents were unwanted in a recovering New Orleans. Within weeks of the storm, HANO announced plans to demolish four large-scale public housing projects because of "flood damage," including units with no water intrusion at all.[3] Many of these undamaged apartments were slated for demolition previously,[4] making Katrina an opportunity to move the plans along faster without the need to formally relocate the families. As a result, the reconstruction timeline effectively required residents to rebuild their lives outside the city, reinforcing the notion that they, exclusively poor and Black, were simply not wanted within the "new New Orleans."

Despite residents' protests and a public outcry against the demolitions, including condemnation from the United Nations Human Rights Committee,[5] in December 2007 a unanimous City Council approved HANO's plans. The housing authority would build 3,200 new units of subsidized housing to replace 4,500 units.[6] The families who could have lived in the demolished 1,300 public housing units would have to find new homes elsewhere. And yet the plans included housing for 1,765 affluent families in order to create a "mixed income" environment—a model borrowed from the existing HOPE VI federal housing program.[7]

A national trend in redevelopment, this transition to economically diverse communities privatizes the management of public housing to attract profitable, middle-income families, leaving the poorest, least stable families homeless.[8] In New Orleans, mixed-income housing policy means that at least one-third of poor families will not be able to return to subsidized housing in the city. This displacement pattern parallels citywide population loss, as 118,000 African Americans have not returned since the storm.[9] Instead, low-income families must build new lives in new locations—without sufficient financial resources to do so.

HOUSING ASSISTANCE PROGRAMS

Women displaced from public housing attempted to reinvent their pre-Katrina housing security while living *outside of* New Orleans. To do so, the women in this study drew on three housing programs: (1) FEMA's Individuals and Households Program (IHP), (2) the Katrina Disaster Housing Assistance Program (KDHAP), and (3) the Section 8 Housing Choice Voucher Program. Both the IHP and KDHAP offered short-term assistance to help

Table 5.1. Housing Programs before and after Hurricane Katrina

Type of Program	Rent Provision	Duration	Other Provisions
I. Federal Housing Programs			
Traditional Public Housing	Determined by the housing authority	Unlimited	Rent includes utilities such as electricity, water, sewerage, and cable
Section 8	HUD's fair market rent rate minus 30% of the tenant's income	Annual renewal	Tenant pays 30% of income for rent; tenant pays full utilities
HOPE VI	Determined by the housing authority	Unlimited	Tenant pays full utilities
II. Disaster-Related Housing Programs			
FEMA IHP/DHAP	100%	12 months	Can include utilities, determined on a case-by-case basis
KDHAP	HUD's fair market rent rate	18 months	Tenant pays any difference between rent cost and voucher value; tenant pays utilities

families recover, while Section 8 is a traditional form of public, voucher-based housing assistance.

INDIVIDUALS AND HOUSEHOLDS PROGRAM (IHP)

FEMA's IHP, the standard federal disaster-response program, provides rental assistance and trailers, money for housing repairs, and compensation for lost property or vehicles, and covers other basic expenses.[10] When families qualify, their rental assistance lasts for twelve months, and FEMA pays the rent directly to the landlord. Families did not pay anything, but had to document how they spent the money if they received a cash payment, a common FEMA practice after Hurricane Katrina.[11]

In 2007, this program received more funding and a new name: the Disaster Housing Assistance Program (DHAP). Since there was continued need for housing assistance two years after the storm, FEMA transferred administrative power to the Department of Housing and Urban Development (HUD).[12] Within HUD, the DHAP was run by individual housing authorities across the nation that already housed thousands of families in similar programs such as Section 8. By dealing directly with evacuees, the local housing authority could provide immediate assistance to Katrina families still in need.

THE KATRINA DISASTER HOUSING ASSISTANCE PROGRAM (KDHAP)

To qualify for KDHAP, a family needed to live in public housing or be homeless before the storm.[13] Under KDHAP, families received a rental voucher for eighteen months and did not have to meet income requirements. The only cost to families was any excess in the price of their rent beyond HUD's determination of what fair market rent for the area should be.

Like the IHP, in January 2006 KDHAP also received an extension and a new name to become the Disaster Voucher Program (DVP).[14] Like its predecessor, the DVP had no income eligibility requirements or rental payments and lasted for eighteen months.[15] The only notable change was that families who were homeless (those living in shelters or on the street) before Katrina became ineligible, while public housing families already in KDHAP continued to receive rental vouchers in the new program.

THE SECTION 8 HOUSING CHOICE VOUCHER PROGRAM

The Section 8 Housing Choice Voucher Program is a standard form of public housing assistance. Under Section 8, a tenant pays 30 percent of his or her income toward rent, with the housing authority paying the remainder directly to the landlord. The tenant also pays for utilities. For each community, HUD establishes voucher funding limits, called "fair market rents." If an apartment's cost exceeds the fair market rent, it falls to the tenant to cover the difference. Vouchers are allocated to specific housing authorities and can only be used within their service areas.

THE STUDY

At the time of the hurricane, I was a graduate student living in New Orleans, preparing to research the effect of the HOPE VI housing program on the lives of women living in two developments in the city: St. Thomas (now

River Gardens) and Desire (now Abundance Square). To recruit my sample, I received a list of resident names from HANO in early 2005. However, before I could begin interviews, Katrina struck. Unable to study HOPE VI's effects, I decided to locate those same residents and alter my research focus to investigate their disaster recovery experiences. Since the women of my study and I were all displaced by the storm, I used phone interviews to overcome our physical distance.

I interviewed women between October 2005 and December 2006. It took fifteen months to locate respondents, who were scattered in Louisiana, Texas, Mississippi, Georgia, Alabama, and Florida. To find the women, I used telephone calls to their last known phone number and Internet searches for new telephone information. I e-mailed social service providers and churches in New Orleans, Atlanta, and Houston and hung flyers throughout the Desire, Lafitte, and St. Thomas neighborhoods and within local convenience stores. In New Orleans, I left leaflets in the mailboxes of all units at the St. Thomas/River Gardens development. Finally, I sent hand-addressed letters to the last mailing address I had for each woman. My recruitment letter discussed the research purpose and the consent information required by the university's institutional review board and included my New Orleans cell phone number. Overall, the hand-addressed letters and a list of names secured from a social service provider, whom I knew before the storm, produced the most responses. The women I interviewed also provided a few additional contacts.

The conceptual foci of the interviews included an initial section of closed-end questions on evacuation, employment, assistance before and after the storm, and demographic characteristics. This section generally took between five and fifteen minutes to complete. A second, and more informative, qualitative section asked women to describe their evacuation and recovery experiences in their own words. These responses typically took between thirty and ninety minutes and told a vivid story about how each woman and her family survived the storm. Because I chose not to audio-record the women, to protect their anonymity, I typed their replies during the interview and edited them afterwards. In appreciation, women received a twenty-dollar gift card and, if they wanted them, two hotline numbers for free counseling services.

The fifty-one women who spoke with me were all Black and living as stable public housing residents. On average, the women had lived in their current homes for nearly six years before the storm, with many in public housing for much longer. As a group, their mean age was just over fifty. A majority (n = 28) were single, while eight were divorced, six were married, and six were widowed. A few were separated or cohabitating. Almost half (n = 24) had a high school degree or a GED, while most of the rest (n = 21) had no degree. Five women had earned an associate's or bachelor's degree, and just one woman had earned a graduate degree. Finally, almost every woman (n = 46) earned below twenty thousand dollars in 2004, the year before the hurricane. The rest had household incomes between twenty and forty thousand dollars. Since limited income and resources were something they shared with nearly a third of the city, these women's disaster experiences are in many ways representative of a typical Black working-class or poor New Orleans family.

CHALLENGES TO HOUSING SECURITY

The post-disaster housing struggles of poor and low-income families are more acute than those from other socioeconomic groups, primarily because low-income families have fewer resources to prepare for or respond to a disaster.[16] The women I interviewed were among the least likely to have savings for rental deposits, funds to purchase basic furniture, or access to job transfers that would ensure a steady stream of income. While twenty-one women were employed the month before Katrina, only four were employed following the storm. In part, the drop in employment occurred because nearly half of the previously employed had worked in healthcare in capacities such as nursing assistants and home help aids that require certification and verification of skills—documentation of which was unavailable following the storm. The remaining women who were employed before the storm worked in government institutions, such as the police department and the school system, and two were employed in the tourism industry.

Every woman relied on some form of economic assistance following the storm, and all but one received varying amounts of aid from FEMA. The one exception was denied aid because a family member had already filed a claim using her New Orleans address. For everyone else, FEMA aid offered the first opportunity to obtain clothing, food, and shelter. A typical benefit package included a onetime payment of $2,000, followed by a second payment of $2,358 for housing, with additional funding determined on a case-by-case basis. All but one woman received cash-based assistance from the American Red Cross, and sixteen women received money or gift cards from religious organizations in their receiving communities.

Even with assistance, however, meeting individual housing needs was often a significant and persistent challenge. While all of the women in this study were in independent households before the storm, only thirty of the fifty-one women found a home of their own during their evacuation and displacement from the city. Nearly one-third (n = 16) stayed with friends and family, and four remained in hotels or shelters. Notably, nearly a fourth of the women evacuated to locations with housing markets flooded by other evacuees, including Houston, Baton Rouge, Atlanta, and Dallas–Ft. Worth. Others began in these locations, but left to live in smaller places that were less crowded with evacuees and offered better social services, including Corpus Christi, Conroe, and Tyler, Texas.

To locate a stable housing situation, many women moved multiple times during their displacement, with most having lived in three or four homes at the time of our interview. By May of 2006, less than a year after the storm, one woman had lived with her grandchildren in *nine* homes— moves triggered after FEMA rescinded her voucher because the rent was too expensive.

> INTERVIEWEE: [W]hen they set up an apartment, the apartment was supposed to be for a year, I signed a lease for a year, and was living there for five months. That put the most stress on you, 'cause you have to find a place to live. Before, I was feeling like "I'm on lease for a year, that will give me a chance to pull it together," just feeling like 70 percent better, even though everybody was separated . . . but only five months lasted and we had to find somewhere else to go.
>
> PARDEE: But didn't you have a lease?
> INTERVIEWEE: FEMA stopped paying for it.
> PARDEE: Why did FEMA stop paying for it?
> INTERVIEWEE: They stopped paying for it because the rent was so high. They told me I have to find somewhere else to go, and I've been going from house to house ever since then.

This woman's housing struggle resulted from a high demand for private market housing, which drove rents higher in areas flooded with evacuees. As she relocated to other "evacuee flood zones," her chances of finding housing were greatly reduced. Everyone in the study experienced these problems, which center on two main themes: interactions with private rental actors and with assisting institutions.

PRIVATE RENTAL ACTORS

For women working to establish stable housing situations, navigating encounters with private rental actors was one of the most challenging processes. Landlords, property management agents, and administrative assistants could enable or prevent women's access to housing. Many took advantage of the confusion following Katrina, while the women they hurt had little or no recourse. Landlords had a unique opportunity to create discriminatory barriers to housing stability by specifying how and to whom they would rent their units. For one forty-seven-year-old woman who worked full-time as a security guard before the storm, finding stable housing was a constant problem. In the three months after the storm, she moved between residences and shelters *six* times. After working to secure a FEMA IHP voucher, she was surprised when the landlord refused to accept it. She described her frustration:

> INTERVIEWEE: I got a voucher, but the landlords didn't want to take the FEMA voucher. . . . So, I got the voucher, but I can't find a home. Then I found a place, but the landlord wouldn't take the FEMA voucher. They wanted a KADI voucher.
>
> PARDEE: What's the KADI voucher?
>
> INTERVIEWEE: It's the Texas Section 8 voucher, so I got one of those instead. See, I had found a place where I wanted to live early on and was told, "Honey, I'm sorry, I don't take FEMA, I take Section 8." And I got a Section 8 voucher, found a place, and everything is in process now. The HANO people in Houston, they said deposits and things should be waived. But I don't know, so I'm just going to pay them anyway because I need a place.

In all likelihood, she was denied access to the first apartment in favor of a renter with a Section 8 voucher. Because they are renewable, Section 8 vouchers create the potential for longer-term residency and rent revenue. By contrast, the disaster housing programs are limited to twelve or eighteen months and are founded on the assumption that residents will return to their home communities—an inaccurate policy assumption in the context of the large-scale post-Katrina displacement and severe housing loss in New Orleans. As a result, Katrina evacuees were less desirable tenants because they were short-term, while local residents had the potential to be steady sources of income.

Economics and the intricacies of post-disaster housing programs do not fully explain the unwillingness of some landlords to rent to an evacuee. In particular, race, class, and gender stereotypes may have discouraged landlords from renting to otherwise responsible and motivated people.[17] A woman whom I will call Vivienne, for example, is a mother of one and the caretaker of her blind mother, and was a full-time teacher for a parochial school before the storm. Learning about housing and other assistance available in Tyler, Texas, from a friend, Vivienne quickly moved there to stabilize her housing situation and establish care for her mother. After weighing her immediate assistance options against her family's need for long-term stability, she chose to use the KDHAP voucher for its eighteen months' worth of assistance. Locating a house, she signed the lease, moved in, *and* provided a deposit for two months' rent, only to have her landlord refuse to rent to her when he learned that she was a "public housing" recipient. She explained the situation as follows:

We lucked up and found a lease. I found a house, signed a year lease. Once I signed a year lease, I went to Baton Rouge, and got my mom. Then, when it was time for the [housing authority] people to come out . . . the landlord thought it'd be just him filling out forms, or whatever. I explained that I'd be getting assistance. I had paid out of my pocket, the deposit and two months' rent, out of my own pocket. Once we were there a week and a half, they [the local housing authority] said, "We put you on [KDHAP], here are the steps you have to take." They inspect the house. Once they came out, the house passed. When it was time for the landlord to fill out his part, he went crazy. He didn't want to deal with this.

Once I went to him with that, he was like, "I never heard of that." He was looking for FEMA, he knew FEMA was going to help, but the housing authority, he didn't want to deal with that. He like, "Why didn't you tell me? . . . I hear in Houston, in Dallas . . ." FEMA came to me, they trying to give me assistance. FEMA was staying twelve months, and housing offers eighteen months. Under this program [KDHAP], it's even better. FEMA sent $2,353 every three months, automatically, with the rent being paid. It's a different program. I chose to go to this program. I didn't want his house under that program. I had already paid rent until December. I paid the deposit! But when I said it was actually through the housing authority, he said, "I don't want anything to do with this crap." "But you're already assisting me." He like, "I don't want anything to do with this." All I can think is like, "Okay, you're tripping." So, I broke the lease. I got up looking for another house.

Wondering if this was an issue of racism, I questioned Vivienne about the interaction with her landlord:

PARDEE: Was he white?
VIVIENNE: He was a white man, you have to be there to see where he

was coming from. He was saying stuff like "you people," "you from this housing," "you from the projects," "you people." I went from being "Miss Jones," to "Katrina victim," to "you people." He don't want to deal with nothing. I went from "Miss Jones" to "you people." He like, "I wasn't aware you came from a program like this." . . . Then he kept talking about "you people" and "those type of programs." We went backwards and forwards. Your rent due January first—why he care as long as you paid it? The next day, I was out looking for another house. I didn't care if he take me to court.

This exchange made Vivienne feel as if the landlord believed that she was a lower-quality tenant because she had previously required public housing assistance in a tight and limited New Orleans housing market. Yet she was a full-time teacher, responsible mother, and dedicated caretaker. Ironically, neither race, gender, nor evacuee status alone prevented the landlord from selecting her as a renter when he believed that FEMA would be covering the monthly rental payments. It was only at the prospect of housing a "public housing resident" that he refused to accept her fair market rate rental voucher. Fortunately, a sympathetic housing authority employee was able to assist Vivienne in locating a new house, and she moved within two weeks of the incident. Since she had signed the lease, she lost her deposit and two months' rent. She also lost some additional assistance from a community charity group that had sent money directly to the old landlord on her behalf.

One of the complicating requirements of both the KDHAP and Section 8 programs was a required property inspection of the rental unit. In Vivienne's case, a problem arose because the local housing authority did not inspect the unit before the lease signing. While Vivienne's lease fell through because of discrimination, had the inspectors visited sooner, the landlord's bias might have been exposed before she paid the deposit and the rent. This policy practice of inspecting a unit after a binding legal agreement had been entered into was illogical, counterproductive, costly, stressful, and entrapping. In the end, Vivienne was left in a lease for which she was legally liable and that eliminated valuable financial resources needed to care for her kin. While Vivienne technically could have sued the landlord for her money, she did not, instead focusing on finding another home immediately.

The continual negotiation with private rental agents, pervasive in the recovery experiences of low-income evacuees, made it seem as if whatever voucher a woman managed to secure was never the "correct" one. Despite having a stable Social Security income from her husband, for example, one fifty-six-year-old married woman and caretaker of her nine-year-old grandson found accessing her new housing in Baton Rouge, Louisiana, nearly impossible.

> INTERVIEWEE: It took a long time to get where I was. You try to do one thing, and always get a kick back.
> PARDEE: Could you give me an example of a "kick back"?
> INTERVIEWEE: Here, it went on a month. You get up, you call 9:00 or 9:30, it [the unit] wouldn't be ready. You call Tuesday, Wednesday, Thursday. Something else, it's not finished. Those people wasn't trying to help people. They tell you, "You need a FEMA number," you ask why, and they say, "because you're a New Orleans evacuee, you need a FEMA number." Why, if you can pay your own rent? I had to go back, go to a computer. I couldn't get [the FEMA number] on the computer. I just gave up. . . .
>   Finally, they called, told me to bring in the deposit. They kept the deposit for two weeks before we could have the apartment. They're saying they was trying to help people from New Orleans, but not really.
> PARDEE: Why did they hold the deposit?
> INTERVIEWEE: First, they said they were fixing the plumbing, then they had to put down a carpet. We can't really say anything, we had nowhere else to go. It's the same old dirty carpet. We've had no stove for two weeks. Oh honey, it was a mess. I'm telling you.

Collectively, these women were treated as if their money, deposits, vouchers, time, and energy were less valuable than they really were. And these challenges were not simply isolated in the private housing markets. Barriers to housing security originated with the administrators of the assistance programs themselves, especially FEMA and local public housing authorities.

INSTITUTIONALIZED HOUSING INSECURITY

One of the most disappointing realities of Katrina's aftermath was that many of the institutions whose job was to help evacuees actually made their experiences worse. Whether working with FEMA or local housing agencies, women dealt with a range of complications. This section highlights four of the most problematic: (1) removal of vouchers without notification, (2) incorrect implementation of the KDHAP program, (3) HUD's failure to adjust voucher values to reflect increased rental costs in places with significant evacuee populations, and (4) the failure of housing authorities to provide HUD-funded moving assistance for evacuees. Together, these factors impeded women's recovery from the storm.

REMOVAL OF HOUSING VOUCHERS

The removal of housing vouchers without notification overwhelmed evacuees' recovery efforts. The loss of a FEMA voucher left one woman and her children homeless and triggered a period of instability during which they stayed at *nine* different homes in nine months. For a fifty-two-year-old married woman, the loss of her brother's IHP voucher initiated eviction proceedings. As the leaseholder, the brother was trying to transition to the new KDHAP voucher. However, once FEMA recognized him as an applicant to KDHAP, it terminated IHP rental payments, leaving him *without any assistance* until the new voucher was processed. So by applying to a recovery program, evacuees could accidentally undermine the housing security they were working toward.

INCORRECT IMPLEMENTATION

Despite housing program designs that did support evacuees' needs, assisting institutions undermined their effectiveness when they failed to implement the programs correctly. As the family above was being evicted, the fifty-two-year-old woman and her husband secured a KDHAP voucher of their own for an apartment. Located in Texas, the new housing was very expensive, and their rent contribution increased by nearly $500 per month. Yet, according to the KDHAP program rules, they should not have been paying rent at all.

> You see, I had Section 8 before the storm. When I was in New Orleans, I paid $135 rent. I'm living on Section 8 now, but it's still $605. They prorated it.
>
> With my housing, I'm worried about being put out. I'm worried about the electric being turned off right now. I have KDHAP instead of rental assistance. My rent is $605. It's $895 before the voucher. I need to find out what HUD can do. I'm gonna find out tomorrow.

In this case, the local housing authority was keeping a large portion of the HUD money for itself. At the time of the interview, HUD's fair market rents for Tarrant County, Texas—where the couple was staying—were $589 for a one-bedroom unit and $725 for a two-bedroom unit.[18] So their $895 apartment should never have cost the couple more than $306 a month in rent. This mistake, intentional or otherwise, defrauded the couple of a minimum of $3,588 for a one-bedroom apartment, and up to $5,220 for a two-bedroom apartment, annually. As a result, they struggled to pay other bills, including electricity, water, and groceries.

FAILURE TO ADJUST VOUCHER VALUE

Following Katrina, HUD also created housing insecurity by allocating insufficient dollar values for rental vouchers. A fifty-eight-year-old Katrina survivor who initially sought shelter in the Superdome, for example, described how rapid rental increases plagued New Orleans and other major evacuee cities:

> My mama's friend, Miss Marie, she paying $1,127 for a little apartment. It's only got three rooms. She pays $1,127 per month for that. Plus she pays her own utilities. Every month her light bill is like $400 to $500. Entergy lost millions, so now they double the price. Why people can't come home? It's the rent, lights and the rent. How can you come home and pay $1,200? You call on the phone, then they said they want $1,500 for a one-bedroom apartment. You don't have that. You don't need to talk. They don't give a damn. They just don't. First they say you can come back, then they send you a letter saying you may not qualify. But you still had to send a deposit. So, you eligible because you in the system, but you may not qualify. You still have to have X amount of dollars, and you have no money! How can I move back if I can't afford to rent a truck? I have no money!

To contextualize the increase in rents, fair market rent in New Orleans for a one-bedroom apartment was $531 dollars in 2004, increased to $578 in 2005, and ballooned to $831 in 2006.[19] As demonstrated by an older woman who stayed with her daughter in Gretna, Louisiana, this rapid increase was not incorporated into local values defining "fair" market rent:

> I'm trying to find a house. I have Section 8, but I can't find a house because they hiked up the rent so much. It's too high for a voucher. A one-room studio is like $1,100, plus I need money for utilities and medicine because I'm diabetic.

In the "new New Orleans," Section 8 came to represent an unfulfilled promise of assistance in hard times. If vouchers had not been restricted to a specific city or township, many evacuees could have sought housing outside the city limits where there was no catastrophic flooding.

In fact, virtually all of the women I interviewed who returned to New

Orleans came back to the same housing units they had occupied before the storm; the Housing Authority required it. Those who could not afford to return to nonflooded homes lost their apartments. For those whose homes were damaged, the remaining choice was one of the few, very expensive private apartments.

FAILURE TO PROVIDE MOVING ASSISTANCE

Beyond inadequate housing aid, lack of money to cover the cost of moving prevented some women from coming home. While HUD offered allocations for moving expenses for low-income residents,[20] none of the women in this study mentioned receiving help or information, even when they actively contacted the local housing authority. In the absence of this aid, many public housing residents openly questioned whether HANO really wanted to bring them home at all. As a thirty-three-year-old resident of the Lafitte complex explained:

> I felt I was being encouraged to not return. And they kept saying it would be many years before we could come back, but I wouldn't just take their word for it. They didn't want us to come back so they could do what they want to do, and tear down what they want to tear down.

At the time of our interview in 2006, this woman was paying $1,600 a month in rent, with assistance from a KDHAP voucher, in post-Katrina New Orleans.

The woman's belief that the Housing Authority of New Orleans purposely kept people out to ease the process of demolition at Lafitte, Iberville, C.J. Peete, and St. Bernard was commonplace. And her situation reflects the failure of post-storm housing policy to adequately address the desperate housing situations of the poor. Without long-term assistance or a right to return to their homes, without employment or permanent housing, these families were left adrift, with no idea of what would happen when their assistance ended.

CONCLUSION

In an ideal scenario, the rehousing process would have been simple—find a place, sign a lease, get an inspection, submit the voucher, and . . . Welcome home! In reality, the women in this study faced multiple barriers imposed by private rental actors and assisting institutions—the people charged with "helping" them after the storm. These women were almost always left after

Katrina with less money than they had before to pay the rent or for other needs.

In the broader context of American housing policy over the last twenty years, the trend has been to engage residents in negotiations over how to improve their communities with HOPE VI grants, but then to keep those same residents from moving back into the new homes. In the decade before Katrina, HANO demolished nearly five thousand public housing units, even though it had nearly twenty thousand families waiting for assistance.[21]

Now, four massive housing developments have also been demolished, and only a select group of families will be allowed to return. These families will face rigorous application requirements, criminal background checks, employment stability requirements, and hefty application fees. They will be whittled down to a minority, while existing policy loopholes allow empty units to be filled with middle-class families. That process is already in motion at the St. Thomas/Abundance Square complex and has been praised as *the* model for redevelopment in New Orleans.

Over half a decade after Katrina, a loud, clear message remains. The women who shared their stories with me, once contributing citizens and residents of the city, are simply not wanted as part of the "new New Orleans."

NOTES

1. U.S. Department of Housing and Urban Development, "Current Housing Unit Damage Estimates: Hurricanes Katrina, Rita, and Wilma" (Washington, DC: HUD Office of Policy Research and Development, 2006), p. 23; Jessica W. Pardee and Kevin Fox Gotham, "HOPE VI, Section 8, and the Contradictions of Low-Income Housing Policy," *Journal of Poverty* 9, no. 2 (2005): 1–21.

2. Greater New Orleans Community Data Center, "Fair Market Rent Report: 2005–2007," http://www.gnocdc.org/reports/fair_market_rents.html, accessed June 15, 2008.

3. States News Service, "Fact Sheet: Redevelopment That Respects New Orleanians" (Washington, DC: States News Service, 2007).

4. Gwen Filosa, "Wrecking Crews Start Tearing Down St. Bernard Complex; Replacement Slated to Be Ready in 2010," *New Orleans Times Picayune*, February 20, 2008.

5. David Hammer, "HUD Rebuked over Katrina Response; U.N. Panel Sees Race Disparity in Housing," *New Orleans Times Picayune*, March 8, 2008.

6. David Hammer, "Tenants in Poll Don't Want Old Units; And Most Who Do Are There Already, HUD Says," *New Orleans Times Picayune*, March 7, 2008.

7. HOPE VI is a program that provides funding to demolish dilapidated public housing, while replacing it with mixed-income units. It provides on-site social services and allows housing authorities to use private funding for construction and

management. In most instances, the number of subsidized units is reduced by approximately 50–70 percent nationwide, leaving many families to accept Section 8 housing vouchers or simply manage without any assistance at all. National Housing Law Project, "False HOPE: A Critical Assessment of the HOPE VI Public Housing Redevelopment Program" (Oakland, CA: National Housing Law Project, 2002); Daniel Anderson and Mitchell Thompson, "Public/Private Partnerships: A Key to Success," *Journal of Housing and Community Development* 56, no. 3 (1999): 11–15; Andrew E. Finkel, Karin A. Lennon, and Elizabeth R. Eisenstadt, "Hope VI: A Promising Vintage?," *Policy Studies Review* 17, nos. 2/3 (2000): 104–119.

8. Susan J. Popkin, Larry F. Buron, Diane K. Levy, and Mary K. Cunningham, "The Gautreaux Legacy: What Might Mixed-income and Dispersal Strategies Mean for the Poorest Public Housing Tenants?," *Housing Policy Debate* 11, no. 4 (2000): 911–942; Pardee and Gotham, "HOPE VI, Section 8"; National Housing Law Project, "False HOPE."

9. Campbell Robertson, "Smaller New Orleans after Katrina, Census Shows," *New York Times*, February 3, 2011, http://www.nytimes.com/2011/02/04/us/04census.html?_r=1&ref=population, accessed February 24, 2011.

10. Federal Emergency Management Administration, "Fact Sheet: Individuals and Household" (release number: 1497-01–FactSheet), September 30, 2003, http://www.fema.gov/news/newsrelease.fema?id=5404, accessed June 18, 2008.

11. Ibid.

12. Katy Reckdahl, "Red Tape Choking Post-K Housing Program; Rents Unpaid, Storm Victims, Landlords Say," *New Orleans Times Picayune*, June 10, 2008.

13. U.S. Department of Housing and Urban Development, "Katrina Disaster Housing Assistance Program (KDHAP) Application. User Guide" (Washington, DC: HUD, December 2005).

14. U.S. Department of Housing and Urban Development, "Housing Choice Voucher Program FY 2006 Appropriations Implementation" (Washington, DC: HUD Office of Housing Voucher Programs, 2006).

15. Ibid.

16. Alice Fothergill and Lori Peek, "Poverty and Disasters in the United States: A Review of Recent Sociological Findings," *Natural Hazards* 32, no. 1 (2004): 89–110.

17. Also see Peek, this volume.

18. HUDUSER, HUD Fair Market Rent Calculator, "Final FY 2006 FMR Summary for Tarrant County, Texas," http://www.huduser.org/datasets/fmr/fmrs/2006summary.odb?INPUTNAME=METRO19100MM2800*Tarrant+County&county_select=yes&state_name=Texas&data=2006&statefp=48.0&fmrtype=%24fmrtype%24, accessed July 24, 2008.

19. Greater New Orleans Community Data Center, "Fair Market Rent Report: 2005–2007."

20. Hammer, "Tenants in Poll Don't Want Old Units."

21. Pardee and Gotham, "HOPE VI, Section 8."

6

WHEN DEMAND EXCEEDS SUPPLY
DISASTER RESPONSE AND THE
SOUTHERN POLITICAL ECONOMY

Before Hurricane Katrina struck, the Gulf Coast states of Louisiana, Mississippi, and Alabama had among the highest levels of race, class, and gender inequality and the worst quality-of-life indicators in the nation for their poor, people of color, and women. The extreme inequality in these states reflects a Southern legacy of a government/elite/corporate alliance that promoted slavery and the plantation system; postslavery agricultural peonage; the convict lease system; emerging agribusiness; and, more recently, the nonunion, low-wage, and internationally driven industrial/retail sector.[1]

Since the political realignment of the 1980s, this alliance, which historically defined the Southern governing philosophy, came to dominate the nation as a whole. Often labeled "neoliberal," and yet fundamentally conservative, this governing philosophy calls for cutting social spending deeply, including spending on welfare programs and benefits, and selling off government assets and functions to private corporations, while reducing or eliminating regulations on profit accumulation.[2]

One outcome of the long-term, widespread application of this governing model has been rising inequality across the nation, but especially in the historically poor and racially divided South. Despite hopes that the influx of Katrina recovery money into the Gulf Coast states would improve the status of the disadvantaged and ameliorate inequalities, the emerging consensus is that the storm and the response to it simply exacerbated these preexisting social ills.[3]

This chapter presents findings from a study of Katrina evacuees' reception in Columbia and West Columbia, South Carolina. Interviews with community members, volunteers, service providers, and evacuees themselves reveal how people coming to and living in these two Southern towns—seven hundred miles away from New Orleans—responded to and made sense of the massive disaster of Hurricane Katrina and the local resettlement it pre-

LYNN WEBER

cipitated. When Katrina's evacuees came to South Carolina, they entered a state that had the same high levels of poverty and poor quality-of-life indicators as New Orleans and the Gulf Coast. But in part because South Carolina had more systematically and comprehensively embraced neoliberal governing ideas than had even other Southern states, evacuees to South Carolina negotiated post-disaster displacement in a place whose affordable housing, public transportation, and employment options are among the least available in the nation and whose social welfare policies and benefits are among the nation's most restrictive and punitive and least generous. The story of the evacuees' reception in South Carolina highlights the ways in which political, economic, and social conditions in cities and towns across the country affected their ability to respond to the crisis and the ways that the crisis itself magnified the long-term consequences of government disinvestment in such critical needs as infrastructure, social programs, and services.

I begin with a brief overview of the socioeconomic-political context of the Midlands South Carolina region, including Columbia and West Columbia, and a description of the initial reception of Katrina evacuees in September 2005. Then, after describing data collection, I analyze the reception and resettlement processes associated with housing, transportation, and social welfare benefits and the impact of these processes on the evacuees. Finally, I present evidence that the evacuees' reception in the Midlands was also shaped by, and locally understood in relation to, its history of race relations and its experience with other recent migrants to the area: Latinos, Eastern Europeans, and Somali Bantu refugees.

THE RECEIVING COMMUNITIES: COLUMBIA AND WEST COLUMBIA, SOUTH CAROLINA

The Midlands area of South Carolina is situated in the center of the state, less than two hours from both the Upstate area of Greenville and the growing suburbs of Charlotte, North Carolina, and the Low Country, including Charleston. Columbia, the capital of South Carolina, is situated in the Midlands and is the largest city in the state, with a population of approximately 123,000 within city limits and of over 700,000 for the Metropolitan Statistical Area (MSA). Major employers in the area include government, healthcare, the University of South Carolina, and the largest US Army training base in the nation, Fort Jackson.

West Columbia, a small and largely working-class town of 13,000 in adjacent Lexington County, is separated from Columbia by the Congaree River. In the early nineteenth century, West Columbia was established as a mill town that housed workers who ferried across the river to work in Columbia's textile mills, until the first bridge was built in 1827. A century of textile production in Columbia ended in 1996 with the closing of the Olympia and Granby Mills, and those sites have since been transformed into apartment complexes, grocery stores, museums, and art galleries. More recently, West Columbia has become home to Columbia's growing workforce, University of South Carolina students, and young professionals and their families because it has more affordable housing than Columbia. West Columbia and its neighboring communities of Cayce and Springdale, the West Metro Area, also host a major hospital, the regional airport, and a variety of storage and distribution facilities and employers, including United Parcel Service.

Table 6.1 presents some demographic characteristics of Columbia, West Columbia, and, where comparable data are available, New Orleans and the United States. Data on poverty and median household income for 2000 demonstrate some basic similarities among the three Southern cities. All have poverty populations ranging from 4.4 (West Columbia) to 11.3 (New Orleans) percentage points above the national median and household incomes ranging from $10,853 (Columbia) to $14,861 (New Orleans) below the national median for all groups—Blacks, Whites, and Hispanics. Hispanics in West Columbia appear to have both higher numbers in poverty and higher household incomes than Hispanics or Blacks in Columbia or New Orleans, figures that likely reflect the larger number of earners in a single household in West Columbia.

Table 6.1 also presents population change data based on local government surveys conducted in 2006.[4] The data illustrate the more rapid growth of West Columbia, increasing by 8.5 percent since 1990 while Columbia increased by only 5.5 percent. More important, in the last two decades, the population of West Columbia, as in much of the South, has undergone major transitions in race, ethnicity, and class composition—a significant increase in African Americans and in documented and undocumented Hispanics.[5] By 2004, South Carolina's Hispanic population had the fourth-fastest rate of increase in the country, and since 1990, Lexington County (including West Columbia) has consistently been among the ten South Carolina counties with the highest Hispanic population.[6]

As Table 6.1 indicates, from 1990 to 2006, the Hispanic population in West Columbia grew by over 1,000 percent, while the Hispanic population of Columbia, just across the river, grew by only 94 percent.[7] Likewise, West Columbia's African American population grew by 24.8 percent, while

Table 6.1. Demographic Characteristics of the United States, New Orleans,
West Columbia, and Columbia

	United States	New Orleans	West Columbia	Columbia
% Individuals Below Poverty, 2000				
Total	12.4	23.7	16.8	22.0
White	6.7	11.0	11.4	9.8
Black	23.5	33.8	33.0	26.1
Hispanic	22.0	21.9	32.7	13.2
Median Household Income, 2000				
Total	$41,994	$27,133	$31,000	$31,141
White	$44,687	$40,049	$34,558	$39,877
Black	$29,423	$21,461	$18,813	$21,393
Hispanic	$33,676	$28,545	$34,558	$31,079
Total Population*				
1990			12,541	116,405
2006			13,604	122,819
% Change 1990–2006			8.5	5.5
Hispanic Population				
% of Total Pop, 1990			0.6	1.8
% of Total Pop, 2006			7.3	3.5
% Change			1116.0	94.0
Black Population				
% of Total Pop, 1990			14.9	45.8
% of Total Pop, 2006			18.6	45.3
% Change, 1990–2006			24.8	−1.0
White Population				
% of Total Pop, 1990			84.1	51.8
% of Total Pop, 2006			76.1	50.0
% Change, 1990–2006			−9.5	−3.5

*Sources: U.S. Census Bureau, American Fact Finder Demographic Profile Highlights (2000): United States; Columbia, SC; West Columbia, SC; and New Orleans, LA, available at http://factfinder .census.gov, accessed January 16, 2011. Since census data are not available for West Columbia beyond 2000, 2006 population data for Columbia and West Columbia are from Central Midlands Council of Governments surveys (CMCOG 2007), available at http://www.centralmidlands.org/pdf/West_ Columbia.pdf and http://www.centralmidlands.org/pdf/Columbia.pdf, accessed January 16, 2011.

Columbia's declined by 1 percent. As the presence of people of color grew in West Columbia, the White population declined by 9.5 percent, although it still constituted three-fourths of the community. And Whites maintain strong political dominance in the city, holding seven of the eight seats on the city council, as well as the mayoral and city-administrator positions.

THE RECEPTION OF KATRINA EVACUEES

In the weeks after Katrina hit the Gulf Coast, the South Carolina Midlands became an emergency relief center for relocation efforts. Columbia received over 4,000 families, some 10,000–15,000 people, 2,053 of whom arrived on airplanes nine to ten days after the hurricane. These 2,053 evacuees were among the last to leave New Orleans. Most had spent days in shelters or on highway overpasses before the evacuation, had left their hometown involuntarily, and had no earlier connection to South Carolina.[8] For the first six months, the displaced were largely accommodated in hotels, but by the end of February 2006, all who remained had moved into rental houses and apartments or to Section 8 housing. But another year later, eighteen months after their arrival, 800 families in the Midlands area were still receiving FEMA assistance. West Columbia was the receiving site for many of the displaced both during their hotel stays and as they moved to more permanent housing arrangements.

Political leaders in South Carolina made the initial decision to receive evacuees, including the 2,053 who were airlifted out of the New Orleans area. Congressman James Clyburn (D-SC), the ranking African American and then the majority whip in the US House of Representatives, and Bob Coble, Columbia's mayor at the time, organized the local response, calling on about forty leaders from city government, social services, education, labor, the nonprofit sector, business, law, healthcare, and religion to meet and coordinate activities. The coalition of Midlands leaders and volunteers that emerged to manage the reception named itself South Carolina Cares. Dubbing the evacuees "South Carolina's guests," the coalition did its best to reflect that designation in its treatment of the "guests." The model it developed had three core elements:

- creating a one-stop point of entry/reception center—designed to address all of the guests' immediate needs, including making contact with family members, FEMA registration, healthcare, schools for the children, clothes, food, and legal advice and assistance;

- placing evacuees in hotels and apartments paid for with private funds raised by South Carolina Cares, not in shelters;
- matching hotels and individual evacuees with volunteer "hosts" to assist in the relocation.

When Gulf Coast residents began arriving, especially the airlifted group, they were disoriented and upset, having not been told where they were being taken. Many were sick and had gone days without access to food, clean water, and regular medications for chronic conditions. And all were under intense psychological strain. South Carolina Cares arranged for food to be donated and delivered to the hotels and provided shuttle buses to and from the center. The reception center operated for two months, and local agencies ran two centers for four more months. Among the people we interviewed who had worked in or had been received by South Carolina Cares, the overwhelming consensus was that the center and the initial reception were a success. People's immediate needs were met, and the evacuees were treated with dignity and respect. Research conducted during the early reception period suggested that the evacuees were largely satisfied with the social climate in the hotels and surrounding neighborhoods and with their "host" relationship, and that each of these factors had positive effects on mental health outcomes (e.g., post-traumatic stress disorder, depression, anxiety).[9]

THE STUDY

In 2007–2008, I had been involved for five years with colleagues in Women's and Gender Studies at the University of South Carolina in a multiyear, multipronged program of community-based participatory action research in West Columbia. Because many of Katrina's displaced had been "temporarily" housed in West Columbia in 2005 and still resided there and because the initial relocation and reception process locally had been largely deemed a success, I initiated a study of the local context of reception. I was particularly interested in how West Columbia residents came to view and to incorporate the displaced, and, conversely, in how Katrina's displaced experienced Columbia and West Columbia.

Three major sources of in-depth interviews inform this multimethod research project, including interviews with forty-eight Black, White, and Hispanic English-speaking and twenty-one Spanish-speaking community leaders and residents of West Columbia; twenty-three people who led and worked in the Midlands relocation efforts; and twelve evacuees residing in West Columbia. Interviews lasted between 45 and 120 minutes and were conducted between May 2007 and September 2008.[10]

WEST COLUMBIA LEADERS AND RESIDENTS

Initial interviews with forty-eight English-speaking community leaders assessed their perceptions of the displaced in their community, their level of involvement, if any, with the relocation process, and their perceptions of how new residents' decisions to remain indefinitely might affect the community. Over the summer of 2008, using a slightly modified interview schedule, team members conducted twenty-one additional interviews in Spanish with Latinos in West Columbia.

The English-speaking sample included thirty-two (67 percent) men and sixteen (33 percent) women aged twenty-six to seventy-eight, with a median age of fifty. The racial composition of the respondents was twenty-nine (60 percent) White, thirteen (27 percent) African American, three (6.25 percent) Latino, and three (6.25 percent) Mixed Race. These proportions approximate the racial composition of West Columbia (see Table 6.1). The Spanish-language interviews were with sixteen women and five men, with a median age of thirty-two. Eighteen were employed full-time in occupations including domestic, Hispanic-focused business owner or employee, landscaper, and tax preparer. As part of this project, we also gathered demographic, economic, political, and organizational data on West Columbia.

MIDLANDS RECEPTION/RELOCATION LEADERS

To explore the experiences of, reactions to, and reflections about the local reception and relocation effort, we identified people through Katrina-related public records, newspapers, and personal contacts,[11] as well as through snowball techniques. Beginning in summer 2007 and extending through spring 2008, data were collected from twenty-three people substantially involved in the relocation effort—either intensely in the early effort through volunteering or working at the reception center, hotels, hospitals, and the like or through volunteering or working for an agency or group involved over an extended time (e.g., housing authority, social services). This sample included eight men and fifteen women aged thirty-two to sixty-four, with a median age of fifty. Nineteen were White, one was Asian American, and three were African American. Although this sample is largely White, it is in line with the perceptions of reception coordinators, as well as with the actual overwhelmingly White composition of South Carolina and the Midlands government, business, and education leadership. Responder interviews focused on the roles responders and their agencies played in the emergency response and relocation effort, their assessment of the strengths and weaknesses of the response effort, and their perceptions of the displaced, their needs, and potential contributions to the community.

DISPLACED PERSONS

We identified displaced persons by visiting apartment complexes known to have housed evacuees, as well as through snowball techniques. The twelve interviews conducted included five Whites (two women and three men) and seven African Americans (two women and five men). Interviewees ranged in age from thirty-five to seventy-eight, with a median age of fifty-two. Three of the displaced were employed, four were disabled and on fixed incomes, and five were unemployed. All were among the evacuees who were airlifted out of New Orleans nine to ten days after the storm and were largely poor and low-income, unemployed, elderly, and/or disabled.

Displaced persons were asked to discuss their lives before the storm, their evacuation experience and reception in South Carolina, and their lives (e.g., family life, supports, health, employment, housing) and plans since arriving.

FINDINGS

Despite the similar and even slightly worse economic conditions in New Orleans compared to Columbia or West Columbia, Katrina's displaced came to see that the conditions of life and the resources available to them were not always better than they had been in New Orleans. In part these differences derived from the more conservative history and political climate in South Carolina. Although Columbia is a Democratic stronghold, West Columbia is in one of the most consistently Republican counties in the state. Further, South Carolina politics have been solidly dominated by Republicans since the 1960s, and the state is nationally noted as one of the most conservative states in the union. The governor's office and both branches of the legislature are controlled by conservative Republicans—a fact that has made the state a testing ground for the national Republican Party's conservative policies, policies designed to lead the nation toward their conception of free market capitalism and social conservatism.[12]

In a state that in February 2009 had the highest unemployment rate in the nation, Governor Mark Sanford, then head of the Republican Governor's Association, led the charge of Republican Southern governors to oppose President Obama's American Recovery and Reinvestment Act of 2009, better known as the stimulus bill. Twice he refused the portion of the stimulus over which he had authority, especially objecting to increases in unemployment and Medicaid benefits that the state might have to continue without federal aid two years later.[13] This stance reflected a long history in the state of enacting unusually punitive social welfare policies and diminishing social spending to support the poor and working classes, including investments in affordable housing and public transportation. Housing subsidies, food stamps, child welfare benefits—all paid less and/or had stricter eligibility requirements than in New Orleans. Public transportation, at least as necessary in South Carolina, was less available than it had been in New Orleans.

HOUSING

Well before Katrina and before the US housing/mortgage crisis officially began in 2007, local, regional, and national housing and economic policies had contributed to a serious shortage of affordable housing along the Gulf Coast and in the receiving communities across the nation.[14] For middle-class home owners displaced to South Carolina, finding temporary housing, dealing with insurance companies and the government, and deciding on their long-term housing plans were stressors that, though extreme and prolonged, were nonetheless, for most, surmountable. But the housing crisis was doubly intensified for low-income New Orleanians, especially the elderly and people with disabilities, who had rented or lived in subsidized housing.

On the one hand, New Orleans and the entire Gulf Coast placed the lowest priority on rebuilding rental housing units, fifty-two thousand of which were destroyed by the storm. By 2010, five years after Katrina, all four of the major public housing units, formerly housing five thousand residents, either had been destroyed or remained slated for destruction. In short, years after Katrina, tens of thousands of low-income displaced people still cannot return to New Orleans because there is no place to return to. Several of our respondents expressed sentiments similar to a thirty-five-year-old African American evacuee who had found part-time employment in Columbia. When asked in April 2008 if he had been back to New Orleans, he said, "I'm just waiting to see what the outcome's going to be. I wanna see how they rebuild New Orleans as far as the people. That's what I wanna see. Yeah, I'm just waiting for the rebuilding of New Orleans."

On the other hand, Columbia and West Columbia had an affordable housing crisis of their own that had been exacerbated by a 10 percent cut in Section 8 housing vouchers (339 vouchers) between 2004 and 2006, a cut attributed to funding formula flaws.[15] Further, in 2004, the West Columbia City Council blocked a developer's proposal to build a low-income apartment complex in the city. The developer and the National Association of Home Builders sued the city in 2005 on the grounds that the decision had an unfair impact on minorities, and the city paid $600,000 in 2008 to the developer to settle the suit—without a requirement that the complex be built.[16] A manager of homeless programs for the area described the housing shortage succinctly:

> [It] probably wouldn't have made any difference if they had thought about this ahead of time, but, you know, we don't have some of the resources that folks need. So the idea that you need suddenly a whole new batch of affordable housing—good luck to you. We don't have it to start with.

And a manager for the local housing authority described not only the public housing situation when the displaced arrived, but also its deterioration since:

> South Carolina Emergency Management thought we could just go and take people in, and I said, "You've got to be kidding me." I said, "You don't understand." At that time, we had about 1,700 units of housing. Maybe about 1,650 is what we had gotten down to, but we were 700 units down [from demolition/rebuilding projects in process]. We had about 5,000 on our waiting list at that time [2005], and my waiting list right now, as of January 14, 2008, just hit 10,000. So I've got about 5,000 units of housing that I can either do through the voucher or the public housing program, but a waiting list of 10,000. So it's the highest in the thirty years I've been here. It's gonna be three to four years if you apply today.

Evacuees living in public housing in New Orleans were eligible for public housing in South Carolina. But eligibility and availability are two different things. And there is the further hurdle of affordability, because many people cannot afford housing officially designated as "affordable." In 2006, for example, the fair market rent for a two-bedroom apartment in South Carolina was $615 per month. The wage necessary to afford this two-bedroom apartment was estimated to be $11.82 per hour for a person working a forty-hour week.[17] Yet with the exception of registered nurse, the eight highest-growth jobs in South Carolina that year were unlikely to provide full-time, year-round employment. And five of those eight high-growth jobs—food prep and serving workers, waiters and waitresses, janitors and cleaners, retail salespeople, office clerks—provided wages below $11.82 per hour.[18]

Beginning in fall 2005, FEMA periodically issued lists of families still eligible for housing assistance. And each time the lists came out, some families were left off even though local caseworkers and the displaced themselves knew they were still eligible. Between September 2007 and March 2008, fourteen families in Columbia were dropped, despite continued eligibility, and decided to return to New Orleans. A social service caseworker conveyed the frustration that the evacuees felt:

> Some of them got so frustrated they left and went back. Because they knew they were FEMA-eligible, but they weren't on the list . . . and I really don't blame them for leaving. Many of them paid rent [in New Orleans] anywhere from $250 . . . and the rent they're paying now is probably $600 . . . on a fixed income. You know, the question is where are you more comfortable, here or there? And it's easier to be homeless there than to be homeless here.

In September 2007, two years after their displacement, eighty families in the area were still receiving housing subsidies. After having demonstrated a continued need for housing assistance and having requalified several times, these remaining families were told that they were going to be "weaned" from subsidies over the next eighteen months. Beginning in March 2008, these families were asked to pay $50 toward the monthly rent and to increase that amount by $50 per month up to $250 or one-third of their gross monthly income. By April 2008, the rolls had been reduced from eighty to forty families. While most were still in apartments, some found individual homes to rent from landlords, one a trailer, and one a Habitat for Humanity home. Ten moved to HUD foreclosure homes, living rent-free but with the possibility of removal at any time without notice. And some, facing eviction, returned to New Orleans to uncertain employment and housing options.

All of the evacuees we interviewed were living in Section 8 apartment complexes in West Columbia at the time of the interview. And all but one were concerned about their long-term ability to afford to stay in the apartment, especially as their contribution to the rent was to increase. People with disabilities and on fixed incomes also lamented that they paid higher rents in Columbia than in New Orleans. According to one White woman respondent, even though she and her husband, both living with disabilities, liked the apartment in West Columbia, the rent was $650 a month—more than double what they had paid in New Orleans:

[W]hen I lived in New Orleans, I was paying $300 a month for a room, no stove and no icebox and no bathtub. This here is not really worth what they want for it. I'd say this here is worth like $250 or $275, that's all.

As long as the FEMA or the Katrina Disaster Housing Assistance Program (KDHAP) emergency housing programs were paying all the rent, she was satisfied. But at the time of her interview in December 2007, the "weaning" plan had already begun, and upon follow-up several months later, we were told that she and her husband had been evicted and had returned to New Orleans after housing assistance ran out.

In March 2008, three months after the initial interview, one of our research team members talked with another of our respondents at the homeless shelter in Columbia. A middle-aged White man who had had great difficulty finding employment, he was also evicted when full housing assistance ran out. In New Orleans, he had at one time worked in a laundry for a homeless shelter. He described his plight and what he saw on the horizon for the nation:

I did laundry for them people [homeless] in New Orleans. . . . I worked there in the daytime. I'd get up at 5:00, going to work 5:30, get done at 4:00. I would do the laundry for the homeless. I never thought of me being homeless, never, and yet I lost my house because the insurance company wouldn't cover it. . . . [I've] never been homeless, and it shocked me. I always had a good job, I had three jobs, and that's all gone, it wiped it all out. I believe with all this banking crap that happened, there's gonna be a lot of people out of work, a lot of people, and where are they gonna put 'em? They better build something that size six times over [referring to the size of Columbia's shelter].

TRANSPORTATION

Because West Columbia is for many people the bedroom community of Columbia's workforce, and many services used by residents of West Columbia are located in Columbia and the surrounding area, transportation is a critical need. Yet public transportation is abysmally inadequate. A United Way needs assessment in 2004, for example, cited transportation as the most significant barrier to health and human services in the Midlands.[19] In 2002, the Central Midlands Regional Transit Authority (CMRTA) was created as a public entity to manage and operate bus and paratransit services in the Midlands area. At the time it was created, projections were that it would not be fiscally solvent after 2009 without significant infusions of funds from local governments of Richland County, including Columbia, and the West Metro Area.[20]

In 2006, facing insolvency and drastic cuts in services, the CMRTA began petitioning city and county governments in Columbia, Richland County, and the West Metro Area for a dedicated source of funding from each municipality. By 2008, the three Lexington municipalities had still earmarked no funds for the Authority and had cut multiple routes over the years. West Columbia's bus service included only two early morning and two rush hour evening routes, placing a special burden on people with disabilities, the elderly on fixed incomes, and even women escaping domestic violence, who most need access to daycare and transportation. The reduction in bus routes brought low ridership, since the few routes remaining were simply not workable for those who most needed them. West Columbia's mayor and city council cited the low ridership as evidence that the service is "not needed" and as justification for continuing to opt out of CMRTA support.[21]

For Katrina's displaced who owned no car and were living and/or seeking employment in West Columbia, transportation posed major problems. When asked how her daily routine had changed since coming to West Columbia, a middle-aged woman with disabilities described her lack of familiarity with the area and the transportation obstacles confronting her:

> Oh, it changed a lot 'cause when I was in New Orleans, I could get out, you know, I know New Orleans like I know the back of my hand. Here I don't unless I got a way to get around, and that I don't have. Unless I pay five dollars for a cab—five dollars I don't have all the time. See, some people can get a ride for nothing. I can't unless I come up with some money . . . and I can't afford it.

Others echoed her frustration: "We don't have no transportation." "I travel much further to go to work." "Here it's too hard to find a job 'cause the stores and everything are two miles away." "Everything is spread out, and the bus service sucks."

Service providers in the Midlands heard that story repeated many times over. One provider described the biggest challenge facing the displaced in the area as "public transportation . . . everything is so spread out. We're not a major city. We're a large town in a rural state. And we don't have—get on the bus for seventy-five cents and go everywhere you need to go." Another service provider, working in the housing authority, said:

That was the biggest complaint that we had from the clients in that they were so used to the New Orleans transportation system that coming here was an absolute nightmare. They couldn't believe that there were so many areas that they had no transportation to get to. You'd go and find a place to live, but . . . you'd be stranded out there. . . .

We had one client one night who was staying in a hotel out by the airport [West Metro Area]. He was a computer programmer. He got a job with Blue Cross/Blue Shield. . . . Of course, that's twenty-five miles or twenty miles or whatever, which required two different bus transfers. . . . So evidently, he got off on Two Notch Road at the wrong bus stop and had no idea where he was—had nobody he knew he could even call. . . . It was like in October or November, and it was cold, and a policeman finally stopped and said, "Where are you?" He had that nervous breakdown kind of . . . all of a sudden it just came crashing in on him.

The transportation problems for evacuees were seen as so extreme that one evacuee, who had a car and a job, has been fighting local authorities to increase bus service to the West Metro area:

I'm trying to help to fight for the bus line to get back here. . . . There is no buses back here at all for these poor people. And how do you take a bus off a line that goes to a hospital? So they got two buses come back here twice a day, early in the morning and then from four to seven at night. So that's what? That's two trips per bus.

A self-described "old rebel" who began his commitment to community activism in the civil rights movement of the 1960s, he earned the title of "Mayor," when he and other evacuees were living for months in hotels, because of the way that he advocated for them and with them. He has been particularly adamant about access for people with disabilities, some of whom miss work because there are too many wheelchair riders for the spaces on the bus and the routes run too infrequently.

The lack of public transportation has drastically changed the lives of people with disabilities who have chronic conditions requiring regular visits for medical care. One evacuee in the study needed dialysis three times a week in a place that could not be reached by bus from his home, requiring a fifty-dollar cab ride. Missing treatments because of the lack of transportation, he was forced to visit the emergency room several times. An elderly African American couple, both living with disabilities, described becoming very isolated and depressed. They repeatedly said that the hardest thing for them about living in Columbia was "getting around. We can't get around." They described their typical days as sitting in the apartment. They could not afford to return to New Orleans, but wondered what would happen when the rent subsidies ran out.

The lack of public transportation made finding employment especially difficult for low-income displaced people. For single mothers, the lack of affordable and accessible childcare exacerbated the problem of employment. In New Orleans, those who lived in particular communities for years had many more options for accessing childcare. One caseworker described the difficulties of one of her clients, difficulties that she said were characteristic of several of her clients:

> This woman lives in an apartment complex, and behind her complex, she can literally walk her kids to daycare, and she works at a hotel that is within walking distance. She has a neighbor who helps her watch her kids when she has to work late. But the cost of her childcare was just . . . I don't know what she's gonna do. . . . Her income doesn't cover her living expenses for herself and her four-year-old daughter. She already works full-time and, I know, overtime when she can.

If the woman moves closer to less expensive childcare, transportation to her job becomes an issue. Further, no aid is available from any source to address clients' needs for transportation to employment.

SOCIAL WELFARE/SOCIAL SAFETY NET

Since all Deep South states share a variety of population indicators—high poverty, low socioeconomic status, poor health—it was reasonable for evacuees who were welfare recipients in New Orleans to expect that they would receive similar benefits when they applied in South Carolina. What they realized, however, was that in many ways South Carolina—in part because of its extremely conservative, neoliberal economic and social policies—is much more restrictive than New Orleans. A recent study of public assistance in South Carolina summarized the state's harsh position on welfare:

> South Carolina's Family Independence Program [FIP—i.e., its TANF program] is one of the strictest, least generous, and most work-oriented welfare programs in the country. While most states have adopted the federal five-year time limit on assistance, South Carolina imposes time limits of

24 months of participation in a ten-year period and five years in a lifetime. . . . After the fourth month of employment, only the first $100 in monthly earnings is disregarded; beyond that, benefits are reduced by 32.4 cents for each additional dollar. The meager benefits levels, low disregard, and high reduction rate mean that families lose their eligibility for cash assistance after earning just a small amount of money.[22]

In 2005, the maximum monthly benefit for a family of three with no other income was $241 per month. FIP benefits in South Carolina are so low that a family with full benefits and no other income qualifies for the maximum food stamp allotment—$349 for a family of three.[23] In 2003, a family of three receiving only FIP and food stamps was at 27.8 percent of the federal poverty level. No child support is provided for FIP recipients, and benefits are disallowed for children conceived while a parent receives FIP. It is no surprise that South Carolina ranks fiftieth in per capita child welfare expenditures per month and forty-sixth in overall child welfare in the United States.[24]

In part because of the confluence of limited funding, strict qualification criteria, and a high poverty population, there were already long waiting lists to obtain not only subsidized housing but also welfare benefits in South Carolina. "The Mayor," who had been active in advocating for mass transit, recounted problems in his encounters with others who resented the Katrina evacuees' preferential treatment in welfare services—even if the services were to be used for only a short time:

A lot of people here was upset with us because they felt that we were getting treated, getting treatments that they should've gotten. . . . like far as for housing and stuff like this. Far as for food stamps, some of these people had been on the list for months and months and months and years and years.

Having to requalify without documentation and personal records, and doing so in a state that provided less support, meant that many evacuees on public assistance had different and much more difficult experiences than in New Orleans. One woman with a disability compared her experiences:

I'm having problems about my food stamps, you know. . . . And then sometimes I have it hard paying my utilities because I have so many bills to pay. This month paying all my bills doing everything, I had seventy dollars left to go a whole month on. I cannot go on just seventy dollars. I need help with that. I've called these organizations, a lot of them say we don't have the funds for this, we don't have the funds for that, but I'm trying to do the best I can, you know. So I'm trying to get somebody to help me with my utility bill . . .

Back in New Orleans I was getting the same thing on SSI [Supplemental Security Income] that I'm getting now, but I was getting more food stamps, see, and I'm not getting it here. . . . I feel if we're disabled, why don't you pay our utility bills for us because you know we can't do it out of that small little check and try to pay rent too. We can't do it.

In a joint interview, two social service case managers who worked with evacuees expressed shock at how much assistance some of the evacuees had been receiving in New Orleans. These caseworkers' comments illustrate the personal responsibility/self-sufficiency, welfare-to-work orientation that guides the state's programs:

South Carolina is not so forthcoming with saying, "Here's your welfare check. Here's your food stamps." I mean we had a lot of people who received assistance in New Orleans and were not able to get it here because they didn't meet the criteria under South Carolina's laws.

They received a ridiculous amount of money in food stamps, and then they come here and there's—the criteria is very different . . . and it was like, "Okay," and . . . I mean, I'm looking at them thinking, "What prevents you, really, from getting a job?"

A COMMUNITY IN TRANSITION

Besides negotiating difficulties in the housing, transportation/spatial location, and social services contexts, evacuees to West Columbia entered a community undergoing significant change in its racial and ethnic makeup—rapid growth of the Latino, mostly Mexican, population and increases in the African American population and in young White and Black families. In our interviews with West Columbia leaders and residents, these changes were characterized as unsettling by some, a challenge by others, and a welcome addition by still others.

When local communities are asked to embrace newcomers, especially racial/ethnic minorities or transnational populations who are driven from their homes by disasters such as weather, war, economic crisis, and political repression, the displaced people enter an environment that is already shaped by the community's perceptions of the previous migrants to the area. Despite the fact that Katrina's displaced in West Columbia were almost solely Black and White United States citizens, over one-third of West Columbia's leaders framed their perceptions of Katrina evacuees in the context of recent working-class and low-income migrants from Mexico, Central American countries, Russia, and Somalia. And in many of their comments, these leaders made specific connections between the ability and desire of West Columbia to incorporate new migrants and the perception of strains on an already stressed social infrastructure. In the words of a White woman adult education teacher:

> I think people get along fairly well, but I think there's a clearer line between African Americans and Whites. . . . Some of the older community are very much not liking the growth of the Hispanic population. . . . I think, again, the older population is resentful for maybe the shift in the population and perceived problems the shift has brought, and they [Hispanics] have brought shifts, and they've brought a need for infrastructure in the sense of federal housing, more use of the hospital system, more department of social services—and those entities promptly have been stretched or challenged with the movement of the population. . . . All in all, the shift will help; it'll help the community grow—and change isn't bad. . . . But it does tax your infrastructure if it's not prepared to handle it.

Others said that Hispanics were not accepted as they "should be" by others and that they are struggling in West Columbia. But the West Columbia natives also put these struggles in a national context, arguing that the issue isn't just a local one. Much like many cities around the globe, West Columbia is experiencing a transnational migratory stream that is affecting the local environment in many ways. As an extension agent, who was herself mixed-race, described it:

> I'll tell you who exactly is working in the West Columbia Wal-Mart are Russian immigrants. . . . They do all the cleaning and the maintenance. They come in in crews. So there's a strong Russian population in West Columbia. I don't know where they're living. I wasn't aware of that at all. He [my husband, who manages a Wal-Mart] said they did speak English . . . but they would spend the night at Wal-Mart cleaning . . . you know, buffering the floors . . . because you don't have to be able to speak English to buffer floors. So that's definitely a competition for the Hispanic market and anybody that's looking for a minimum-wage job.

Few people know of the existence of Russian immigrants in West Columbia, but most people are aware—because their relocation to South Carolina received so much attention, especially in the press—that 125 Somali Bantu families were resettled in West Columbia and its neighboring communities in 2004.[25] Lutheran Family Services had agreed to resettle 125 Bantu families as part of a US State Department plan to accept 13,000 political refugees from Somalia. Although the number of people was relatively small, some, including a schoolteacher and the city manager, feared that the Somalis would not have the resources to manage. And West Columbia and Cayce were among the few cities in the country (including Holyoke, Massachusetts) actually opposed to their resettlement.[26]

This resistance received media attention and is still highly visible in the minds of leaders in West Columbia, most of whom were not involved in the resistance but who saw the negative publicity as a problem. So when we asked about how the community leaders felt Katrina's displaced would be received in West Columbia, over one-third of the leaders spontaneously made a comparison to either the Bantu or to the much larger Hispanic migration or to both. For example, in the words of a White male Community Health Center executive:

> There was a lot of concern in the Cayce and the West Columbia community about having these Somali Bantu families come into their community and the impact it would have upon their community. And we knew this was a very small group of people and that there were thousands of Hispanics in an underground way just kind of melded into the community. We're saying you kind of—what is it? Strained to the gnat and swallowed the camel, you know. It was—the community wasn't really in touch with what was going on.
>
> Well, these people were literally sort of persecuted in their African nation. They were literally banned from the country, and they have no country, they have no home, they have nothing to cling to. And I think . . . many Bantu people came in, but there was lots of doors closed everywhere because of their huge needs, and they were welcomed into West Columbia, lived close by here in the apartments, and everyone wasn't on board by any means, but those who were, were really into and very receptive to this refugee resettlement idea.

When we asked about the challenges posed if Katrina's displaced chose to remain permanently in West Columbia, comments such as this, which came from a White male director of a school program, were common:

We made it through the Bantu and life went on, so same here. . . . The challenge is that we already have a plate full of those with social services needs, and I'm sure some people say, well, why do I want to bring more of that into my area? What for? We have enough problems.

While the receiving community's leaders pondered the strain on social services, the evacuees who lived in West Columbia were in daily contact with Latino migrants, many of whom lived in the same apartment complexes as the evacuees in our study. Yet the contact did not lead to mutual understanding and support—in large part because language and cultural barriers made communication impossible. Only one of the twenty-one Latinos we interviewed had any knowledge of or contact with Katrina's displaced, and he cleaned in a hotel where many evacuees had once resided.

Even in the same apartment complex, the isolation felt by Katrina's evacuees seemed to be heightened by the presence of Latinos, whom they could not understand. One African American couple, for example, lamenting their isolation from the familiar people and places of home, discussed how they felt "cut off" in West Columbia and how the presence of Hispanics in the apartment complex heightened that sense. When asked about any friends they had made, the husband said they hadn't made any: "Most people around here is Spanish. They say 'Hey' and move on." And a similar response came from a White male evacuee: "Making friends? I don't know nobody around here. . . . They're all Mexican."

CONCLUSIONS

Since the political realignment of the 1980s, the South has led the nation in implementing the conservative economic and social policies that now largely structure the conditions of life across much of the United States. Southern states have vigorously embraced these policies: privatization/outsourcing of government functions, reduced taxes, especially on the wealthy, deregulation of private business, and deep cuts in social spending. But South Carolina has been more successful than even most Southern states in reducing taxes, limiting infrastructural supports for public life, and severely restricting and dismantling social welfare programs. Consequently, the most vulnerable of Katrina's displaced found West Columbia and Columbia, South Carolina, despite some racial and cultural similarities to their home, to be a particularly harsh environment:

- Housing: A shortage of affordable housing was exacerbated by the loss of Section 8 vouchers, public housing that was demolished before new housing was built, and West Columbia's refusal to allow a Section 8 apartment complex to be built.
- Transportation: The grossly inadequate, underfunded public transportation system has never met the needs of the community, especially of West Columbia, with its rapidly growing population.
- Welfare system: In addition to its draconian eligibility requirements, South Carolina's support levels are so low that a family of three receiving full FIP and the maximum food stamp allowance is at only one-fourth of the federally defined poverty level.
- Intergroup relations: The movement of the labor force across national borders has meant that what was a Black/White divide in South Carolina only twenty-five years ago is now a multinational, multicultural complex of groups and families competing for scarce resources.

In expressing their concern about potential strains on the infrastructure and social services, many West Columbia natives framed their response to the Katrina evacuees in the context of the Somali refugees and Hispanic immigrants settled there. And in addition to experiencing difficulties in making a life for themselves in West Columbia, the evacuees met resentment from some of the local poor, whose wait for housing and social services was extended because the evacuees received priority.

In part because they recognized that the federal government was failing in its response to Katrina, people in the South Carolina Midlands worked hard to provide a welcome for their "guests." Hundreds of people volunteered, and local leadership committed not just to receive the displaced people of Katrina, but to do so with respect—to contradict the disrespect and inhumane response of the federal and state governments. But because volunteer work cannot be sustained for extended periods, the basic needs of healthy and thriving communities—jobs, healthcare, housing, transportation, and so on—cannot adequately be met without reliable, substantive, and ongoing government engagement.

The harshness of the economic and social policies embraced by South Carolina's political leadership was made visible by the most destitute of Katrina's survivors displaced into the Midlands' social, economic, and political landscape. The magnifying glass that the evacuees placed on the Midlands also revealed already existing community needs. When hotel rooms, meals, and clothes were made available to the displaced, people already homeless in Columbia showed up too. The heightened awareness of existing problems and the success of South Carolina Cares led a coalition of business leaders and homeless advocates to propose a $15 million center for the city's approximately 1,600 homeless that is modeled on the Katrina reception center. Although they faced substantial political opposition—particularly around the proposed location—the new, multiservice Transition Center opened in 2011.[27]

The experiences of Katrina's displaced in South Carolina highlight the ways in which conservative social and economic policies have rendered our cities incapable of dealing with the ongoing needs of poor populations and have weakened our infrastructure and supports for family life. Because they are unequipped to deal with their own poor, our communities are not equipped to deal with displaced disaster survivors for an extended time. Despite the phenomenal outflow of generosity, time, and expertise from individuals to international aid groups, Katrina is still a disaster—for both the poor still in New Orleans and the poor in the Katrina diaspora.

ACKNOWLEDGMENTS

In addition to recognizing the important and multifaceted assistance of the SSRC Research Network in providing feedback at all phases of this project, I wish to thank the graduate assistants who worked tirelessly on these research projects. For conducting interviews, Steve Hardin, David Asiamah, Manju Tanwar; for coding, data analysis, and other research, Jenny Castellow, Beth Fadeley, Uma Kandasamy, Christina Griffin, Joanne Rinaldi Stevenson. Finally, I greatly appreciate feedback on the manuscript from the Women's and Gender Studies core faculty reading group and especially from DeAnne Messias, who gave me advice throughout the process.

This research was partially supported by the National Science Foundation under Grant CMMI-0623991. Any opinions, findings, and conclusions or recommendations expressed in this material are those of the authors and do not necessarily reflect the views of the National Science Foundation.

NOTES

1. V. O. Key, Jr., *Southern Politics in State and Nation* (New York: A. A. Knopf, 1949); Joel Williamson, *The Crucible of Race: Black and White Race Relations in the American South* (Oxford: Oxford University Press, 1984); Michael Goldfield, *The Color of Politics: Race and the Mainsprings of American Politics* (New York: New Press, 1997); Jeffrey S. Lowe and Todd C. Shaw, "After Katrina: Racial Regimes and

Human Development Barriers in the Gulf Coast Region," *American Quarterly* 61, no. 3 (2009): 803–827.

2. Lowe and Shaw, "After Katrina"; Naomi Klein, *The Shock Doctrine: The Rise of Disaster Capitalism* (New York: Metropolitan Books, 2007).

3. Lowe and Shaw, "After Katrina"; Klein, *The Shock Doctrine*; Lynn Weber, "Intersectionality, Gender, and Health: What Katrina Reveals," paper presented at Social Science & Medicine, Gender & Health Special Issue Workshop: Relational, Biosocial, and Intersectional Approaches, Mailman School of Public Health, Columbia University, New York, 2010; Mark M. Smith, *Camille, 1969: Histories of a Hurricane* (Athens: University of Georgia Press, 2011).

4. Central Midlands Council of Governments, *Region Report: West Metro Area* 3, no. 1 (2006), http://www.centralmidlands.org/pdf/caycewcola06.pdf, accessed February 17, 2011.

5. Center for Research on Women, *Across Races & Nations: Building New Communities in the U.S. South* (Memphis, TN: University of Memphis, 2006); State of South Carolina Commission for Minority Affairs, "South Carolina Hispanic/Latino Report" (Columbia: South Carolina Commission on Minority Affairs, 2006), http://www.state.sc.us/cma/data/FINDINGS%20REPORT2006.pdf, accessed February 21, 2011; Heather A. Smith and Owen J. Furuseth, *Latinos in the New South: Transformations of Place* (Burlington, VT: Ashgate, 2006).

6. Brenda Vander Mey and Ashley W. Harris, "Latino Populations in South Carolina, 1990–2002," working paper (Clemson, SC: Department of Sociology, Clemson University, 2004).

7. For a variety of reasons, the Hispanic population is undercounted by census enumerators. The most common factors associated with the undercount of Hispanics in the census include complex household makeup or cultural differences in defining households, individual/family mobility, legal (authorized versus unauthorized) status, fear or distrust of government, and language barriers. See Elaine Lacy, "Mexican Immigrants in South Carolina: A Profile" (Columbia: University of South Carolina, 2007).

8. Bret Kloos, Kater Flory, Benjamin L. Hankin, Catherine A. Cheely, and Michelle Segal, "Investigating the Roles of Neighborhood Environments and Housing–based Social Support in the Relocation of Persons Made Homeless by Hurricane Katrina," *Journal of Prevention and Intervention in the Community* 37, no. 2 (2009): 143–154.

9. Ibid.

10. Trained graduate-student research assistants and I conducted the interviews, and participants provided informed consent beforehand. All interviews were audiotaped, professionally transcribed, and coded for analysis.

11. Because I had been director of the Women's Studies Program at the University of South Carolina for the nine years before Katrina and because the campus is located adjacent to the state capitol grounds, I had had many opportunities to work with activists, nonprofits, and government leaders both in the state and the city on

critical issues related to women and girls. So I knew several of the people who played key roles in the relocation effort. For example, the director of South Carolina Cares, the organization established to manage the relocation, had been a member of the Women's Studies Community Advisory Board for three years, and his wife was the state school superintendent.

12. Laura R. Woliver, "Abortion Conflicts, City Governments and Culture Wars: Continually Negotiating Coexistence in South Carolina," in *Culture Wars and Local Politics*, ed. E. Sharpe (Lawrence: University of Kansas Press, 1999), pp. 21–42; Laura R. Woliver, *The Political Geographies of Pregnancy* (Urbana: University of Illinois Press, 2002).

13. Richard Fausset, "South Carolina's Governor May Turn Down Stimulus Money," *Los Angeles Times*, February 21, 2009; Editorial, "Courting Disaster in South Carolina," *New York Times*, March 30, 2009.

14. Sheila Crowley, "Where Is Home? Housing for Low-Income People after the 2005 Hurricanes," in *There Is No Such Thing as a Natural Disaster: Race, Class, and Hurricane Katrina*, ed. C. Hartman and G. D. Squires (New York: Routledge, 2006), pp. 121–166.

15. Center on Budget and Policy Priorities, *Housing Vouchers Funded in South Carolina under Pending Proposals*, November 1, 2006, http://www.cbpp.org/files/11-1-06hous-sc.pdf, accessed February 17, 2011.

16. John O'Connor, "West Columbia Accused of Blocking Apartments," *The State*, February 18, 2005; Tim Flach, "West Columbia Paying Out $600,000," *The State*, March 4, 2008; Tim Flach, "Builders Urge More Attention to Low-Income Homes," *The State*, March 13, 2008.

17. Child Welfare Leagues of America, "South Carolina's Children 2008," http://www.cwla.org/advocacy/statefactsheets/2008/southcarolina.htm, accessed February 17, 2011.

18. South Carolina Department of Commerce, "High-Growth Jobs in South Carolina: Labor Market Information," July 2008, http://www.workforcesouthcarolina.com/media/3163/highgrowthjobs072008.pdf, accessed February 21, 2011.

19. United Way of the Midlands, *Facing Facts: United Way of the Midlands Update for 2004: A Study of Issues That Shape Our Region* (Columbia, SC: United Way of the Midlands, 2004).

20. Shalama Jackson, "Lexington County—Public Transportation Dilemma— Bus Service Cuts Thwart Disabled," *The State*, February 2, 2007; Shalama Jackson, "Funding the Transit System: Low Ridership Might End Services—Lexington County," *The State*, June 5, 2007.

21. Jackson, "Lexington County—Public Transportation Dilemma"; Jackson, "Funding the Transit System."

22. David C. Ribar, Marilyn Edelhoch, and Qiduan Liu, *South Carolina Food Stamp and Well-Being Study: Transitions in Food Stamp and TANF Participation and Employment among Families with Children* (United States Department of Agriculture, April 2006), http://hdl.handle.net/10113/32788, accessed February 16, 2011.

23. Ibid.

24. Child Welfare Leagues of America, "South Carolina's Children 2008."

25. Jenny Burns, "No Pressure: Bible Belt Families Welcome Muslim Refugees, *The State*, March 12, 2004; Joy Woodson, "Open Arms Missing to Greet Refugees: Sponsors Lacking as Charities Welcome Persecuted People to New Lives in Columbia," *The State*, August 24, 2006; Joy Woodson, "Yesterday's Refugee, Tomorrow's Architect," *The State*, April 20, 2007.

26. "Federal Agency Calls Off Bantu Resettlement in Cayce," *The State*, October 9, 2003; "U.S. City Refuses to Admit Somali Bantu Refugees," *The State*, October 13, 2003.

27. Adam Beam, "Group Plans 15 Million Dollar Homeless Center," *The State*, June 26, 2008; Adam Beam, "Neighbors to Fight Homeless Shelter," *The State*, October 5, 2008.

7

KATRINA EVACUEE RECEPTION IN RURAL EAST TEXAS
RETHINKING DISASTER "RECOVERY"

There was an outpouring of love and graciousness: Anything
these people needed, all we had to do was ask. I think that's why they
loved Huntsville, Texas, so much. [The] outpouring of sharing and
caring they got, they'd never seen that in Louisiana.

LOCAL FIRST RESPONDER

People fleeing Katrina began to arrive in Huntsville as soon as the main shelter opened on August 30, 2005. This shelter, which is actually the Family Life Center of the First Baptist Church of Huntsville, is located two blocks from the town square, featuring the county courthouse surrounded by businesses and restaurants. Across the street from the Center is the First Baptist Church, one of the largest churches in the city at the time. Both are in the shadow of the Texas Department of Criminal Justice's Walls Unit. The Sam Houston State University campus is four blocks away.

The shelter is a two-story brick building with meeting rooms, a gymnasium (basketball court and indoor track), a racquetball court, kitchen, bathrooms, formal parlor, and a youth recreation room with computers and musical instruments. It is a well-appointed, clean, well-equipped private church facility normally used for youth group activities, vacation Bible school, Bible study meetings, and other social events hosted by the church.

Displaced people came in shifts and stayed in hotels, motels, and private residences, as well as shelters. At first people trickled in, arriving in private vehicles with some supplies. These 70 or so people were able to get themselves out of harm's way. Most of the evacuees in this first wave did not stay long. As news spread about conditions in the New Orleans Superdome and the need to relocate survivors to other locations, the first group of evacuees moved out of the main shelter either to local hotel rooms or other locations altogether. A middle-aged employee of the church who acted as the coordi-

LEE M. MILLER

nator of the main shelter—I will call her Sarah here—reported that those in this first wave of displaced did not want to remain in a shelter slated to receive such desperate people.

In the dark, early morning hours of September 3, 2005, five yellow school buses pulled into the parking lot of the Family Life Center. Aboard were 340 people who had been evacuated from the Superdome and routed to Houston's Astrodome and Reliant Center. However, upon arrival in Houston, the buses were turned away and encouraged to continue their journey to Huntsville. Sarah told the story of how the main group of evacuees—exhausted, hungry, confused, and traumatized—was greeted by the pastor of the church. As he boarded each bus, his message was one of welcome and hope: "You've been through hell. Welcome to heaven." Tossed about by the winds and waters of Katrina, they were finally offered the comfort of clean beds, bathrooms, food, and safety. As the evacuees disembarked, they were also met by representatives of local law enforcement and given the opportunity to surrender anything prohibited in the shelters. The combined message was immediate and clear: We are here to help; you will be well taken care of; but there are rules and they will be enforced.

Since people were housed in many locations and stayed different lengths of time, it is hard to know with any certainty how many people stopped in Huntsville as a result of the storm. Estimates ranged from five to seven hundred, with the largest, most visible group being the over three hundred people who stayed in the main shelter.

To fully understand the experiences of evacuees, it is critical to first understand the social, cultural, and economic character of the host environment and the reception it offers. Is the place similar to their home or very different? How do the hosts feel about the new arrivals? Will they be treated well or with suspicion? Will they be ignored? Is the community willing to encourage them to stay? Does it offer jobs, schools, housing, healthcare, and faith-based charitable organizations? All of these factors influence the reception evacuees receive and their decisions about what to do next— stay in one host community, move to another, or return home.

To describe the evacuees' arrival and the local area's reaction, I draw on the voices of the people responsible for managing one East Texas community's response to Katrina evacuees. Through their narratives, we gain insight into how the community viewed the evacuees and how attitudes and community involvement in the reception and relocation process changed over time. The perceptions of emergency response managers about Huntsville itself and about the evacuees critically affected how the community, in turn, came to view the newcomers. This change happened in phases. The first lasted about two weeks, the second about a week, and the third began about three weeks after the shelters opened and lasted about six months. The fourth phase is harder to measure, since, regarding those evacuees who cannot return home and have no real stability, it is still ongoing. Below I describe how key responders' perceptions of the evacuees gradually shifted from generous sympathy to suspicion and even rejection, shaping the experience of evacuees and the wider community's response to them.

THE STUDY

At the time of the storm, I was living in Huntsville, Texas, the town I grew up in, and teaching at Sam Houston State University. When Hurricane Katrina devastated New Orleans, national media covered the event extensively, and Huntsville's newspaper and radio station did so as well. As I moved through my daily life, the reactions that I encountered to the news included both shock and compassion. When I discussed Katrina with relatives, friends, or neighbors, everyone mentioned the desire to help in some way. Yet, uncertainty about *how* best to help left us frustrated. News traveled quickly when evacuees began to arrive in Huntsville several days after the storm. Radio announcements, newspaper articles, and church phone trees called for volunteers and donations. The response was overwhelming. In fact, the large numbers of volunteers and donations created unforeseen organizational strains.[1]

By the time I arrived at the shelter with my load of pillows, bleach, paper towels, batteries, and toiletries, there was no room to store them. I was asked to keep them until further notice. The same was true for volunteering. Despite attempts to help, I was turned away because so many people had already arrived. The church I attend was one of a team of churches that took turns providing meals to evacuees in hotels. My rush to the sign-up sheet after the Sunday morning service paid off, and I was able to get my name in to donate, but the line was long and some were turned away there, too. I was fascinated by the community's response and began to study it.

From October 2005 through March 2006, I conducted an ethnographic study of the community's response to, and reception of, the evacuees who arrived in Huntsville. The research included twenty-four in-depth interviews with community responders, surveys of twenty-one emergency response managers, and reviews of secondary sources, including newspapers and county, regional, and state emergency management plans and reports. Conversations with responders ranged from informal discussions with volunteers to lengthy formal interviews with emergency response coordinators and local officials. Questions focused on interviewees' roles in hosting people displaced by Hurricane Katrina, their evaluations of the local response, and their perceptions of the evacuees. Since the community is small and many of the research participants will be easy to identify locally, descriptions of respondents are intentionally general and all names are pseudonyms. Although many people provided helpful information concerning the process of hosting the displaced from New Orleans, I have selected several people who were able to eloquently express their perspectives to represent this community's experience of hosting evacuees from Hurricane Katrina.

For a broader picture of how key emergency responders connect to the community, I surveyed twenty-one key responders in the spring of 2006 to understand their feelings about the community and their social positions in it. (Two people participated in both the interviews and the survey.) The survey included questions about the individual's length of residence, type of community involvement and connections, and employment information. Family and household structure and general attitudes about the community were topics included as well. The sample included first responders (police, firefighters, and paramedics), county and city personnel, and social service providers.

THE RECEIVING COMMUNITY

Portes and Rumbaut use the expression "context of reception" to refer to the environment in which migrants "land."[2] What was that context in the case of Huntsville, Texas, and how did the reception unfold over time?

Huntsville is the county seat of Walker County. The population of the county in 2005 was 62,735 (64 percent urban, 36 percent rural).[3] According to the 2000 census, the city of Huntsville registered 35,078 residents.[4] However, these census data do not provide an accurate picture of the true population of Huntsville, because it is inflated by the presence of the Texas Department of Criminal Justice and the university. There are five prison units within the city limits and four others within a twenty-five-mile radius.[5] The institutional population of the correctional facilities within the city limits is approximately 9,000.[6] If this population is excluded, the number of community residents shrinks to 26,078. Sam Houston State University's student population of nearly 16,500 is also a significant presence in the community, but dormitory residents are not reflected in census population counts.

To evacuees from New Orleans, the people of Huntsville must have seemed very different: much less urban, whiter, somewhat wealthier, more likely to work in government jobs, and far more conservative both socially and politically. In 2005, Orleans Parish had a population of over 450,000.[7] The percentage of people living in poverty was 24.5 percent. Median household income in 2005 was $30,711. Non-Hispanic Whites accounted for 27 percent of the population, Blacks 67 percent, and Hispanics 3.1 percent. Workers were employed mostly in private wage/salaried jobs (74 percent).[8] Walker County, on the other hand, was 60 percent non-Hispanic White, 23.9 percent African American, and 14.1 percent Hispanic in 2005.[9]

Although the racial composition of the two locations was almost reversed, there were class similarities, with 21 percent of the Walker County population living below poverty.[10] So only a portion of the Huntsville community shared race and economic status with the evacuees, who were overwhelmingly low-income minority group members. Portes and Rumbaut argue that in areas where immigrants have been present long enough and are represented at all socioeconomic levels, the integration of new arrivals of the same ethnicity is facilitated.[11] However, despite the historical presence of African Americans in Huntsville, there are relatively few minority-owned businesses, and the inroads into the middle and upper-middle classes have been few. Therefore, Katrina evacuees in Huntsville did not benefit from the dynamics enjoyed by new immigrants when well-established immigrant communities are present.

Like most small cities and towns in the United States, Huntsville, located in the piney woods of East Texas, does not have city buses or other forms of public transportation. Walking is difficult, as there are few sidewalks, and hills make bicycle riding strenuous. The hot temperatures and high humidity in the summer can also make outdoor activities unpleasant. Before the arrival of Katrina evacuees, few taxicabs were available for hire. Retail and service establishments are dispersed over a relatively wide area, with the large, low-price, big-box stores located across the interstate highway from residential areas. The physical layout of the city is therefore not conducive to living without a car. In 2000, 94 percent of Walker County residents reported using a motor vehicle, either alone or carpooling, to go to work.[12]

Texas is not known for generous social programs. State and federal social services are habitually stretched especially thin in this small rural city. People in need of assistance in the local community therefore rely on the network of nonprofit and faith-based organizations to fill the gaps between government assistance and local needs.

Overall, local responders and volunteers looked different from the evacuees in the shelter in some important ways. While most of the Katrina evacuees in the second wave, from the Superdome, were Black, most of the volunteers and responders were White. Most first responders, as is typically the case, were men, while the majority of evacuees in the shelter were women and children. The majority of volunteers were women, although both men and women were involved with the process at all levels. However, in 2005 there were perhaps more women directly involved in emergency management in this county than is historically the case.[13] In Huntsville in 2005, women occupied important positions, including chief of police, city representative to the Emergency Operations Center, president of the Chamber of Commerce, and the primary dispatcher at the sheriff's office communications center. Furthermore, women held leadership positions in most local nonprofits. Women, therefore, were key players in managing resources and sheltering activities. Volunteers in the shelters came largely from the faith-based community and were organized into teams through local churches. In terms of socioeconomic status, most responders and volunteers were working, middle, or upper-middle class, whereas most of the shelter evacuees were perceived as government-supported "poor people."

City and county officials were ready to host evacuees. Just prior to Hurricane Katrina, in June 2005, Walker County was designated as a shelter community by the Governor's Office of Emergency Management. The official policy was that the community would be ready and willing to receive evacuees in the event of a major storm affecting the Texas Gulf Coast. Training sessions were conducted that summer, and two local churches received Red Cross shelter certification, while others were undergoing the certification process. However, the state plan was based on a partnering system, with coastal areas assigned to inland evacuation jurisdictions. Huntsville was paired with, and prepared to receive evacuees from, Galveston, Texas. In the wake of Katrina, the established shelter communities were called upon by the governor of Texas to open their doors to those from New Orleans who were seeking refuge.

Local economic factors also condition how newcomers will be received and whether or not they will be integrated into the receiving community.[14] Unemployment in Walker County at the time of the arrival of the evacuees was 5.6 percent. This was slightly higher than the average unemployment rate for the state, but low-skilled and unskilled service-sector jobs were available.

In addition to its demographic composition, other less visible factors, such as how the people of a community fit together and interact with one another, also influence how they react when receiving outsiders. The people I interviewed all referred to Huntsville as a close-knit community, and they attributed the community's generosity and outpouring of assistance to that characteristic. By one estimate, at least five hundred volunteers from Huntsville participated in the relief efforts at one shelter alone.

Explanations for that extensive involvement were traced to the nature of the community itself. A representative of the local business community and longtime resident—I'll call her Mary—mentioned the "desire to keep our warm, hospitable community intact," noting that it was "about commitment to each other" rather than to the incoming group. A city representative stated that "overall, most people feel a sense of responsibility, a village mentality." Sarah, the main shelter coordinator, spoke of people volunteering in order to support the people working at the shelter and make it easier for them. She, too, attributed the warmth of Huntsville's response to the web of connections people weave while living together in a small community over a long period of time.

When people move to Huntsville, they tend to stay. In a 2005 survey, 50 percent of respondents reported having lived in Huntsville for over twenty years, and in 2007 that number had increased to 55 percent. All of the Katrina responders I surveyed had lived in the area over ten years and 81 percent for over twenty. Sarah repeatedly mentioned people's overlapping connections as key to the effectiveness of the response effort, saying that people "came together so well because it's a small community."

Recognition of the importance of social structure and social ties to community disaster response is certainly not new to the disaster literature. Dynes and Quarantelli, for example, pointed out that when responding to an emergency, a community's "primary resource is its predisaster social organization."[15] As the emergency response managers in Huntsville talked about their experiences hosting people displaced by Hurricane Katrina, they explained that when a need surfaced someone knew a local resident who could furnish the item or service. Knowledge of local material and human resources is developed over time and through organizational interconnections. Strong attachment to community and the numerous overlapping social ties of the responders and volunteers contributed to the collective response to Katrina evacuees.[16]

CULTURE AND RECEPTION

How a community receives a group of outsiders is also influenced by local culture—values, beliefs, and customs. To deepen understanding of the cultural context Hurricane Katrina evacuees encountered, I explore several characteristics of Huntsville as a community, with a special focus on community satisfaction, religion, and self-sufficiency.

First, one factor contributing to local culture is how residents feel about living there. Individual and collective involvement in community events is presumably influenced by the level of attachment to, and satisfaction with, the community. In 2005 and 2007, surveys of residents showed that 90 percent of respondents were satisfied or very satisfied with the community. Not only did people report satisfaction, they also reported being regularly involved in community activities—76 percent of those surveyed in 2005 and 74 percent in 2007.[17] Satisfaction with and pride in community were each commonly cited by the emergency response managers when explaining why so many people volunteered and made donations to help the evacuees. The desire to keep the community strong, to preserve it, was also mentioned frequently. One businesswoman noted that people acted to "keep the community the place we know and love, but improve upon that." Volunteering and helping were seen as a continuation of community traditions that have made Huntsville a nice place to live. One experienced first responder referred to this pride of place when he commented that the evacuees "saw how Texans treated Texans and what Texans could do."

Second, Huntsville and Walker County boast numerous churches. I counted eighty in 2007.[18] An expectation in the community is that residents are Christian and belong to a local congregation. An unaffiliated new resident will typically be invited to attend Sunday services at a variety of churches. The strong presence of faith organizations formed the foundation for the community response to Katrina evacuees, since the shelters were churches. Service teams were organized through the nonshelter churches to help at the shelters. Churches also coordinated assistance to people staying in hotels and motels. A veteran law enforcement officer and emergency coordinator explained: "Faith-based organizations, you know, those people, when God touches them to do stuff, it's just unreal. They were calling us saying we can take people." Sarah mentioned that the "churches came out [and asked] what they could do to help us, fellow Christians." Gas cards, phone cards, and bus and plane tickets were all donated by members of local congregations.

Finally, the local culture of Huntsville emphasizes work, community participation, and self-sufficiency. Particularly during the third phase of sheltering, local residents began to feel that some of the evacuees' behaviors did not reflect an appropriate commitment to local values. After several months, Mary began to feel that "some people haven't done a thing for themselves since they got here." She went on to express frustration that "some still don't get it, they are just handed everything. When the money's gone, they are still waiting for the next handout." Many in the community began to feel, along with Mary, that "we are willing to do our part as long as you meet us halfway with your part."

These comments reveal a difference between the expectations of the evacuees and of their hosts. Expectations on both sides had been similar during and just after evacuation, but they soon changed.

PHASES OF COMMUNITY REACTION

The community response to the arrival of Katrina evacuees varied over time and can be divided into four principal phases. In the first phase, lasting about two weeks, the "therapeutic community" described in classic works by Fritz[19] and Barton[20] was evidenced by generosity: overwhelming offers to donate time as well as supplies, money, and services. Over time, though, volunteers became weary as it became more and more difficult to put their normal, day-to-day activities on hold. This shift occurred in about the third week. From this time, after the initial relief and appreciation for the shelter, evacuees began to realize that the shelter was really just another temporary stop on what was to be a long, difficult journey. Frustration and resentment on the part of both volunteers and evacuees characterized the following months, or the third phase. The fourth phase began about six months after the shelters opened and was the period of leaving the emergency assistance system. For many evacuees the process of resettlement has taken much longer—even years. What follows is a description of how the context of reception after Hurricane Katrina changed over time in Huntsville.

The first phase began when evacuees arrived in Huntsville, many of them with only the clothes they had on, the same clothes they had been wearing for four or five days. All had stories of extreme hardship. One family had been stranded on a bridge in New Orleans for three days with no shelter or provisions. One mother had been separated from two of her children. In the middle of the night these people were dropped off at the Huntsville shelter, after more than sixteen hours on the bus, needing food, showers, and clean clothes. With the help of the nearby prison, the shelter could process large quantities of laundry at one time and provided alternate clothing (prison issue) to wear temporarily while the Katrina survivors' clothes were cleaned.

Consensus among the interviewees was that evacuees received very special treatment in Huntsville, and far superior to the perceived conditions in Houston. Not only were basic necessities provided, but by the third day the children in the shelter were registered in local schools, and the shelter was added to the school bus route. The Texas Department of Criminal Justice held a seminar encouraging people to apply for open correctional positions. The local university donated computers to the shelter so that evacuees could register with FEMA and locate loved ones using online databases. A van sponsored by the local Chamber of Commerce transported people to Houston to reunite Huntsville evacuees with family members at the Astrodome and Reliant Center. The city government arranged for a public shuttle bus route to locations evacuees needed to frequent, such as the grocery store and the Laundromat. A retired phone company representative had three additional phones installed in the main shelter. Inmate trustees from the nearby Walls Unit cooked and helped with daily cleaning. Volunteers served food, registered people, sorted donations, procured and distributed supplies, and helped with other vital tasks. Fire department personnel parked a pump truck outside of the shelter so kids could play in the water, since city pool facilities were closed for construction.

One volunteer stated that the community's "response was really overwhelming, phenomenal, [we received] over 450 calls in three days" with offers of food, donations, services, and so on. Another said that it "amazed me that everybody was willing to do whatever you asked them to do." A third commented that "people came out of the woodwork." When asked about the motivation behind the community's generosity toward the evacuees, another volunteer explained that "We wanted to make them feel that they had come to a community that welcomed them, that would not turn their back and say take care of yourself."

Huntsville's evacuee population was not limited to the shelters. Hotels, motels, and many guest rooms in private residences were also full to capacity. A local elected official noted that not all the evacuees were in shelters and asserted that "it would be a mistake if we focused only on the people arriving by bus." He went on to say:

> The Sunday after Katrina, the family sitting in our pew was a family from St. Bernard Parish, and they had come here under their own means, but they were getting a little bit desperate. I mean, yes, they had a car. Yes, they had credit cards, but they didn't really know how much they would have to go back to.

The second phase of the sheltering experience began about two weeks after the shelters were opened and was characterized by physical exhaustion and a marked decline of the collective "high" on the parts of both the evacuees and the volunteers. Sarah offered one analysis of the unfolding situation. She said that a woman in the shelter she managed told her that she "just want[ed] to tell you the good job that you're doing and she said, you know, I just want you to know that you're doing a wonderful job and that this place is unlike any that these people have ever been to." Sarah gave some further context to this evacuee's comment:

> You know, she could see on our faces every now and then how stretched we were . . . and how we were really trying to do the best that we could, but we might not have been getting a whole lot of support, not that we needed it, but every now and then you need some, you know, encouragement.

The shift in energy and attitude of the second phase was noted by the emergency response coordinators, too. One man mentioned that volunteers were beginning to say, "Okay, I'll come in again" somewhat wearily, with hesitation. One of the most involved managers of the response effort commented that "it was hard to set boundaries," that she was receiving calls at all hours of the day and night, even on her cell phone. Another volunteer observed that the ongoing sheltering "did take a huge toll on volunteers: it was exhausting."

The third phase, which began about three weeks after the opening of the shelters, was marked by shifts in expectations and the exposure of cultural differences between volunteers and evacuees. Evacuees began to be seen as from an entirely different "culture." The interviewees who addressed these differences seemed to use the word "culture" to account for evacuee behavior that they deemed surprising or even inappropriate. Sarah noted, for example, that some of the shelter occupants complained about the food when they tired of cold cereal, asking for things like grits. She reported that they did change the menu. Other instances of evacuee behavior that responders viewed as "questionable" revolved around the accumulation of money and things—selling donated clothing to one another, returning donated merchandise to stores in exchange for cash, and using vouchers for items, like televisions, that did not qualify as necessities in the volunteers' eyes. It is not clear what "culture" means in their remarks, but it seems linked to notions of class and race. While the emergency response managers interviewed were all White and middle-class, the shelter evacuees were overwhelmingly Black and poor.

Mary described the shelter evacuees as the "last to get out of New Orleans. Some were people who didn't do a good job of taking care of themselves before the storm." Volunteers, responders, and other community members gradually began to question whether evacuees were doing enough to move out of the shelter. "You had people who did not want to leave once they were in the shelter," said one worker. She continued:

> These people had experienced real trauma but, again not to sound nega-tive, but these people were perhaps not the best organized people in the world to start with, and so you brought them here, you took care of them.

However, the issue of how to assist people without creating a lasting depen-dency arose when they stayed longer than expected and their needs did not diminish. Another local observer explained:

> Now what do you do? You can't just kick them out of the nest, but you can't just indefinitely take care of them. This proved to be an issue be-cause, once again not being derogatory, but the Baptists sort of felt like they'd done their thing and they were ready to shut down the shelter. Of course, as good Christians you can't just throw them out on the street but, on the other hand, you don't really have the resources to just indefi-nitely take care of them.

The director of a local charitable organization noted that it received a grant for job training, including childcare coverage, but some evacuees did not take advantage of the opportunity. What once had been overwhelming generosity shifted onto a different plane: "Yes, you've been through a hard time, but now what are you going to do?" When evacuees did not make use of the opportunities available, make plans to take the next step toward "normal" life, or return to New Orleans, local people attempting to help were upset. Some reported feeling that they had been taken advantage of. Throughout this third phase, which stretched nearly six months, Huntsville residents began to think, "If you need to be taken care of for the rest of your life, maybe this isn't the best place for you."

In theory, at least, the fourth phase of reception should be a transition from "disaster victim" back to some sort of predisaster status. The expec-tation of local emergency response workers and volunteers was that this phase would begin with shelter closures and the cessation of specially des-ignated assistance funds.

Recipients of disaster assistance (shelter, funds, donations, etc.) were supposed to leave the system and become self-sufficient. Locally, respond-ers and volunteers assumed that evacuees would either return to New

Orleans or get back on their feet and become autonomous local residents. When neither of those outcomes seemed possible, people were encouraged to go elsewhere. In the case of Hurricane Katrina, the typical cycle stalled at the end of the third phase, before the "recovery" phase, and for many the search for a permanent home was still ongoing in the fall of 2008.

CONCLUSION

People fleeing Hurricane Katrina received a generous reception in Huntsville, as in many places across the nation. In the hotels, motels, and private residences, volunteers from the community and churches offered assistance, supplies, and donations. For those in the shelters, all basic necessities were provided. Continued support was available for those who stayed (hotel/motel rooms, rental properties, furniture, gas cards, phone cards, food, job training, childcare, etc.), but help was accompanied by the expectations that its recipients would (1) make clear attempts to help themselves, (2) not work the system to take advantage of people's generosity, and (3) become increasingly self-sufficient. All but a few of those who have stayed met these requirements, continued to benefit from assistance, and came to be seen as full new members of the community. Those who could not meet these requirements, or who did not try to do so, have for the most part left in search of other receiving communities.

Overall, the community seems to have benefited from the experience of providing shelter for the evacuees. One respondent stated that the emergency "gave us cause to see the fabric of our community like you hadn't seen it before. It was a time to be very proud." Similar comments were made by all of the respondents. However, one seemed to recognize that the experience was not completely positive when he stated that the "good news is it all worked out. I don't think we have scars on the community, but I think we learned a tremendous amount," referring to the lessons, both positive and negative, learned about the sheltering process and how the local community works.

One of the most important lessons from Hurricane Katrina is that the assumption that there will be a prompt return home, or at least to some sort of stability, after every disaster should be questioned. For many people displaced by Hurricane Katrina, there is no going back in many ways. Their lives are forever changed. In different but lasting ways, Hurricane Katrina also caused changes in the many people, agencies, organizations, and communities receiving the displaced.

Future research is needed to confirm which factors are most salient to sheltering and resettlement. One crucial area of study suggested by this research is the mismatch between evacuees and responders/receiving communities along race and class lines—which are also gendered—and how differences impact the experiences of displacement from the perspectives of the evacuees and the communities that receive them. For example, differences between evacuee populations and the people in communities to which they are displaced may have contributed to the time limits on empathy. Additionally, displacement was made more problematic because urban evacuees were displaced to rural receiving communities lacking in public transportation, infrastructure, and social services. Future disaster preparation could include matching communities vulnerable to disasters, such as those in coastal areas, with host communities that offer sufficient organizational resources, personnel trained in sheltering, and adequate infrastructure, and that share social, economic, and cultural characteristics. Recognition of the evolution of receiving communities' expectations of evacuee behavior over time is also important to more effectively manage sheltering and relocation processes after events like Hurricane Katrina, which cause such complete devastation—and offer no way home.

ACKNOWLEDGMENTS

This work would not have been possible without the many people who not only generously worked to host people displaced by Hurricane Katrina, but then were willing to take time to recount their experiences. I am grateful for the information and insights they provided. This research was funded in part by the Bill Blackwood Law Enforcement Management Institute of Texas at Sam Houston State University, and this support is gratefully acknowledged. The members of the SSRC Research Network on Persons Displaced by Hurricane Katrina have been a steady source of productive feedback and scholarly input for this work. In particular, Lori Peek, Lynn Weber, and Kai Erikson have provided extensive editorial comments, and this chapter is much improved as a result. I am deeply appreciative.

NOTES

1. Lee M. Miller, "Collective Disaster Responses to Katrina and Rita: Exploring Therapeutic Community, Social Capital and Social Control," *Southern Rural Sociology* 22, no. 2 (2007): 45–63.

2. Alejandro Portes and Ruben G. Rumbaut, *Immigrant America: A Portrait*, 2nd ed. (Berkeley: University of California Press, 1996).

3. City-data for Walker County, Texas, http://www.city-data.com/county/Walker_County-TX.html, accessed February 17, 2008.

4. U.S. Census Bureau, American Factfinder, "Huntsville city, Texas," 2000, http://factfinder.census.gov/servlet/SAFFFacts?_event=&geo_id=16000US4835528&_geoContext=01000US|04000US48|16000US4835528&_street=&_county=Huntsville&_cityTown=Huntsville&_state=04000US48&_zip=&_lang=en&_sse=on&ActiveGeoDiv=&_useEV=&pctxt=fph&pgsl=160&_submenuId=factsheet_1&ds_name=ACS_2009_5YR_SAFF&_ci_nbr=null&qr_name=null&reg=&_keyword=&_industry=, accessed February 17, 2008.

5. Miller, "Collective Disaster Responses."

6. City-data for Walker County.

7. City-data for Orleans Parish, Louisiana, http://www.city-data.com/county/Orleans_Parish-LA.html, accessed February 17, 2008.

8. Ibid.

9. City-data for Walker County.

10. U.S. Census Bureau, "Texas Quickfacts," http://quickfacts.census.gov/qfd/states/48000.html, accessed February 10, 2008.

11. Portes and Rumbaut, *Immigrant America*.

12. U.S. Census Bureau, "Huntsville city, Texas."

13. Elaine Enarson, Alice Fothergill, and Lori Peek, "Gender and Disaster: Foundations and Directions," in *Handbook of Disaster Research*, ed. H. Rodriguez, E. L. Quarantelli, and R. R. Dynes (New York: Springer, 2006), pp. 130–146.

14. Portes and Rumbaut, *Immigrant America*.

15. Russell R. Dynes and Enrico L. Quarantelli, "Helping Behavior in Large Scale Disasters," article no. 132 (Newark: University of Delaware, Disaster Research Center, 1980), p. 347.

16. Multiple formal and informal ties within a community can also facilitate cooperation and organization. See Robert D. Putnam, *Bowling Alone: The Collapse and Revival of American Community* (New York: Simon & Schuster 2000).

17. Huntsville 2005 Citizen Survey (Arlington, TX: Raymond Turco & Associates, November 2005); Huntsville 2007 Citizen Survey (Arlington, TX: Raymond Turco & Associates, October 2007).

18. Miller, "Collective Disaster Responses."

19. C. E. Fritz, "Disaster," in *Contemporary Social Problems*, ed. R. K. Merton and R. A. Nisbet (New York: Harcourt, Brace & World, 1961), pp. 651–694.

20. A. H. Barton, *Communities in Disaster: A Sociological Analysis of Collective Stress Situations* (Garden City, NY: Doubleday, 1969).

8

PERMANENT TEMPORARINESS
DISPLACED CHILDREN IN LOUISIANA

Over one million children lived in the Gulf Coast counties most directly affected by Katrina's winds and waters. Early estimates suggested that 372,000 school-age children evacuated as a result of the storm,[1] and 163,000 children between the ages of zero and nineteen years remained displaced months later.[2] Like adults, those children were scattered throughout the Gulf Coast region and across the United States. Some ended up in the homes of relatives or friends; others found refuge in temporary shelters and hotels. Over 5,100 children were reported missing in the aftermath of Katrina, and the last child was reunited with her family in March of 2006.[3] Thousands more children were separated from members of their immediate and extended families in the evacuation.[4]

According to Abramson and colleagues, in the two years following Katrina, between 81,595 and 94,650 formerly displaced children returned to their home state or home communities, while approximately 70,000 children remained displaced.[5] Those children and families who returned to the city of New Orleans faced severe shortages of affordable housing,[6] unsafe environmental conditions,[7] high rates of violent crime, and a lack of classroom space and an insufficient number of qualified teachers in an already deeply troubled public school system.[8] One administrator estimated that in 2006, up to 2,000 school-age children were turned away from the public schools due to lack of available space.[9]

Many children and families along the Gulf Coast were living in crisis well before Hurricane Katrina made landfall. Mississippi and Louisiana were the two poorest states in the nation. The typical household income in both of these states was far below the national average, which meant that hundreds of thousands of people in the direct path of the storm had limited or no excess resources available to prepare for or cope with disaster. In Mis-

ALICE FOTHERGILL AND LORI PEEK

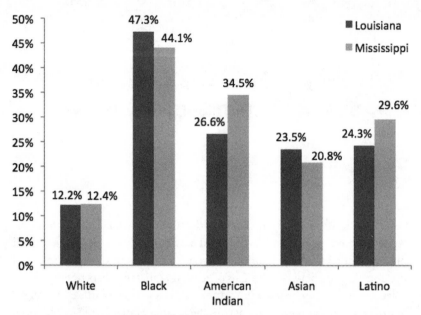

FIGURE 8.1. Percent Poor Children by Race in Louisiana and Mississippi

sissippi, over 227,000 children were living below the poverty line in 2004, and in Louisiana, that number surpassed 343,000.[10] Nearly one-third of all children in these states were impoverished, although the percentage of poor children varied significantly by race, with disproportionately high percentages of African American, Native American, Latino, and Asian American children living below the poverty line (see Figure 8.1). These children were especially vulnerable to the various problems that often accompany poverty—diminished educational achievement, neighborhood disorganization, food insecurity, abuse and neglect, physical and mental ailments, and limited or no access to healthcare—and these issues had reached epidemic levels in some of the hardest-hit areas.[11]

The limited research available on children who remain displaced, as well as those who have returned "home," indicates that the youngest survivors of Katrina have faced many serious physical and emotional challenges since the storm.[12] What is less well understood, however, is how the process of displacement has affected these young people's lives, relationships, and overall well-being. In our previous work, we examined children's post-Katrina experiences from the perspective of adults.[13] While the adults' observations and interpretations are obviously important, hearing children's voices adds critical information to the overall discussion of how children fare in disaster. In a great deal of the research on children in both psychology and sociology, the voices of children are often overlooked, and have been almost entirely absent in the scholarship on Katrina.[14]

This chapter focuses on children's stories and their perspectives on loss and displacement. We argue in the following pages that the children are in a state of "permanent temporariness." This term, borrowed from scholars Bailey, Wright, Mountz, and Miyares, refers to being constantly in flux, living in between two worlds, and floundering in "perpetual limbo."[15] While they used this concept to understand the legal, economic, and political situation of immigrants and asylum seekers, it is also applicable to children of the Katrina diaspora. Listening to the children's stories of evacuation, multiple displacements, and continued disruption reveals how unsettled they remain, how uncertain they are about where "home" is for them.

LISTENING TO CHILDREN'S VOICES

This ethnographic project began as an effort to learn how children and families fared in the immediate aftermath of Hurricane Katrina. Over the five-year period of this research, we studied hundreds of individuals. Because we had varying levels of contact with the participants in the larger sample, we divide these individuals into core, secondary, and tertiary groups.

Our core sample includes twenty-five children whom we interviewed and observed several times; we examined them *over time*. Within this core group, we interviewed the children and the children's family members, teachers, and/or other adults who knew them. In addition, sixty other children constitute our secondary sample, whom we formally or informally interviewed and observed at one point in time. The data from this group include field notes and/or transcriptions from audio-recorded interviews. Finally, a group of well over two hundred children whom we observed but did not interview formally comprise our tertiary sample. We watched them, and sometimes engaged in informal conversations, in classrooms, on playgrounds, in school lunchrooms, in disaster relief shelters, and so forth. When observing these children, we recorded systematic field notes regarding their behaviors and interactions with other children and adults.

All of the children we interviewed and observed were between three and eighteen years old.[16] Our interview sample was split evenly by gender: half males and half females. The children were all originally from New Orleans, and the racial composition of the sample—approximately two-thirds African American and one-third White—reflected the pre-Katrina demographics of the city. The children came from low-income, working-class, middle-class, and upper-middle-class families.

We conducted interviews with the children in our core and secondary samples in one-on-one as well as small-group settings. The group interviews typically included between two and five children who were siblings, neighbors, or classmates. Thus, all of the children were familiar with one another before the group interview, which seemed to put them at ease.[17] Both the one-on-one interviews and group interviews were audio-recorded. We also spent many hours speaking informally with children, sharing lunches and dinners, and joining with them and their families in their daily activities.[18]

We gathered observational data at various locations throughout Louisiana in the months and years following the storm.[19] In the immediate aftermath of Katrina, we observed operations at a large mass shelter in Lafayette and at a much smaller shelter in a Baptist church in Baton Rouge. We visited the Goodwill food and clothing distribution center for hurricane evacuees in Lafayette and later spent time at the Federal Emergency Management Agency (FEMA) Welcome Home Center in New Orleans.[20] We conducted interviews and observations at two childcare centers located in shelters and at a private daycare center in Lafayette. We observed and interviewed students and several teachers at nine schools, including: a temporary school for displaced students in New Iberia, which was formed by two teachers and a group of parents following Hurricane Katrina; a private Catholic school in Metairie; two charter schools in New Orleans; a state-run "Recovery School" in New Orleans; a private school in New Orleans; a public high school in New Orleans; a public high school in Lafayette; and a public elementary school in Baton Rouge. We spent afternoons and evenings in FEMA trailer sites in Baton Rouge and Scott, visited the flood-damaged homes of families in New Orleans, and attended church services with displaced families.

During the months between our fieldwork visits to Louisiana, we communicated with children and adults through telephone calls, e-mail messages, and cards and letters.[21] In the subsequent sections we present some of our findings from this project; throughout the chapter we privilege children's voices in telling their story of what happened during and following Katrina and examine how a wide range of factors resulted in a state of permanent temporariness.

EVACUATING AND BECOMING DISPLACED

All of the children in our study faced the coming of Katrina with members of their immediate families. Some of the families were able to leave New Orleans before the levees broke, but some were not. For the children we interviewed who were still in the city when it began to flood—all of whom were African American and working-class or poor—the situation was frightening and dangerous. Children of all ages expressed to us their fears of being in the city as it filled with water and increasingly desperate survivors awaited rescue and life-sustaining resources.

During three separate group interviews, a classroom of African American teenagers at a New Orleans middle school described their experiences after the levees broke. Over half of the students did not evacuate prior to the storm, and they were struggling to make sense of the horrifying things they saw and experienced. One recounted her intense fear as she and her mother watched the water engulf their home; another woke up and thought she must be dreaming as she saw the water continue to rise and rise. A third student described his terrifying experience evacuating after the city had flooded:

> And I was scared. After I fell in the water, you know how the water was dirty? That water was dirty. We was walking from my house on the bridge, and they had my sister's hand, my sister was eight months, and I was holding her, she couldn't walk. She was only eight months. And you couldn't see the curb. And everybody else was big, my mom and my brother, just me and my little sister. And we walking, and I ain't seen the curb. You can't see that in the water. I ain't seen the curb, and I stepped down and my little sister almost died, and I don't know how to swim. My brother jumped in there and got me and he got my little sister.

Some of the children in our study had to receive shots for their health after they had been in the floodwaters; waters which were considered especially dangerous for persons with more vulnerable immune systems. The children, understandably, complained to us about both the water and the shots. An African American five-year-old who was separated from his mother and had to evacuate out of New Orleans with his older sister could only remember that the storm was "really big" and that "the water was very high."

During a group interview, several adolescent African American boys recounted their experience with the evacuation. One of them explained how officials separated the members of his family in the Superdome: "My dad and my mama went with my auntie, and my cousin and my sister, they all went to Tennessee. Me and my two brothers and my one older cousin, we stayed behind." Another stated: "I knew how to swim, but I wasn't going to get in the water because of the alligators and the snakes." His friend responded: "I swam to the Superdome. My uncle couldn't swim, so I went down and got him a piece [of foam] and I came back and gave it to him."

A few children and youth who did not evacuate said that they were not scared of the storm and the water. One seventh grade African American boy, for example, told his dad that he wanted to stay because he had been informed by others that his housing project would not be harmed by a hurricane; later, when the waters came after the levees were breached, he explained that he was not worried because he knew how to swim. He did, however, have trouble with what followed: their homes were looted, and in the Superdome the hallways smelled of urine, the food was rotten, the military mistreated the evacuees, and some people died.

Some of the children who were trapped in the city for days discussed the things they did to survive, including taking supplies from stores. A fourteen-year-old African American girl who sought shelter with her family at the Convention Center related:

> We broke into the store and took stuff. The police came around and had shotguns and all that. We was taking real stuff that we needed. They shot the gun off. We was getting it for the elderly people, water and stuff. They shot at my cousin, because he tried to take this car for this lady so he could take her to the hospital. He took the car and they shot him in the head.

Her friend quickly responded:

> That's not breaking in, that's called surviving. And I'm not trying to be mean, but when Black people do it, they say, "They're stealing, they're stealing," and when Caucasian people do it, it's like, "They're surviving. They're trying to survive." And I'm like, that's not fair. Just because we are Black don't mean we're stealing. We're trying to survive just like the other people are trying to survive. And all they show was Black people killing and looting.

Subsequent conversations with these and other youth revealed similar astuteness regarding race, the media, politics, and the disaster.

Other children evacuated with their families before the levees broke, and thus their evacuation experience was less dangerous, but still anxiety-producing. One eight-year-old African American boy evacuated with his mother before Katrina made landfall, and he told us how they had to hurry and run in and out of the house loading up essential belongings. He explained: "I wanted to take all my toys, and I was sneaking them in my pants." His mother caught him, however, and made him put his toys back in his room. A number of children described long, hot, crowded car rides as their families evacuated the city.

For the most part, the children were not involved in the family decision to leave and felt little control over the situation. As we noted in our earlier work, however, mothers and fathers indicated that they evacuated because of their children.[22] In fact, several parents said that they would not have evacuated at all had it not been for their children.

The children in our study spoke of the people, pets, and belongings that they had to leave behind when they evacuated. While past research has shown that adults, and especially the elderly, suffer from losing the possessions of a lifetime in a disaster,[23] there has been little focus on what these losses mean to children. Our interviews demonstrate how difficult it was for young people to come to terms with some of the important things they had to leave behind and ultimately lost in the storm, such as toys, clothing, pictures, and school awards. The boy we described who tried to "sneak out" his toys in his pants ended up losing all of those toys when his home flooded. One African American middle school student was particularly upset about the loss of her favorite "cute" shoes, prompting her classmates to tease her. One of her friends mentioned missing her room and a small rug she had hand-made. And a White five-year-old told us how scared he was that he had lost a favorite shell that his grandmother (who died less than a month after Katrina) had given him.

It is not surprising that children's fates in Katrina were tied to their families' fates—especially their mothers'. This was true in terms of whether children evacuated, where they ended up, what types of shelter or housing they occupied, and what sorts of schools they attended during the evacuation. The children's emotional states were also affected by their parents' reactions to the disaster. Although parents often tried to hide their emotions, the children were keenly aware of how their parents were responding to the immense loss caused by Katrina. For many of the children, one difficult experience was seeing their mothers or fathers crying after Katrina, as described by this white nine-year-old boy:

INTERVIEWEE: They [his mom and dad] were sad, like, once they thought about it, they would start crying and stuff.

AUTHOR: How did you feel when they started to cry a little bit?

INTERVIEWEE: Uncomfortable, you know?

Outside the family context, children reflected on the unsettling experiences in evacuation when they found themselves in new communities that were demographically and culturally quite different from their former neighborhoods in New Orleans. In one of the focus groups with African American seventh graders, the students explained how they had evacuated to many locations, including Georgia, Arkansas, Texas, and Mississippi. Two of them proceeded to playfully argue over who was in the "lamest" town. Then they explained, more seriously, how they encountered racism in the places where they evacuated. One of the students described his encounters:

Some people was prejudiced. They were worse than the people down here. It was a White person—no offense. A White person would walk up to you, and they'll be like, "Hey!" and if you don't speak back, they'll shoot you right there. And the police, they don't care. Yes, indeed. At first, [they would] say, "You-all is niggers, you need to go back where you belong." And I would say, "You-all are crackers," or whatever.

Some of the Black children, who had previously attended segregated public schools in New Orleans with student bodies overwhelmingly made up of African American youth, ended up in similarly segregated schools in the cities where they evacuated. These schools, like those in New Orleans, tended to be seriously underfunded and had inadequate human and material resources. Other African American youth entered schools where they were in the minority. Most White children in New Orleans and the surrounding suburbs attended predominantly White schools before the storm and also during their evacuation. However, several of the White children in our study attended diverse public schools in New Orleans, and they had to adjust to attending schools and living in communities that were much less diverse than New Orleans. The White nine-year-old we quoted a moment ago, for example, attended a predominantly White school in Houston, whereas he had attended an elementary school in New Orleans that actively promoted and celebrated cultural and racial diversity. The diversity was one of the many things that he missed about his old school in New Orleans.

Children—both Black and White—spoke of feeling unwanted or disliked in their new schools due to their city of origin, New Orleans. However,

African American children, in particular, faced the most hostile responses. This was likely a result of the racial framing of Katrina, as well as preexisting prejudices against African Americans that are prevalent in US culture.[24] An African American teen described a falling out she had with a friend she met at the school she attended in Texas during the evacuation:

> A girl was friends with me for a whole week without knowing where I was from. Once I told her where I was from, she just completely stopped hanging out with me. That's weird. I was like, "You can't do that just because I'm from New Orleans."

An African American thirteen-year-old who evacuated with his mother and two-year-old sister to Baton Rouge found that in his new public school, which was predominantly African American, students were cruel and sometimes violent toward him. He explained why kids at the school threatened him:

> Like my first day of school, the first word that appeared out of this person's mouth is that New Orleans is s-h-i-t, New Orleans is this, New Orleans is that. A lot of cursing and putting New Orleans down. If you got to know us better than what you hear on the news, you would see that we are not that type of person. . . . [But] our reputation is "the highest killer rate in Louisiana."

In addition to being burdened with the stigma of New Orleans that led to his being bullied, this particular teen also found that the school was a rougher and more dangerous place than his school back home:

> Guns, knives, drugs in the back of the school. I saw it all. . . . If you normally go to school in New Orleans, you know that the schools in New Orleans, you don't even need the police. This school had police in the back, police in the front, security at the door. They pat you down at the door every morning.

The school that this teen attended in Baton Rouge was in a racially segregated and low-income part of the city. He ended up in the school because it was the only option in the district surrounding the FEMA trailer park where his family relocated. Over time, the bullying that he faced escalated to a point where he and his mother felt that it was no longer safe for him to attend the school. He was not able to transfer to another district, because his family did not own a car and they had minimal resources. He eventually dropped out of seventh grade and started caring for his little sister while his mother worked.

Families with more resources were able to exert more control over the entire evacuation process, including the decision about where their children would attend school. Moreover, the middle-class and White families in our study were more likely to have extended family and friendship networks in other cities, which further eased the transition for their children.

Some of the White middle-class children who evacuated to the homes of family or friends were able to view the evacuation as an enjoyable adventure. A number of these families even tried to treat the evacuation like a vacation and hence called it their "hurrication." One White five-year-old, who lived during evacuation with his family and two other families, thought "It was cool. There was a pool and a hot tub . . . and seven hundred billion dogs." While his friend corrected him that there were actually "only six dogs," it did not curb his enthusiasm about the experience. At the same time, even these children who had safer and more secure evacuation experiences were well aware of, and upset by, the devastation caused by Katrina. A White elementary school student at a Catholic school in Metairie watched media coverage of the storm and later stated, "I saw on TV that Katrina was a big hole and it destroyed all the houses." A White nine-year-old boy succinctly described Katrina as "Terrible. Heartbreaking."

Although African American youth faced more significant challenges in the evacuation, several relayed positive experiences, including seeing new places, meeting new people, and getting to travel outside of New Orleans—which, for some, was their first time. One of the middle school students, an African American girl, remarked:

> A good thing about Hurricane Katrina is that I went exploring from one state to another. When we were about to go to Georgia, my mom was scared and I was excited to go to Georgia. We went there anyway, and it was fun. . . . Well, I'm glad to be back, but I miss Georgia. It was a nice place . . . it was kind of fun there. I really liked it. My mom liked it, but she was very homesick, so after about, like, a couple of months we came back to New Orleans.

Some African American students, in contrast to many of those who faced stigmatization and hostility, found that students welcomed them to their new cities. A student who attended school in Houston commented:

They like the way we talk. Because everybody was like: "You-all got a different accent from us. Your accent is cute." Or they kept saying, "Say fried chicken." I'd be like, "Fried chicken." And then they walk around, they be like, "Fried chicken." They'd be trying. . . . And they would actually come to school dressed like how I was dressed. . . . I didn't want to leave that school. I didn't want to leave for nothing.

Children had a wide range of views on the evacuation, and while some liked traveling and meeting new people, others did not. In a group interview, for example, one student remarked, "I met new friends," and a classmate quickly chimed in, "I don't like new friends." These examples illustrate that while race and class were often the most significant factors in determining how children experienced the evacuation, many other factors such as family circumstances, the context of the receiving city and school, and individual personality also shaped their interpretations and feelings.

When reflecting on the storm, several of the African American teenagers displayed a strong racial consciousness and were more political in their analysis than younger children. This was also seen earlier in their discussion about looting. In one exchange in a middle school, a group of students expressed their anger at the government and their belief that the levees were intentionally destroyed. Each paragraph is a different speaker, although some students speak more than once.

I knew it all would happen. Katrina did none of that stuff. I'm talking about people doing that. Katrina [in the] Gulf, she was a Category 6. When Katrina hit New Orleans, it was a Category 1. The day Hurricane Katrina came, I mean, water and rain and everything. Next day, sunny and pretty outside. Next day water rising. Ain't nobody stupid? Come on! Next day sunny, next day water. *They blew the levees.*

Look what Bush did. Bush pushed the button. He sure did!

He pushed the goddamn button! [laughter]

Bush did it! I know he did it! 'Cause when everybody was outside on the bridge and stuff, they could have sent them somewhere. They waited about five days, and then Bush decided, "Well, look, send them here, send them there." How would he feel if somebody sent his daughter somewhere and his wife and he don't never get to see them in two years?

His daughter's an alcoholic.

Author: How do you feel about the government right now?

Down, babe.

It was Blanco, too.

Backstabber.

It was Blanco, too.

Bush's daughter is a drunk.

She [Blanco] was talking about "Who gonna pay for this? Who gonna pay for that?" while we out there dying. It was Blanco and Bush. And then he gonna come. . . . He gonna come and look around in New Orleans and act like he crying.

He [Bush] gonna ride around in an army truck and pretend he was crying. He wasn't crying. He did that. I'm telling you. He did that because he wanted to stop crime and nobody else would do it. The jails were getting too full.

They showed it, Bush and Blanco did that. Even Ray Nagin tried to help them [blow the levees].

No, he didn't!

Yes, he did. . . . Ray Nagin even tried to help them.

When the levees broke, we saw it on TV, because it was like far distant. They had the men on the bridge and they had the stuff, and everybody got out of the water. And when he pushed the button on the bridge, it just blew up, boom! Explosives everywhere. Katrina did not do that.

Other work has indicated that African American adults were much more likely than White adults to believe that the government had blown the levees.[25] These beliefs among some African Americans have been shaped by historical experiences with overtly racial responses to potential flooding and because of a profound mistrust of historically racist government authorities. Our research documents that some youth also came to share this perspective on Katrina and that they believed political leaders, especially President Bush and Louisiana Governor Blanco, attempted to feign empathy after a delayed response that led to the deaths of many people. We can surmise that these views were likely shaped by the adults in the children's lives, as well as by their peers.

In the years following Katrina, tens of thousands of individuals did not return to New Orleans for a wide range of economic, social, and personal reasons. During this time, many of the children and families in our study had to begin the long and arduous process of making a new home in a new place. Yet many felt that New Orleans was still "home" and not returning there meant a continuing a state of displacement; this "permanent temporariness" involved living in one place while thinking constantly about another. The children talked to us about the many difficulties they faced as they adjusted to new surroundings and went through many simultaneous transitions. However, with these challenges also came new opportunities.

For some youth who grew attached to people—both volunteers and fellow evacuees—at shelters, moving out of shelters to a trailer, apartment, or house was bittersweet. A twelve-year-old African American girl explained her emotions when she left the Cajundome shelter in Lafayette and moved with her mother into their own FEMA trailer:

> I was happy because we were moving and we had a little bit more freedom. We had our own shower, and we don't have to wait, like, a bunch to get in the shower after other people. But it was sad because that was my home for, like, some months, and I was getting attached to a lot of people, and I was getting attached to Mr. Brad and Miss Sue and Miss Renee.

A thirteen-year-old African American boy expressed a similar feeling about leaving a church shelter in Baton Rouge and moving to a FEMA trailer:

> At first I really wanted to stay at the church. Because it was like, at church I knew everybody. I didn't want to leave. I just got settled in. Just the thought of being around people who went through the same thing with me, it was, like, a peaceful place. Nobody got into it. It never was, never caused commotion or stuff like that. . . . I really did want to stay at the church as long as I could.

Once families decided to settle in new cities, rather than return to New Orleans, children faced significant adjustments at their new schools. An eight-year-old African American boy in our sample moved with his mother, infant brother, and maternal grandmother to Lafayette, where he was attending a new public school. His mother was pleased with the school, but the boy was not. There were several other displaced children from New

Orleans in his new school. They might have helped each other adjust, but the school required that the evacuee students be placed in separate classrooms.

In addition to school upheavals and losses, children also faced losses associated with family relationships, particularly their grandparents and fathers. Most of the African American children in our study were from single-parent families and lived with their mothers before Katrina. However, almost all of them saw their fathers frequently—in many cases, several times a week—before the storm. After Katrina, the children relocated to new cities with their mothers, while their fathers returned to New Orleans or settled elsewhere. One boy told us how much he missed his father, and then he said, "Sometimes I be crying over my dad." Another girl noted that she was "not very close" to her father before the storm. However, she saw him at least "every other weekend." After Katrina, when her father relocated to Texas, the visits dwindled to once a year at family reunions. He also began calling less often and missed birthdays and other key moments in his daughter's life. She eventually steeled herself and decided to try to love her father, but "from a distance":

> I don't want to say I don't need him, but I mean, I'm better without him and the disappointment, like, he tells me he'll come pick me up and then he doesn't. Sometimes it's disappointing. . . . It's better to just—like, sometimes you just have to love people from a distance, just so you won't destroy yourself in the process.

In the disaster aftermath, children in families headed by single African American mothers were more vulnerable to the loss of fathers and extended family members and the support and resources they provided. In many ways, the separation from fathers and other family members represented an "invisible loss," since those relatives did not live with them before the disaster.

Children clearly missed many things about New Orleans, but they often noted that they were glad that they were far from the crime there and the threat of more hurricanes. When we asked one boy what he liked about Lafayette, he thought for a minute and then stated: "Let's see. They haven't had a hurricane in a long time." He went on to explain that he would want to live in New Orleans again "if they didn't have all that killing there."

Children who settled in different cities encountered new opportunities, such as extracurricular activities at school that they did not have in New Orleans. Initially, children hesitated to dive into new things, not knowing if they would be staying long. One African American girl, after at first resisting joining any clubs, was voted head cheerleader at her new school in Lafayette and later joined the local 4-H club. She proudly showed us the dress that she had sewn for her 4-H project and had modeled at the county fair. She was also nominated by one of her new teachers to attend a national leadership conference in Washington, DC, and she was invited to participate in a beauty pageant. She indicated that she could not have participated in these same activities in New Orleans:

> I feel that, like, in New Orleans we didn't get a lot of chances. Kids, they didn't get a lot of chances. They didn't have stuff like Washington, DC, trips. It was a once-in-a-lifetime chance. I was also accepted to be in a beauty pageant. I had to pick either Washington, DC, or that. I'm going to Washington, DC, but next year they're gonna save my spot [for the beauty pageant].

Similarly, a young African American boy who had fought the idea of relocating permanently did eventually join a local Little League baseball team and a junior football league in Lafayette and found enjoyment in the sports and his teammates.

One of the most significant changes for a number of the displaced youth in our study was related to their housing situation post-Katrina. Two of the families we interviewed in Lafayette, both headed by African American single mothers, were able to acquire newly built Habitat for Humanity houses. The mothers, as well as their children, worked on these houses as part of the required "sweat equity" hours that new homeowners must contribute. This led to a strong sense of pride and accomplishment among adults and children alike.

Families we interviewed that had moved into FEMA trailers in Lafayette and Baton Rouge in the months following Katrina were also grateful to have new homes. One thirteen-year-old African American boy who had been in and out of homeless shelters and was living in a run-down apartment with his mom and baby sister before the hurricane described how he felt when they arrived at their FEMA trailer:

> My mama told me that the man gave her the keys and she broke down in tears . . . because we never had anything this big before. She let me open the door with the key. And when I got in, I was like, "Do we have to share with roommates or something like that?" She was like, "No . . ." I said, "It can't be all mine." I've never imagined having a big house like this under

the circumstances, before Katrina and even after Katrina. So we came in, she let me unlock the door, and she let me choose which room I wanted. And then I chose that room, and then I went in, and I couldn't believe that I had my own room to myself. That was the first time ever having my own room to myself. There was just peace of mind, stuff like that. . . . [Before Katrina] the place we were living in, it was a sewer. . . . And we couldn't pay the rent. We've been having it hard, before Katrina, going from pillar to post, from shelter to shelter. And it was just a blessing just to have our own [home] and not worry about where we are gonna sleep at or how we were gonna eat, stuff like that.

Other children in our study had also endured poverty and ongoing crises prior to the storm. For example, one boy, who was only five years old at the time of our interview, explained that when they evacuated to Baton Rouge, "My mom didn't have money. We didn't have nothing." As we continued talking, he added that when he was a baby they did not have money then either.

Life in the FEMA trailers brought some level of temporary stability for displaced children like the boys we quoted above, but these units were never intended to serve as permanent housing. FEMA allowed families to stay rent-free in the trailers for twelve to eighteen months, and in some cases for longer periods, although there was often confusing information about the assistance deadline and how much time families would have to find new housing. Some families had no place to go when the FEMA aid ran out. Thus, the families in the most economically precarious situations prior to the storm continued to struggle with immense uncertainty in the aftermath of Katrina. For the children, living in FEMA trailers for several years contributed to their state of permanent temporariness.

RETURNING "HOME": THE UNSETTLEDNESS CONTINUES

Over half of the young people in our study were able to return to New Orleans with their families and either reoccupy their original residences or find new ones in the city. Most of them felt strongly that they wanted to return to the city, yet when they got back they found that there were many difficulties associated with returning to the "new New Orleans." These children and youth thought that it no longer felt like "home."

We asked a group of African American teens what their families needed the most when they returned to New Orleans, and they responded as follows. Again, each line represents a different child:

We had to find a house.

Money.

A job.

Shoes. [they all laugh]

These youth and most other children we interviewed were acutely aware of the financial and emotional struggles that their families were facing, even though they did not always articulate their fears to the adults in their lives. An African American adolescent spoke of the frustration of having a fence put up around the housing project where he lived before Katrina. Another student returned to his family's apartment in a different housing project, but officials would not allow the other units to be reoccupied. He stated, "I think the whole project should be open. They just got, like, a hundred or some families, and they got so many vacancies. They want a lot of people to come back to New Orleans, but I think that if they opened up the projects, they could get everybody back." Another teenager observed that rebuilding efforts were focusing on people who could afford houses, but for African American families like his who used to live in the housing projects, "We didn't get nothing." Later in the conversation, we asked the students what they missed the most from before the storm, and one boy responded: "I miss my [housing] project. . . . I miss the people, I miss the project, I miss everything about it." These African American youth were also facing the politics and inequities involved in the large-scale housing project demolition initiated by the Housing Authority of New Orleans, which clearly was a source of stress and sent messages to them about their race, class, and place in the city.

Besides confronting the life-sustaining needs of families as they returned to New Orleans, the children also were forced to adjust to new or changed schools. As has been widely documented, the schools of New Orleans were underfunded, in physical disrepair, short-staffed, and wracked with problems before the storm, and these issues were amplified after Katrina.[26] Many thousands of children found that their original schools were destroyed or were closed permanently after the storm; others who were able to return to their former schools found them unfamiliar and unwelcoming, since the hallways and classrooms were filled with strangers. An elementary school student in New Orleans described being back in his old school this way: "It has people leaving, people going, people coming, people staying, people coming back."

Children of all backgrounds felt the stress in New Orleans school settings. In private schools, for example, White children from families with resources were also struggling with the loss of teachers, friends, and community and other drastic changes to their school situations. Yet, while children shared these losses across race and class lines, the school setting was particularly problematic for low-income children, as there were far fewer resources available to support them. For example, many low-income African American children were enrolled in schools without a single social worker or school counselor to come to their aid. In addition, the Recovery School we studied had no drama or art program or outdoor playground, was racially segregated, and had a severe shortage of qualified teachers. It is not surprising that children told us that they "hated" their school or wished they could do experiments in science instead of just sitting in their seats.

Another challenge for youth who had returned to the city was feeling vulnerable to future hurricanes. As is apparent in their evacuation stories, they had every reason to be terrified of being in that situation again. Perhaps as a result of their fears of storms, children and teens exhibited an uncanny awareness of weather patterns and the state of the levee system surrounding New Orleans. In one of our focus groups with seventh graders, several of the students said they were scared that another big disaster could happen. In fact, when we asked how they felt about future hurricanes, a student quickly and nervously asked, "Are we gonna have a hurricane?" Another student explained that she had a breaking point: "[If a] hurricane comes, I'm so sorry. I like New Orleans, but I ain't coming back. After a while, I say, if three good more hurricanes come—" A fellow student then interjected, "*One* more!" and then the girl continued, "No, I'm gone if *three* more big ones come, New Orleans gonna be off the map completely. It ain't gonna be no more New Orleans. New Orleans gonna be abandoned." Younger children also expressed their fears about future storms and often felt anxious when it rained or if there were storm warnings.

Children of all backgrounds who returned to New Orleans articulated serious concern over the increase in property crime, assaults, and murders in the city. Their knowledge about crime came from television, listening to their peers and the adults in their lives, and in some instances, firsthand experience. One African American adolescent described the ways that violence was affecting his ability to function in the city:

I miss having to come outside and you-all got to be scared to be outside. Before Hurricane Katrina, we would just come outside and [talk] to everybody, but not everybody all over the world, in different parts, we want to know what they is, what they do, how they do. But now, you can't go outside no more. Just sitting on the porch. You can't chill no more. It's just dangerous. Yesterday somebody was shot in my mama's backyard. They don't only come at you at night now, they kill you in the broad daylight now. They just don't care.

Another African American boy, twelve years old, explained that certain neighborhoods have more crime than others, "Just make sure [tourists] stay downtown. They can't come uptown." When we asked him where he lives and goes to school, he said, matter-of-factly, "This is uptown."

Perhaps the most difficult problem for the children who returned to New Orleans was dealing with life *without* the family and friends who did not return. It was often the case that extended-family members, and sometimes the case that immediate family such as an older sibling or parent, stayed elsewhere. This loss was profound. When we asked middle school students how they coped emotionally, one African American girl explained, "We try not to talk about it," and, as several of her friends nodded, she added, "because it makes us cry."

Children frequently talked about friends who were permanently displaced to places like Arkansas, California, Georgia, Kansas, Mississippi, Oklahoma, Nevada, Tennessee, and Texas. One boy, who was in second grade when Katrina made landfall, returned to New Orleans after the storm, but his best friend relocated to Atlanta. This was difficult for him, and he said, "I asked him if he was gonna come back, like when he grows up, and he said, 'Maybe.'" A White nine-year-old said that she was "really excited" to come back to her house in New Orleans, but when she got there her friends were gone and the neighborhood had changed:

It was freaky and it was really quiet . . . nobody was back, and it was really weird seeing that nobody was out in the school. All my friends were still gone. I remember on Friday [before the evacuation], my friend and I were going to have a sleepover on Saturday. Before we evacuated we said, "If we can't have the sleepover, I'll see you on Monday!" And I didn't see her for, like, a year.

Later in the same interview, she brought up the feeling in her neighborhood again:

It was weird, because, like, there weren't any cars out, and all the trees were dead. At night it was just really quiet and none of the streetlights were on, so it was really dark and kind of spooky. And you didn't hear all the noise outside and the cars running by. It was just kind of a weird feeling.

CONCLUSION

The children's individual experiences and perspectives, taken as a whole, tell a larger story: all the children in our study, regardless of whether they returned to New Orleans or remained displaced, felt and continue to feel unsettled. Their story is one of permanent temporariness.

Permanent temporariness means a life of limbo. Past research has shown that living such a life can lead individuals to resist developing new relationships or getting involved in new activities, since it is unclear how long they will be in a particular setting.[27] It also can result in frustration, stress, disillusionment, depression, and changes in identity.[28] Perpetual limbo for immigrants and political asylum applicants means a fear of sudden deportation and a loss of their new lives. For the children of Katrina, living "lives in limbo" meant that every place felt unstable, transitional, impermanent.

While all the children in our study experienced some degree of permanent temporariness, children who were marginalized, whose families had fewer resources, who were poor, and who were Black, were likely to experience this state more profoundly. Indeed, children's pre- and post-disaster experiences were clearly shaped by their racial background and class status. Before the disaster, factors such as where children lived, the type of housing they occupied, and the quality of the schools they attended were correlated with their race and class. In the disaster, children's access to transportation and their likelihood of evacuating, ending up in shelter, attending a "safe" school, and reestablishing stable housing were all influenced by race and class. The way in which people treated the children and youth during displacement was often based on class, race, and city of origin, and this treatment manifested itself in particular ways based on age—such as some children being bullied or taunted by older children or youth at a new school.

Age is sometimes left unexamined in analyses of vulnerability and social inequality. Yet age, like race and class, is a social category or structure attached to power and privilege; these categories and many others overlap and shape experiences and relationships. We found that race, class, and age interacted in important ways. Through listening to children's voices, we were able to learn about their experiences in the disaster and its aftermath, the challenges they faced during the evacuation and relocation, and their struggles with the loss of their homes and schools and separation from their family members.

In some cases, children suffered from increased vulnerability because of their age and stage of development. For example, younger children were physically vulnerable to the floodwaters due to their smaller size and still-developing immune systems. Older African American children and teens were keenly aware of the racism that led to a delayed and inadequate response to the disaster. They were also forced to confront unjust treatment from authorities and inequalities in their schools and neighborhoods. Children of all ages were affected by their parents' emotional states, and children and youth expressed extreme sadness at the loss of teachers, friends, and important possessions. Children had little or no control over where their families evacuated, how long they stayed, and if or when they returned to New Orleans. They also had little or no control over what schools they attended.

It is important to understand that children are relatively powerless members of society: they do not vote, they do not determine policy, they usually do not make decisions for their families, and they are often exploited or their voices are silenced.[29] While children and youth have agency and are capable of contributing to society in meaningful ways, their exclusion from positions of authority and decision-making processes often renders their experiences and needs invisible in disasters.

Research on the impact of disasters on children has documented the environmental, social, economic, and familial factors that place children at particular risk: experiencing a life-threatening event, losing a loved one, witnessing scenes of destruction, suffering severe loss and damage to home and community, having a parent who is depressed or absent, experiencing persistent uncertainty, and becoming displaced or homeless.[30] Children displaced by Katrina experienced most, and in some cases all, of these risk factors. Research on children and disasters has shown that most children, when faced with adversity, are capable of coping with one or two major risk factors in their lives without significant detrimental consequences.[31] However, children are highly susceptible to developmental damage and troubling life outcomes when a number of risk factors accumulate.[32]

For the children who survived Katrina, and especially those low-income and minority youth who were living in crisis before the storm, there has been no clearly identifiable "end" to the disaster. Instead, children who have returned to New Orleans, as well as those who live in new cities, continue to struggle to make sense of the loss, disruption, and state of permanent temporariness caused by Katrina. Indeed, the losses children have suffered are profound and have had an enormous impact on their everyday lives and their perspectives on the future. It is our hope that the needs of these children are acknowledged and addressed and that their stories are not forgotten.

ACKNOWLEDGMENTS

We would like to express our sincere gratitude to the children who participated in this study. Their honesty and thoughtfulness helped us understand the impacts of Hurricane Katrina from their perspective. We would also like to thank Jennifer Tobin-Gurley and Megan Underhill for their assistance with data collection. The members of the SSRC Research Network on Persons Displaced by Hurricane Katrina have offered invaluable insights and many significant contributions to our work. We are especially thankful for the many thoughtful suggestions that Kai Erikson provided on an earlier draft of this chapter. This research was supported by the University of Vermont's College of Arts and Sciences Dean's Fund and the Colorado State University College of Liberal Arts Professional Development Fund, which are gratefully acknowledged.

NOTES

1. Michael Casserly, "Double Jeopardy: Public Education in New Orleans before and after the Storm," in *There Is No Such Thing as a Natural Disaster: Race, Class, and Hurricane Katrina*, ed. C. Hartman and G. D. Squires (New York: Routledge, 2006), pp. 197–214.

2. David Abramson, Irwin Redlener, Tasha Stehling-Ariza, and Elizabeth Fuller, "The Legacy of Katrina's Children: Estimating the Numbers of Hurricane-Related At-Risk Children in the Gulf Coast States of Louisiana and Mississippi" (New York: Columbia University Mailman School of Public Health, 2007).

3. National Center for Missing and Exploited Children, "National Center for Missing and Exploited Children Reunites Last Missing Child Separated by Hurricane Katrina and Rita," press release (Alexandria, VA: National Center for Missing and Exploited Children, 2006).

4. Olivia Golden, "Young Children after Katrina: A Proposal to Heal the Damage and Create Opportunity in New Orleans" (Washington, DC: Urban Institute, 2006).

5. Abramson et al., "The Legacy of Katrina's Children."

6. Eric N. Weiss, "Rebuilding Housing after Hurricane Katrina: Lessons Learned and Unresolved Issues" (order code RL33761) (Washington, DC: Congressional Research Service, 2006).

7. Manuel Pastor, Robert D. Bullard, James K. Boyce, Alice Fothergill, Rachel Morello-Frosch, and Beverly Wright, *In the Wake of the Storm: Environment, Disaster, and Race after Katrina* (New York: Russell Sage Foundation, 2006).

8. United Teachers of New Orleans, Louisiana Federation of Teachers, and the American Federation of Teachers, "No Experience Necessary: How the New Orleans School Takeover Experiment Devalues Experienced Teachers" (New Orleans: United Teachers of New Orleans, 2007).

9. Children's Defense Fund, "Katrina's Children: A Call to Conscience and Action" (Washington, DC: Children's Defense Fund, 2006).

10. Ibid.

11. Abramson et al., "The Legacy of Katrina's Children."

12. David M. Abramson, Yoon Soo Park, Tasha Stehling-Ariza, and Irwin Redlener, "Children as Bellwethers of Recovery: Dysfunctional Systems and the Effects of Parents, Households, and Neighborhoods on Serious Emotional Disturbance in Children after Hurricane Katrina," *Disaster Medicine and Public Health Preparedness* 4, no. 1 (2010): S17–S27; Carl F. Weems, Leslie K. Taylor, Melinda F. Cannon, Reshelle C. Marino, Dawn M. Romano, Brandon G. Scott, Andre M. Perry, and Vera Triplett, "Post Traumatic Stress, Context, and the Lingering Effects of the Hurricane Katrina Disaster among Ethnic Minority Youth," *Journal of Abnormal Child Psychology* 38, no. 1 (2010): 49–56.

13. Alice Fothergill and Lori Peek, "Surviving Catastrophe: A Study of Children in Hurricane Katrina," in *Learning from Catastrophe: Quick Response Research in the Wake of Hurricane Katrina*, ed. the Natural Hazards Center (Boulder: Institute of Behavioral Science, University of Colorado at Boulder, 2006), pp. 97–129; Lori Peek and Alice Fothergill, "Reconstructing Childhood: An Exploratory Study of Children in Hurricane Katrina," Quick Response Report #186 (Boulder: Natural Hazards Research and Applications Information Center, University of Colorado, April 2006), http://www.colorado.edu/hazards/research/qr/qr186/qr186.pdf.

14. Lori Peek, "Children and Disasters: Understanding Vulnerability, Developing Capacities, and Promoting Resilience," *Children, Youth and Environments* 18, no. 1 (2008): 1–29.

15. Adrian J. Bailey, Richard A. Wright, Alison Mountz, and Ines M. Miyares, "(Re)producing Salvadoran Transnational Geographies," *Annals of the Association of American Geographers* 92, no. 1 (2002): 125–144.

16. In addition to interviewing the children, we also conducted qualitative interviews with adults in the child's life: parents and other extended family members; teachers, school counselors, and administrators; and shelter workers and disaster relief volunteers. In this chapter, however, we focus solely on the data from our interviews and observations with the children.

17. We also brought along Play-Doh so that we could engage in an activity with the youngest interviewees while talking to them about their experiences. This gave us something to work on during the interview, and the children appeared pleased when we told them that the Play-Doh was theirs to keep. As the research progressed, we gave the children who were age twelve and younger paper and crayons and asked

them to depict their experiences in the storm, the things that they lost, and the people and things that helped them to recover. This method was particularly effective, as it increased the amount and depth of information that they shared with us.

18. Most of the children were shy initially, but after "hanging out," making trips to Wal-Mart with us, attending church, and receiving piggyback rides through the grocery store, they warmed up to us and were willing to share their stories.

19. These various activities were summarized in a series of written field notes. We each analyzed the field notes and interview transcripts and developed a set of codes based on questions from the interview guide and emergent themes.

20. The FEMA Welcome Home Center, which opened in January 2007 in downtown New Orleans, housed agencies and organizations that provided resources for those affected by Katrina. It was designed to be a one-stop information center for federal assistance.

21. We took numerous photographs during our fieldwork, and we included photos of the families and the children's schools in the cards we sent after our visits. The loss of a lifetime of photographs was traumatic for many of our participants, and thus sending a photo seemed to be one way to offer our gratitude for the time they spent with us. We also mailed books and birthday presents to some of the respondents. We periodically purchased clothes, school uniforms, backpacks, school supplies, blankets, and other necessary items for the children and families that were in dire financial situations.

22. Lori Peek and Alice Fothergill, "Displacement, Gender, and the Challenges of Parenting after Hurricane Katrina," *National Women's Studies Association Journal* 20, no. 3 (2008): 69–105.

23. Lori Peek, "Age," in *Social Vulnerability to Disasters*, ed. B. D. Phillips, D. S. K. Thomas, A. Fothergill, and L. Blinn-Pike (Boca Raton, FL: CRC Press, 2010), pp. 155–185.

24. Michael C. Dawson, "After the Deluge: Publics and Publicity in Katrina's Wake," *Du Bois Review: Social Science Research on Race* 3, no. 1 (2006): 239–249; Michael Eric Dyson, *Come Hell or High Water: Hurricane Katrina and the Color of Disaster* (New York: Basic Books, 2006).

25. Kristina M. Cordasco, David P. Eisenman, Deborah C. Glik, Joya F. Golden, and Steven M. Asch, "'They Blew the Levee': Distrust of Authorities among Hurricane Katrina Evacuees," *Journal of Health Care for the Poor and Underserved* 18, no. 2 (2007): 277–282; Barbara Ransby, "Katrina, Black Women, and the Deadly Discourse on Black Poverty in America," *Du Bois Review: Social Science Research on Race* 3, no. 1 (2006): 215–222.

26. Sharon P. Robinson and M. Christopher Brown II, eds., *The Children Hurricane Katrina Left Behind: Schooling Context, Professional Preparation, and Community Politics* (New York: Peter Lang, 2007).

27. Bailey et al., "(Re)producing Salvadoran Transnational Geographies."

28. Alison Mountz, Richard Wright, Ines Miyares, and Adrian J. Bailey, "Lives in Limbo: Temporary Protected Status and Immigrant Identities," *Global Networks* 2, no. 4 (2002): 335–356.

29. William A. Anderson, "Bringing Children into Focus on the Social Science Disaster Research Agenda," *International Journal of Mass Emergencies and Disasters* 23, no. 3 (2005): 159–175.

30. Inka Weissbecker, Sandra E. Sephton, Meagan B. Martin, and David M. Simpson, "Psychological and Physiological Correlates of Stress in Children Exposed to Disaster: Review of Current Research and Recommendations for Intervention," *Children, Youth and Environments* 18, no. 1 (2008): 30–70.

31. Annette M. La Greca, Wendy K. Silverman, Eric M. Vernberg, and Michael C. Roberts, "Introduction," in *Helping Children Cope with Disasters and Terrorism*, ed. A. M. La Greca, W. K. Silverman, E. M. Vernberg, and M. C. Roberts (Washington, DC: American Psychological Association, 2002), pp. 3–8.

32. Anne Westbrook Lauten and Kimberly Lietz, "A Look at the Standards Gap: Comparing Child Protection Responses in the Aftermath of Hurricane Katrina and the Indian Ocean Tsunami," *Children, Youth and Environments* 18, no. 1 (2008): 158–201.

SOCIAL NETWORKS
SECTION INTRODUCTION

The survivors we meet in these chapters tell of a brutal (and in most cases almost endless) disruption of their everyday lives—a disruption severe enough to threaten their sense of identity, their well-being, and their confidence in the future. In the months and years that followed Katrina, the force of those winds and the rush of those waters were matched by a powerful need to sustain old social networks and to create new ones—to draw individuals back into a center of kin, family, and familiarity. Unable to return to the *place* that had once been home, they tried to reconnect with the *persons* whom they identified with it.

The chapters in this second section of the volume explore displacement through the eyes of Katrina survivors in the locations where they landed after the storm. Most of the voices we hear are low-income African American women, and in one instance, black immigrants from Honduras.[1] They tell of a brutal and, in most cases, unending disruption to their everyday lives and important relationships—a disruption severe enough to shake how they conceived of their identity, physical and mental well-being, and their own and their cities' future.

The chapters report on this economic and social fallout from the disaster and how, in response, the women relied on a combination of informal, formal, and temporary assistance to get them through. As it became clear that a return to New Orleans was a long way off, evacuees developed strategies to remake old social networks in new locations.

The networks that formed after Katrina took shape in the context of entrenched systems of inequality. Women and men occupied different positions in the disaster, while the historic social and economic marginalization of African Americans exacerbated the vulnerabilities they faced in evacuation. In the case of the Garifuna community, highlighted in the chapter by

JACQUELYN LITT

Garza, inequalities in citizenship status interacted with gender and class to shape the evacuation experience.

The studies differ in whether they examine evacuee experiences in *formal* or *informal* networks. The first three chapters in this section focus predominantly on informal networks—how evacuees responded in and through the social relations of their everyday lives. The remaining two chapters focus on formal networks—how organized, purposive groups and institutions responded to and structured displacement.

INFORMAL NETWORKS

The chapters by Fussell, Litt, and Mason focus largely on how informal networks bend and reconfigure themselves to meet the extraordinary circumstance of evacuation and displacement. Beth Fussell's description of evacuees' desire for home signals what most of the authors in this section discovered: "Whether they evacuated before or after the hurricane struck, nearly all of the women explained their preparation for the hurricane as a social network–based strategy with the goal of remaining together while coping with the hurricane's effects." Fussell was writing about evacuation, but the point continues to be true of the long displacement that was to follow.

Fussell conducted a close analysis of what happens when normal processes of social exchange in networks are challenged by a catastrophe of Katrina's magnitude. She found that women's networks were important for the exchange of resources in the disaster's aftermath and during displacement, but she also makes clear the limits of informal networks for meeting all of a family's basic survival needs. She interviewed a group of young African American women who, before the storm, were enrolled in Delgado Community College or Louisiana Technical College in New Orleans. Fussell found that these women's networks were organized around the principle of homophily—bonding with others who are like you—and were characterized by low levels of material resources. In networks such as these, Fussell discovered that displacement disrupted normal strategies of exchange among network members and stretched these relationships to the breaking point. The principle of homophily compounded the losses, because their closest networks were composed of individuals who suffered similar losses.

Jacquelyn Litt's chapter analyzes how low-income African American women organized an evacuation chain from New Orleans that resulted in fifty-four individuals—including family members, friends, and acquaintances—coming together to live in a two-bedroom duplex in Baton Rouge for six weeks. She describes the importance of two women "anchors" in organizing the network's evacuation and the norms of reciprocity that helped support it. Litt's analysis points to women's informal carework as a significant safety net for evacuees. While evacuees sought and used assistance with food and other expenses from government and other formal institutions, Litt shows how a norm of care among key women dominated the evacuees' responses to kin members' needs. Networks expanded to meet the needs of individuals not yet part of the circle, and caregiving came to constitute the identity of the network anchors. However, the Baton Rouge home was only temporary, and eventually evacuees had to move on. The inevitable dispersal of the individuals from the home in Baton Rouge created deep despair among evacuees, because it meant the beginning of a long journey that pulled them away from "home" and the associated relationships that were the center of their lives. Like Fussell, Litt finds that informal network members eventually faced the limits of their social resources.

Beverly Mason's chapter paints a picture of community dissolution that can occur when long-standing social networks are disrupted. Mason's research took place in FEMA's largest trailer park in Baker, Louisiana. The government's relocation policy, which included partitioning individuals by age and household structure, quickly exacerbated problems of loss and isolation. The women Mason interviewed highlighted their painful dislocation from home, made worse also by being separated from their familiar communities and family members. These women had been "the salt of the earth," the kind of broad shoulders on which so much of New Orleans rested. As the women made their way through the new conditions of the trailer park—including crime and overcrowding—they built new networks of support.

From the research in these chapters one gains an understanding of how women's extraordinary carework and burdens were reconfigured by Katrina's displacement. Women responded to the disruption of their previous patterns of network survival by creating new techniques, finding new resources, and creating new relationships. The chapters highlight the significance of new and old network relationships as a way to capture and make the most of scarce resources, but they also reveal that network ties become fragile when resources are scarce. Women and their families suffered both emotionally and materially when their social networks ceased to function, making their need for new societies of support all the greater. But when those resources declined beyond a certain threshold, women found it increasingly difficult to create new networks and became even more vulnerable.

FORMAL NETWORKS

The chapters by Garza and Jenkins focus on new networks that were organized by religious leaders. These networks were organized not around kin, but around strategies for community building to help heal the social devastation wrought by the disaster.

In these formal networks, gender played a different organizing role than in previously described informal networks, since men were in positions of formal authority and in decision-making positions. The chapters explore how male pastors developed formal social networks. Both highlight the ways in which gendered power relationships within organizations and within family relationships were challenged and disrupted, and thereby made more visible, by the storm and the evacuation process.

Through her research on the Garifuna community, Cynthia M. Garza brings us into a network anchored by a pastor who helped over a hundred evacuees find housing in three apartment complexes in Houston. The pastor's access to and understanding of disaster relief resources in Houston, in addition to his sensitivity to Garifuna culture, made him a key resource for this community.

At the same time, displacement created challenges to the gender order. In the Garifuna community, men traditionally had more authority than women in family decision-making, and that included decisions regarding evacuation. But this authority was thrown into question when men's immigration status interfered with their ability to lead. Undocumented men, in particular, who had been dependent on an informal employment economy in New Orleans, did not have jobs or access to government assistance in the new setting, and they sometimes experienced a disruption of traditional gender norms.

In interviews with thirty displaced persons in Baton Rouge, Pam Jenkins presents a picture of the meaning and function of Black churches for displaced African Americans. The interviews revealed how salient the feeling of uncertainty was for individuals—months and even years after the storm—as they continued to feel "adrift." Testifying to the fundamental place of social connections, Jenkins's respondents said that their greatest need in recovery was spiritual support through community—even more important than their pressing material needs. In this context, the new possibilities of a "home church" helped evacuees reestablish old community ties, feel some continuity with the past, and develop new social connections.

Taken together, the research reported in this section provides a portrait that stands in contrast to the iconic imagery of chaos and desperation in the immediate aftermath of Katrina. Images from the Superdome and Convention Center portrayed disarray and chaos. People were represented on television as desperate, dependent, and, above all, disorderly, disorganized, and, in some cases, violent. However, as these chapters make clear, deep sources of organization were there to be tapped by the powerful call of kin and spiritual community. The analysis in these chapters suggests that the work undertaken by evacuees to preserve existing social networks and to participate in new ones was perhaps the critical means by which they met the challenge of disaster. Behind the apparent disorganization was a complex set of social relationships through which survivors provided each other assistance. Those relationships may have saved them from one of the greatest storms of our time.

NOTES

1. Prior to Katrina, the women evacuees in these studies had, for the most part, been employed in service sector jobs that were generally low-paying: they were housekeepers, cooks, and the like. Some were in community college. Some were retired. Others were disabled and no longer able to work. While covering a range of ages, most had small children in the household, and some were caring for disabled or ill kin as well. Most had spent their entire lives in New Orleans.

9

HELP FROM FAMILY, FRIENDS, AND STRANGERS DURING HURRICANE KATRINA
FINDING THE LIMITS OF SOCIAL NETWORKS

Faced with a disaster like Hurricane Katrina, people invariably turn to close family and friends to assist them in the evacuation and recovery.[1] However, not all networks are equally able to assist those affected by disaster. Disaster researchers have found that racial minorities, the elderly, members of households headed by women, and members of low-income households are more vulnerable to disasters.[2] Since social networks tend to concentrate similar people, networks whose members share characteristics associated with disaster vulnerability are more likely to experience collective as well as individual trauma and loss.[3] Kai Erikson first defined collective trauma as "being ripped out of a meaningful community setting" in which "people put their individual resources at the disposal of the group . . . and draw on that reserve supply for the demands of everyday life."[4] In New Orleans members of these more vulnerable networks quickly reached the limits of the networks' ability to provide assistance precisely because of this concentration of similarly vulnerable people.

In this chapter, I explore the capacity of social networks to assist Hurricane Katrina evacuees by drawing on the stories told by low-income mothers about their evacuations and prolonged dislocations from their homes. These stories come from interviews conducted with fifty-seven low-income mothers who had been enrolled in a New Orleans community college during the 2004–2005 academic year and were participating in a study of community college retention and graduation. Although the interviews were not designed to study social networks, comments about help and support received from family, friends, and strangers arose repeatedly throughout them. These stories illustrate the range of network capacities, as well as the limits of social networks, in providing assistance to low-income mothers in the wake of Hurricane Katrina.

ELIZABETH FUSSELL

Low-income women throughout the world exchange goods and assistance within their networks of family and friends as a way of coping with scarce resources.[5] These exchanges often make up the gap between earned income and expenditures in low-income households and ensure that all members are sheltered, fed, clothed, and cared for. Such exchanges were commonplace in New Orleans before Hurricane Katrina, when 23.7 percent of families had incomes below the poverty line. This level of poverty is not so different from the central cities of the 102 largest US metropolitan areas, where the average poverty rate is 18.4 percent, suggesting that the informal exchanges that occur in New Orleans may also occur in other US cities.[6]

New Orleans is unique, however, in that its residents and neighborhoods are exceptionally stable, thereby facilitating social network exchanges.[7] New Orleanians are particularly attached to their home state, with 77.4 percent of them having been born in Louisiana, while in the United States as a whole only 60 percent of people live in their state of birth.[8] This geographic stability of families and social networks created a deep trust in communities that was necessary for coping with ordinary shortages.[9]

As Hurricane Katrina's arrival was being forecast in late August of 2005, it was natural for New Orleanians to turn to their social networks for advice and assistance. As the disaster unfolded, these same networks were used to exchange information, emotional support, shelter, and in-kind assistance. However, the geographic concentration of social networks within New Orleans, particularly those of low-income residents, led to a common problem: everyone in the network was affected by the disaster.

The low-income mothers who were interviewed for this research were especially vulnerable to disaster because they tended to be members of small, dense, and similarly composed social networks. Usually sooner than later, these women had to turn to non-network sources of support, which were either strangers or formal disaster assistance organizations and volunteers. Support from outside their networks came from the Federal Emergency Management Agency (FEMA), the American Red Cross, their employers, religious congregations and organizations, charities, and concerned and caring strangers. I have selected, first, stories that examine the ways in which out-of-town family and friends were a resource, albeit limited by the overwhelming demand for assistance and shelter by New Orleanians evacuating the city. Second, I relate stories demonstrating how those without geographically dispersed social networks often turned to or received unexpected help from strangers. These stories reveal that those without strong outside networks had little control over their circumstances, often incurring greater costs and facing longer periods of uncertainty in their temporary shelters or homes. The last section shifts the focus from the capacity of social networks to provide shelter and other forms of material assistance to the networks' capacity for emotional support. The stories in this section suggest that many experienced collective trauma, particularly those whose communities had been completely destroyed.

THE STUDY

The interviews used for this analysis come from a study of low-income mothers attending Delgado Community College or Louisiana Technical College–West Bank (LTC). Delgado is the largest community college in Louisiana, enrolling about 15,000 students, of whom 68.9 percent are female, 50 percent are under age twenty-five, and 40.7 percent are non-Hispanic Blacks. Louisiana Technical College–West Bank is much smaller, enrolling about 700 students, of whom 38 percent are female, 42 percent are under age twenty-five, and 56 percent are non-Hispanic Blacks.[10] In the academic year 2002–2003, annual in-state tuition and fees were $1,404 and $484, respectively, for Delgado and LTC, and 36 percent and 77 percent of students received financial aid, mostly from federal sources. Delgado channels its graduates into a range of jobs that concentrate in the city—specifically health and business occupations or general education—while LTC grants mostly certificates in mechanics, repair technologies, and nursing.

The research was part of the Opening Doors Demonstration Study, an experiment carried out by Manpower Demonstration Research Corporation to see if financial aid and academic counseling could improve retention and graduation rates at several community colleges in five different states in the United States. Students eligible for participation at the time of recruitment in 2004 were between eighteen and thirty-four years old, had at least one child younger than the age of nineteen, and had a family income below 200 percent of the federal poverty level. Furthermore, participants had at least a high school diploma or a GED and did not have any other degree or occupational certificate from an accredited college or university. The study's investigators recruited 1,019 students, who were 95 percent female and 85 percent non-Hispanic Blacks. They were on average 24.9 years old, 86 percent were not currently living with partners or spouses, and they averaged 1.8 children. More than half were currently employed, with half of those working thirty to forty hours per week or more. The average hourly wage they received was eight dollars. Among the whole sample of students, 78 percent had graduated from high school, 18 percent had received their GED, and 9 percent had received an occupational or technical certificate from a nonaccredited college or university. They had all completed a baseline phone survey in which they provided information about their current living arrangements, employment, educational participation, their children's circumstances, and their mental and physical health, as well as other topics.

When Katrina struck on August 29, 2005, 492 students had already been surveyed in a second round of phone interviews. Rather than ending the project, some members of the research team reorganized it to study adversity and resilience among these community college students. This research team consisted of Christina A. Paxson, Jean Rhodes, Cecilia Rouse, and Mary C. Waters. I joined the team to participate in the qualitative research component. Eighty-two percent (402 out of 492) of those who had been interviewed just before Katrina were traced using publicly available records. They were interviewed from April 2006 through March 2007, between eight and nineteen months after Hurricane Katrina. Mary Waters and I designed a qualitative study of a subset of the students to complement the phone surveys. Three interviewers, Petrice Sams-Abiodun, Stacey Bosick, and I, conducted intensive in-person interviews with fifty-seven women from the larger sample, and these form the data for this chapter.

To understand how the experience of being displaced for a prolonged period differed from that of having returned to New Orleans, we selected half our interviewees from those who had returned to the New Orleans area and half from those who were living at the time in or around Baton Rouge, Houston, or Dallas. To ensure that we were including those who had been affected by Hurricane Katrina, we selected interviewees who had lived in Orleans Parish at the time of Katrina, or had lived in Jefferson Parish at that time and suffered damage to their pre-Katrina home. All interviewees were women between the ages of eighteen and twenty-nine, and fifty-five of the fifty-seven were non-Hispanic Blacks (one interviewee was non-Hispanic White and another was a Pacific Islander). These interviews typically lasted between one and two hours and covered a range of topics, including the interviewees' childhood and family of origin; their education, work, partnering, and parenting histories; their experiences during and after Katrina; and their expectations and hopes for the future. The interviews were conducted in a mutually convenient location, which may have been the interviewee's home, the interviewer's office, a hotel room, a restaurant, or a library. Still-displaced participants were interviewed in the city in which they currently resided, unless they happened to be visiting New Orleans and it was more convenient to conduct the interview there.

The sample is not representative of New Orleans's population, since it includes mostly low-income Black women with a high school education or more. The sample is interesting, nonetheless, because it includes women who had taken charge of their lives by enrolling in school, even while they also had jobs and were raising children. Having faced these day-to-day challenges, they were perhaps more resourceful in the face of a disaster. Viewed this way, these women have much in common, but their stories reveal a great deal of variation in how they coped with the adversity of Katrina.

RELYING ON FAMILY AND FRIENDS

When the alarming warnings of the threat from Hurricane Katrina were initially issued, social networks began operating in familiar ways. Women in our survey reported that they received warnings from their coworkers, friends, or relatives, which often came with strong advice, if not a demand, that they evacuate. The most persuasive advice came from family members and often included an appeal to their identities as mothers. For example, Rachelle, a twenty-five-year-old Black single mother of three children, is part of a tight-knit family of seven siblings. She was working at a fast-food restaurant and living on her own with her children but in close proximity to her sisters and brothers on the eve of Hurricane Katrina. Rachelle's narrative reveals the powerful influence of her close family members in her decisions to leave New Orleans and, later, to return:

> At first we were going to stay [in New Orleans] but . . . [m]y auntie made us leave. [She said] I better get up and get my children and we better leave. We don't have no choice. . . . [When we got to my uncle's house in Baton Rouge] . . . [i]t was almost fifteen of us altogether. . . . Then my other cousins came. . . . And then my sister came. We found everybody. We left and went to Texas [where my sister had already found a place]. And we stayed in Texas for a year. . . . We all lived in the same apartment complex except my brother and one sister. They lived two miles from us in another set of apartments. I was about to work at Taco Bell. But everybody was deciding they wanted to go home. I really didn't want to leave, because I loved the schools out there. The area was okay. They offered me

a house but I didn't take it. I wanted to come home. But now I feel that I should have stayed. I love New Orleans but I think I should have stayed . . . for my kids.

Later in the interview Rachelle discussed the importance of being physically close to her siblings. Before Katrina, and even now, they exchange childcare, meals, and conversation on a daily basis. Rachelle's dependence on her siblings is characteristic of many women in the study, who regularly exchange goods and services with members of their social networks.

Like Rachelle, Latasha, a twenty-eight-year-old Black single mother of two children, left New Orleans to go to the home of family living out of harm's way. New Orleanians typically had few relations outside of the city, and those relatives' homes were quickly overwhelmed by so many people seeking temporary shelter. Seventeen people ended up staying in a two-bedroom apartment that Latasha's twenty-one-year-old brother shared with his fiancée and a roommate in a small town where he attended college. Latasha described the arrangement:

We were going to stay [in New Orleans], but I thought about my children and I needed to get out. [My brother] told us to come here. He had room for us. The plan was me, my mom, my fiancé, and my two children. But my auntie couldn't find a hotel and that's how [she and her three children] wound up coming with us. [My brother and his fiancée] had three more friends who had to evacuate. We managed. Thank God my little brother had a place for us to stay. Cause otherwise we would be staying in a shelter.

After a week Latasha and the other people in her brother's apartment found separate accommodations with FEMA housing assistance, but they all stayed in the area. The college Latasha's brother attended had become a source of support, with students and staff bringing food, clothes, entertainment, and other types of assistance to the Katrina evacuees. In this way, the overwhelmed family support system was supplemented by more anonymous forms of mostly material support, which helped keep the social network from becoming overburdened.

Other women more quickly reached the limits of their social networks' ability to provide help. For example, Shaina, a twenty-five-year old Black single mother of one young child, went to upstate Louisiana to stay at the home of an elderly great-uncle along with twenty-five other family members. Her uncle lived in a community that was in the storm's path and had lost electricity. Furthermore, the large number of evacuees arriving there had depleted the stocks of local groceries. These shortages raised the temperature in this already overheated social network, straining relations with her uncle so badly that Shaina said she would "rather drive to Seattle and go around and come [home]" than go back to his house in future hurricane evacuations. She was especially upset about this because when he came to New Orleans "he was always treated like a king." While Shaina was angered by her elderly uncle's failure to reciprocate the generosity he received on visits to New Orleans, the demands placed on him after Hurricane Katrina were unforeseeable and overwhelming.

Other women encountered out-of-town social network members who were unable or unwilling to provide them with assistance, and therefore they had to continue traveling until they found social network members who could help. Traci, a twenty-nine-year-old single Black mother living with her two children, moved multiple times until she and her siblings and their families were able to settle together. Here, she explains why she moved so often after Katrina:

> First, I wasn't with my family. I was with [my sister-in-law's family], and they told us that me and my kids had to leave because their family was paying for [their relatives] to stay in a hotel. . . . So we came back to Baton Rouge by my mama's people, [and] after that my sister and brothers [came to] Baton Rouge. We . . . got all together and went back to Dallas. . . . My cousin was there in Dallas and he said they were giving assistance. We needed assistance being that we had kids. We went from Dallas to Denton and from Denton we [stayed] in a hotel for two weeks. They helped us to find housing. From there we got our houses within two weeks. I stayed [in Denton] eight months. My sister [stayed] there five or six months [before returning to New Orleans].

Although Traci had a dispersed social network, she was not close to those individuals. The geographic concentration of Traci's strongest social ties within New Orleans made it difficult for her, and likely for many other New Orleanians, to find out-of-town evacuation destinations with family or friends, so they stayed instead in hotels at first and then FEMA housing.

Many of those lacking strong ties to family or friends outside of New Orleans stayed in the safest place they could find within the city. Ladonna, a twenty-two-year-old Black mother of five, had few family members she could count on, since her mother had died years ago and she was estranged from her siblings. At the time of the hurricane she lived with her boyfriend and their five children. She also relied heavily on Duane, a White man in his sixties, because of the help she had received from him in the past:

> I've been knowing [Duane] for about six years. When my mom died, he took me in. I didn't have a place to go. . . . We didn't evacuate. We stayed at [Duane's] house . . . for two weeks. That was the worst two weeks of my life. . . . [W]e didn't have food. . . . My children didn't have diapers. My children's father had to go into a store and grab some diapers and baby wipes and food, things that we could use. We had a generator but we didn't have gas. We were siphoning gas around here from cars to keep the generator running because we had a newborn. It was really chaos out there. . . . [S]ome guy kicked down the door. He must have thought that we had evacuated. He kicked down the door and was trying to get in here. [Duane] has a couple of rifles around. He was charging after the guy telling him, "I'll shoot you if you come in my house." I was really happy to be at [Duane's] house during the time of the hurricane because . . . [h]e can help himself well.

Ladonna's case illustrates that those who did not evacuate, often because their social networks were small or composed of people with few resources, were exposed to greater dangers than those who were able to evacuate the city.

About four out of five women in our sample evacuated New Orleans before Hurricane Katrina struck. Those who did not often took precautions and joined together with family and friends in two-story homes or in neighborhoods on higher ground or at their place of employment. They sometimes remained in order to maintain contact with important family members. For example, one woman who had the means to get out refused to leave until her son's father returned him to her, two others stayed at the hotels where their relatives worked and where they thought they would be safe, and others stayed because elderly relatives would not or could not leave. Whether they evacuated before or after the hurricane struck, nearly all of the women explained their preparation for the hurricane as a social network–based strategy with the goal of remaining together while coping with the hurricane's effects.

Family and friends were the critical resource for coping with the preparation, evacuation, and displacement, and sometimes, the return to New Orleans. The preceding stories show how, after getting out of harm's way, reconstituting the family in a single place was of utmost concern for the women we interviewed. However, three critical limitations of social networks' capacity to provide disaster assistance are evident. First, local social network members could not offer assistance, because they, too, were displaced. Second, out-of-town members of social networks were often overwhelmed by the demands of so many New Orleanians in their households and communities. This limited the length of time large families could stay together in the homes of family and friends. Finally, many women lacked any network contacts outside of New Orleans, which often meant they spent more money on food and shelter and faced a greater period of uncertainty.

THE ALTRUISM OF STRANGERS

When our study participants' regular social networks became displaced or overwhelmed, many sought and received help from strangers. Samantha, a twenty-seven-year-old Black single mother of two, had gone to her aunt's three-story home on the West Bank instead of evacuating. Although this area did not flood, the wind tore the roof off her aunt's home. Without any electricity, they had no news of what was going on around them, so Samantha used her telephone and created a network of strangers to learn what was happening. She described the situation:

> We still had landline service . . . so we was able to call out. [W]e would just dial numbers, like different area codes, and we would . . . tell them where we were from and [that] we didn't have no TV or nothing. We was asking them to tell us what was going on in New Orleans, and that's how we really found out like how bad it was. . . . [A] lot of people . . . was nice and . . . pretty much was telling us what we wanted to know. . . . We talked to people in California, Tennessee, Oklahoma. . . . [We didn't call family] . . . because . . . everybody had the 504 area code.[11] All their phones was gone because they lived in New Orleans. . . . So we didn't have no way to get in contact with nobody. . . . Like one lady, we bonded real good. [W]e would call back and forth, and she would always update us or see how we doing and stuff like that. And she gave us her number, and she was like, "Well if you all ever need anything, or when you all get out call and let me know . . . that you were okay."

Samantha continued to rely on strangers during this desperate time. She wanted to go to Texas because she thought her family would be there, but her aunt wanted to go to Atlanta. So Samantha and her children got a ride to the highway with her aunt and then parted ways.

I just stood out there [by the road], and [a stranger] saw us with the suitcases and she was asking me what was going on and I went to telling her the story and she asked me did I want to come to her house, and I said yeah. We got in the truck [with her].

Samantha and her children were housed and fed by this generous stranger until the end of September, when she went to Dallas to try to find her brothers and sisters.

Some women had never left New Orleans and knew no one outside of the city. This made them more reluctant to evacuate in the first place and therefore more likely to end up in a shelter. Nicole, a twenty-three-year-old Black married mother of three children, did not evacuate prior to the hurricane, but went to her husband's aunt's home in a safer part of the city. Five days after the hurricane, her family took a bus out of New Orleans. Nicole contrasts her experience of being from a lifelong New Orleans family with her three weeks in an evacuation shelter, in which her family lived with hundreds of strangers:

[During the evacuation] . . . I was kind of a little shaken up because this was all new to me. We were on a bus and tears just began to run out of my eyes because I was going to an unfamiliar place that I have never been. I've been in New Orleans all my life. All my children were born and raised in New Orleans. My entire family, that is where we are from, New Orleans. . . . Then we had to go into a shelter with tons of people that I didn't even know. We are all sharing a bathroom and we are sleeping together. You had to get accustomed to living like this. . . . We were supposed to be on a bus headed to Dallas. Dallas was too packed. Houston was too packed. So we wound up going to Mesquite. . . . [W]e stopped there, we took showers. Did all kind of stuff there and then they took us over to Wylie, Texas, . . . where we stayed in the armory.

Although it was uncomfortable staying in the shelter with so many strangers, the residents of Wylie generously helped the evacuees.

[I]t was a little town, maybe about 18,000 people. They had donated cars. They had school supplies. They had a store where . . . everybody in the town was donating stuff . . . gift cards to Wal-Mart. We were getting three meals a day. There was a chef that was in the armory with us from New Orleans. . . . He was cooking New Orleans food in there. They took the kids school shopping when school came. They had the bus to come pick them up. Anywhere that you had to go, there was somebody that was as-signed to you to help you take care of your business. So that was a bless-ing. They really helped us out.

The residents of Wylie gave the shelter residents housing assistance, and most relocated to larger urban areas. Nicole received six months of rent and utilities on an apartment in Dallas. Nicole's husband also continued to receive pay from his employer, a national package delivery service, during this time. Both these non-network sources of support helped Nicole and her family to settle into Dallas, since they were unable to return to their flooded home in New Orleans East.

These stories illustrate how evacuees who had no family or friends out-side of New Orleans to provide shelter in the immediate aftermath of Katrina had to travel with their immediate family to an unfamiliar place and seek assistance together. Because they did not have free homes to stay in while they were waiting to learn about disaster assistance, they often incurred significant hotel bills and other expenses while waiting to learn if or when they could return home. Alicia, a twenty-one-year-old Black single mother who lived with her daughter, mother, and grandmother be-fore Katrina, decided to go east to Georgia simply because traffic was some-what lighter going that direction by late Sunday afternoon, August 28, the day before Hurricane Katrina struck. Her extended family caravanned, with her daughter, mother, grandmother, and sister in her car, and her cousins and their families in other cars:

We stayed in that hotel [in Georgia] for two nights. It was filthy . . . [s]o I called my job . . . [a national hotel chain] and . . . they gave me an advance pay. We went from that hotel to the hotel next door because it was much cleaner. So we stayed at that hotel for three weeks. . . . [Local] people [were] there helping when the levees broke. And they were just calling hotels saying, "Here's my credit card. I'm going to pay for two nights for three families . . ." Red Cross didn't kick in until later. Then I called my credit card company, they gave me an emergency credit increase, even if I didn't qualify. That's when Red Cross [and FEMA] started kicking in. People talk but it took a long time for the government assistance to kick in. [After three weeks] . . . United Way ran out. We couldn't stay at the hotel anymore. So we left there, went to another hotel. The same thing happened . . . a lot of fraud started going on. So we left there and went to another hotel. We [stayed] in that hotel for weeks. We didn't get into a house because nobody still wasn't giving us houses because we didn't meet the [income] qualifications. . . . They weren't accepting FEMA. We end up working with this church. . . . [T]hey end up putting us in a house and that was at the end of November, right before Thanksgiving. The whole family . . . stayed at the same hotels, went through the same thing, not having money.

Even with Alicia's demonstrated expertise in managing bureaucratic systems, she ended up much worse off after the hurricane. When I interviewed her in New Orleans, she was living in her mother's pre-Katrina home, which they were rebuilding little by little, working in a less suitable job than before Katrina, and trying to pay off a sizable credit card debt. Not having an out-of-town family member or friend to help her get oriented and connected to local resources quickly translated into a large credit card debt and a prolonged period of unstable housing.

These stories illustrate how women in our study looked for safety and shelter for their families without the assistance of a large or spatially dispersed social network. Instead they turned to strangers, employers, credit card companies, disaster assistance organizations, and charities for material help in the disaster aftermath. Their stories suggest that these women without large or geographically dispersed social networks—compared to those who had them—were less likely to evacuate before the hurricane, had less control over their evacuation destination, and were more likely to stay in shelters or incur significant debt while staying in hotels. In short, their experiences were less predictable and often exacted greater costs, especially when these costs were not mitigated by the aid of good Samaritans.

COPING WITH LOSS

Whether the women in our study found shelter with out-of-town family and friends or not, nearly all evacuated with their immediate, and sometimes extended, families, so that their emotional support system remained intact and close. This was a comfort as the news of the levee breaks and the flooding of the city circulated. For example, Dawn, a twenty-one-year-old Black mother of one who was engaged to her child's father, described the comfort of being with family during the months after the disaster:

I just watched shows [about New Orleans] and cried, because it's like that's where I could have been if I would have stayed. But, for the most part, I was all right. [My fiancé] kept me together. And other family members that wind up being close. [I was] living in a house with twenty people. Everybody looking at the news, but they're like, "You're all right. We're here, and we'll just pray for those that we don't really know about yet."

However, for some, this closeness could also be stifling. Lisanne, a twenty-four-year-old married mother of two, evacuated to Houston with her husband, children, and extended family and stayed in a hotel housing evacuees:

Everybody who evacuated with each other, we are all close. [But] we didn't want to see each other when we evacuated because we were around each other too much. My mom's sister's kids and all of us, we are close. And my mom is close to her sisters. So if you see one, you are going to see somebody else with us. . . . I was okay in Houston because everybody was with everybody. But I think I would have cracked up if I didn't have anybody with me.

Other families unraveled during this time. Shannon, a twenty-eight-year-old Black mother of one who was in her seventh month of pregnancy, described the change in her relationship with her boyfriend:

[Before the hurricane] . . . it was like almost the perfect relationship. But after the hurricane, it went downhill . . . [b]ecause he was saying that . . . I treat him bad . . . and he left his family to be with me [during the evacuation]. And I felt like you left your family, but you have a family. . . . I don't know where my family is. . . . I done lost everything. The place where I grew up at, that's gone. My high school—gone. My elementary school—gone. I can't never bring my kids and show them where I come from. You know? And he didn't realize that that was something serious. [He] can always go back to [his] neighborhood and see people that [he] knows. I can't do that. . . . And you don't realize [how special people are] till you can't see them no more. A lot of people right now . . . I don't know if they're dead or if they're alive because I haven't [seen them]. . . . I feel like things not going to ever be the way they were before. . . . And he just didn't understand that and . . . that's the main thing we used to argue about was that, right there.

Shannon's boyfriend's lack of compassion for her losses ultimately undid their relationship.

Some women, even if they were surrounded by family, still felt alone and without support. In some instances it was because of the collective losses suffered by their network, as in the case of Latoya, a thirty-year-old separated mother with five children, whose extended family was concentrated in the devastated Lower Ninth Ward. When Latoya was asked whether her family helped her during the evacuation, she answered:

> Not really, because . . . and I don't think it was because purposely. I just think that everybody was going through it in a different manner. Because all of our family lived in New Orleans, so everybody lost everything. . . . And most of my family lived in the Ninth Ward, where the worst damage was. So they were still traumatized deeply about the loss of everything.

Latoya coped with her loneliness through prayer, though she found it overwhelming being a single parent without family and friends nearby for support. She continued:

> I really dealt with it on my own, because I didn't really know people here. . . . I had friends, maybe two friends, that I can say are my very, very best friends, but neither one of them were here. They weren't in arm's reach. So we was talking together, but of course it's not the same as somebody being physically there. . . . So I really just prayed a lot, and that's what strengthened my relationship with God, because I had nothing and no one else to turn to. . . . And then still having to be a parent, I had to keep my kids with me. I had to like be the strong person, because they needed me so. It was like I would go through the whole day, and I would be okay because I had to be. And then at night, when the house was settled, the kids are asleep, that's when it really hit me. So some days I would just cry. It was hard. So I—I didn't have anybody at that time to . . . [she doesn't finish her sentence].

While the loss of property was difficult to accept, the loss of communality was perhaps more significant. The last two interviewees, Shannon and Latoya, both found it especially difficult to cope with the loss of their homes and neighborhoods, which contained their network of family and friends. Natasha, a twenty-eight-year-old separated Black mother of two children who was living in Houston, was unable to return to the shuttered housing project where she had lived in New Orleans. When asked whether she considered New Orleans or Houston to be home, she replied:

At this point, I still don't believe home is anywhere. . . . I consider wherever I am with my kids as home. . . . It's like Katrina just stripped me of roots. I don't have any roots [in New Orleans] anymore because it's not the same. And I don't have any roots [in Houston].

The loss of place and communality multiplied the trauma of the evacuation and displacement for these women. This collective trauma, like that described by Erikson in Buffalo Creek, West Virginia,[12] could not be overcome by the resources of extensive social networks, the support and assistance of family and friends, organizations offering disaster assistance, or generous strangers.

The stories related here reveal a range of experiences differing in whether and for how long the women in our sample were able to depend on their kin for help in removing themselves and their children from danger and finding temporary shelter. They also differed in whether family and friends were available and able to provide these women the emotional support they so desperately needed in this time of personal and collective loss. Most importantly, these stories show the limits of the small, spatially concentrated, and homogeneous social networks of low-income mothers to absorb the losses inflicted by Katrina and the failure of the levees, and how, for some, those losses were so widespread within their network that they constituted a collective trauma.

This study does not allow us to compare the experiences of these low-income Black women, many of whom are female household heads, to other social groups who are thought to be less vulnerable to the effects of disasters. However, if these women were in fact more vulnerable and therefore experienced longer periods of displacement, more difficulty in returning to their pre-Katrina homes or establishing new homes, and a greater likelihood of having lost their material possessions and homes in the flooding, as research suggests,[13] then we might also conclude that they were at a greater risk of experiencing collective trauma. The stories these women told us about their experiences evacuating and recovering from Hurricane Katrina suggest that differential vulnerability to disaster is compounded as a result of the concentration of vulnerable groups within social networks.

ACKNOWLEDGMENTS

This research was funded by a grant from the MacArthur Foundation's Study Group on Transition to Adulthood. The interviews were designed and carried out by Stacey

Bosick, Elizabeth Fussell, and Petrice Sams-Abiodun, in consultation with Mary Waters. I am grateful to all the participants in the Adversity and Resilience Study who agreed to be interviewed. Their willingness to share their stories reveals the persistently welcoming nature of the city's residents, who generously share their thoughts and feelings with family, friends, and even strangers.

NOTES

1. Thomas E. Drabek, *Human System Responses to Disaster: An Inventory of Sociological Findings* (New York: Springer-Verlag, 1986).

2. Alice Fothergill, Enrique G. M. Maestas, and JoAnne De Rouen Darlington, "Race, Ethnicity, and Disasters in the United States: A Review of the Literature," *Disasters* 23, no. 2 (June 1999): 156–173; Alice Fothergill and Lori Peek, "Poverty and Disasters in the United States: A Review of Recent Sociological Findings," *Natural Hazards* 32, no. 1 (2004): 89–110; Walter Gillis Peacock, Betty Hearn Morrow, and Hugh Gladwin, *Hurricane Andrew: Ethnicity, Gender, and the Sociology of Disasters* (New York: Routledge, 1997).

3. Miller McPherson, Lynn Smith-Lovin, and James M. Cook, "Birds of a Feather: Homophily in Social Networks," *Annual Review of Sociology* 27 (2001): 415–444; Elizabeth Fussell, "Leaving New Orleans: Social Stratification, Networks, and Hurricane Evacuation," Understanding Katrina (Brooklyn, NY: Social Science Research Council, June 11, 2006), http://understandingkatrina.ssrc.org/Fussell/.

4. Kai T. Erikson, *Everything in Its Path: Destruction of Community in the Buffalo Creek Flood* (New York: Simon and Schuster 1976), p. 194.

5. Lourdes Benería, "The Mexican Debt Crisis: Restructuring the Economy and the Household," in *Unequal Burden: Economic Crises, Persistent Poverty, and Women's Work*, ed. L. Benería and S. Feldman (Boulder, CO: Westview Press, 1992), pp. 83–104; Joel Devine and Petrice Sams-Abiodun, "Household Survival Strategies in a Public Housing Development," *Research in Urban Sociology* 6 (2001): 277–311; Kathryn Edin and Laura Lein, *Making Ends Meet: How Single Mothers Survive Welfare and Low-Wage Work* (New York: Russell Sage Foundation, 1997); Mercedes Gonzalez de la Rocha, *The Resources of Poverty: Women and Survival in a Mexican City* (Oxford: Blackwell, 1994); Carol B. Stack, *All Our Kin: Strategies for Survival in a Black Community* (New York: Harper and Row, 1974).

6. Alan Berube and William Frey, "A Decade of Mixed Blessings: Urban and Suburban Poverty in Census 2000" (Washington, DC: Center on Urban and Metropolitan Policy, Brookings Institution, 2002), http://www.brookings.edu/~/media/Files/rc/reports/2002/08demographics_berube/berubefreypoverty.pdf, accessed December 4, 2008; U.S. Census Bureau, "Census 2000 Demographic Profile Highlights for New Orleans (Orleans Parish), Louisiana," American Factfinder, http://factfinder.census.gov/servlet/SAFFFacts?_event=&geo_id=16000US2255000&_geoContext=01000US|04000US22|16000US2255000&_street=&_county=New+Or

leans&_cityTown=New+Orleans&_state=04000US22&_zip=&_lang=en&_
sse=on&ActiveGeoDiv=&_useEV=&pctxt=fph&pgsl=160&_submenuId=fa
ctsheet_1&ds_name=ACS_2009_5YR_SAFF&_ci_nbr=null&qr_name=null&r
eg=&_keyword=&_industry=, accessed December 4, 2008.

7. Devine and Sams-Abiodun, "Household Survival Strategies"; Juliette Land-phair, "'The Forgotten People of New Orleans': Community, Vulnerability, and the Lower Ninth Ward," *Journal of American History* 94, no. 3 (December 2007): 837–845; Petrice Sams-Abiodun, "Missing Data, Missing Men: The Role of Adult Men in Inner-City Neighborhoods" (PhD diss., Tulane University, 2003).

8. U.S. Census Bureau, "Census 2000 Demographic Profile Highlights for New Orleans."

9. Devine and Sams-Abiodun, "Household Survival Strategies"; Sams-Abiodun, "Missing Data, Missing Men."

10. Thomas Brock and Lashawn Richburg-Hayes, "Paying for Persistence: Early Results of a Louisiana Scholarship Program for Low-Income Parents Attending Community College" (New York and Oakland: Manpower Development Research Corporation, May 2006), http://www.mdrc.org/publications/429/full.pdf, accessed May 28, 2008.

11. Cell phones with the 504 area code were mostly inoperable because the network was overwhelmed. Land lines were also inoperable in places where flood or wind damage had disrupted services. The East Bank of New Orleans, where she was taking refuge, was not flooded and apparently didn't suffer wind damage.

12. Erikson, *Everything in Its Path*.

13. Elizabeth Fussell, Narayan Sastry, and Mark VanLandingham, "Race, Socio-economic Status, and Return Migration to New Orleans after Hurricane Katrina," *Population & Environment* 31, nos. 1–3 (2010): 20–42; Jeffrey A. Groen and Anne E. Polivka, "Going Home after Hurricane Katrina: Determinants of Return Migration and Changes in Affected Areas," *Demography* 47, no. 4 (2010): 821–844.

10

"WE NEED TO GET TOGETHER WITH EACH OTHER"

WOMEN'S NARRATIVES OF HELP IN KATRINA'S DISPLACEMENT

While public images of African Americans in the immediate aftermath of Katrina resound with chaos and pathology, hidden stories of social support and mutual assistance challenge these stereotypes. The practices of informal assistance among African American women disaster survivors, for example, have received very little public attention, partly because these practices are organized by networks of support that operate beyond the scope of and visibility to public institutions, and thus they require the rare in-depth research offered in this volume. Inattention to the contribution of these particular survivors is also built into the general disregard for Black women's labor in households and communities.[1] In this chapter I suggest that these less visible women-centered networks of care not only were essential survival resources for the most vulnerable of those displaced by Katrina,[2] but also were the key connections through which survivors identified themselves and measured the success or failure of their recovery.

In the analysis below I identify the practices of carework that defined women evacuees' responsibilities in Katrina's aftermath. "Help" in this context was not individual acts of aid or assistance but sets of actions that were part of and contributed to network relationships. Because evacuees were often shifting between offering assistance and needing it, help also constituted both giving and receiving.[3] New Orleans itself appeared to nurture a commitment to communal interdependence. Indeed, unlike those in any other place I have visited in my studies of women's carework in perilous circumstances, my respondents from New Orleans spoke about having felt cared for and safe in their home city. While displacement after Hurricane Katrina broke up some of those networks of assistance, the fact that families had lived for generations in the city, even on the same street or in the same neighborhood, meant that they knew the value of networks and knew how to form them.

JACQUELYN LITT

This chapter focuses on the narratives of two women—a mother (whom I call Miss Joanne) and her adult daughter (whom I call Wendy)—who sustained a large network of people who escaped New Orleans in the hours before the hurricane hit and for six weeks afterward. Miss Joanne's and Wendy's experiences were similar to the survival stories I heard from other evacuees. The research I report on in this chapter covers the time between August 28, 2005, when Wendy fled New Orleans for Baton Rouge, and mid-October 2005, when she arrived in Missouri to resettle.

Approximately five hundred evacuees came to my hometown, Columbia, Missouri, after Hurricane Katrina.[4] To understand how the evacuation took shape in Columbia, I conducted interviews and attended focus groups with close to eighty people who were involved in the Katrina displacement: evacuees, social service personnel, city leaders, and faith-based volunteers and donors. I conducted participant-observation in many settings where evacuees sought services (e.g., service provider agencies and meetings of evacuees) or found recreation (e.g., church outreach programs and bowling parties for families).[5]

Wendy was born in New Orleans on August 28, 1975. On her thirtieth birthday, she evacuated New Orleans with a caravan of over twenty people. At the time of her evacuation, Wendy lived in her mother's duplex in the Seventh Ward, along with her three young children—Luke, Hisha, and Bill—and her brother. As we toured her neighborhood in early 2006, Wendy described the former occupants of each house, their ties to her, and their fate in the storm. At the time the storm and floods roared in, Wendy was working as a cashier, a service sector job that was common among African American women in New Orleans.

Wendy's mother, Miss Joanne, owned (and still owns) the house. Miss Joanne lived her entire life in this area, and her large extended network had occupied houses in adjacent blocks for decades. She worked for most of her life as a housekeeper at Loyola University. As luck would have it, she moved—temporarily, she thought—to Baton Rouge into a rental house shortly before the storm because her husband took a new job there, through his son's connections, in a welding plant.

During the course of my research, I saw Wendy—and the friends from New Orleans she evacuated with—almost weekly until, in August 2006, she left Columbia to return to Baton Rouge. I also had a close relationship with her children. Since her return to Louisiana, I have visited five times and have regular phone contact. During one of these visits, Wendy took me to meet her mother, whom I have interviewed three times since then, first in February 2007, again in February 2008, and yet again in February 2009.

HELP BEFORE THE DISASTER

The people in my study described their lives back home in New Orleans as being immersed in networks of care. Miss Joanne described her life as a web of connections. For as long as she could remember, daily life was entwined with those closest to her on her street and in the neighborhood. She explains the reasons she bought her house in 1992:

> My mama was right next door. I could never leave my mother. My mother was right next door. . . . I had dinner there every night. . . . She was right in the house next to my house. The house that sits back. The yellow house with the big posts . . . that was my mother's house. And the house next to that was my brother and my sister used to stay on that side. And my sister was staying in the house next to that, and I was staying in the other house before I moved to that house 'cuz it was bigger, so I moved in that house. But we lived down the street, and then we lived over here at the corner over here. We stayed right in that area. I was raised in that area. I seen my classmate and he said, "Where you at now, Miss Joanne?" I say, "Oh God, where am I at? I ain't never moved." [He said,] "Girl, you been living there since . . ." I've been in that area since I was five years old. That area, and I'm fifty-seven. Five years old, I was in that area. 'Cuz I knowed everybody. I felt safe.

Because most members of her social network worked in low-income jobs and were economically vulnerable, the communal ties served, in part, to mitigate the insecurities wrought by poverty. But, as I later came to understand, the networks of care were not only about necessity—they were also about identity. Miss Joanne's, Wendy's, and others' sense of who they were was bound up in both providing and receiving care—emotional as well as material.

Particular needs at any moment determined what help would be offered or sought: family members took in children of kin for a school year or for months or years when such help was necessary; getting children to and from school and childcare was collective work; dinners were shared spontaneously when people stopped by; job information was exchanged and jobs were sought together; and small sums of cash were exchanged regularly.

Below Miss Joanne describes another form of network assistance, one that she considered emblematic of the collective care that defined her life in New Orleans:

> When I used to walk to that bus stop [in the morning to get to work], I used to pray and ask God to get me from one end to the other. Not knowing you could get hurt or anything. 'Cuz I used to leave in the darkness sometimes. Sometimes my husband wasn't there to bring me, I had to walk there by myself. But I always felt secure because even in that lower area where I was staying, I knew everybody. And I'm gonna tell you this, they say about those drugs, those boys on drugs, but many days I walked that street at night. Five o'clock or 4:30 in the morning, catching the bus to go to work at Loyola University . . . They had the boys that was on drugs. [I met one of those boys years later and he said], "Brownie [Miss Joanne's nickname], I saw you and I told your son, I say, I see your mama walking out there but I be watching and she don't see me, sometimes I might holler, but I be noticing what time she be coming out, and I say I'll watch her and I'll look out for you." I pray for that, that child right there is the child that helped protect me. And I didn't even know he was doing it until he said it that day. And when he said that, I knew he was watching me 'cuz he's the one that saw me when I crossed over there. Nobody else was there. Pitched dark. Nobody out there.

Wendy, too, described pre-Katrina New Orleans as a place where "anybody would help you out." She was close and in daily contact with her cousins and aunties, most of whom knew the intricate details of her daily life as well as her children's struggles and successes. When problems arose with the children, kin stepped in, often by phone, but sometimes in person. There was constant visiting in and out of each other's homes. Wendy spent much of her time with her friend Rona (who then got very close to Wendy's mother) doing errands, and sharing childcare, job tips, money, meals, and recreation. When referring to Rona, Wendy said, "When we was in New Orleans, oh yeah, I always help out with her kids and stuff. We always did help each other. . . . We knew them for a lot of years too. They family."

"BRING EVERYBODY OVER":
NETWORKS OF HELP IN EVACUATION

Miss Joanne was awakened on Sunday, August 28, 2005, by a frantic phone call from a relative who had decided that morning, one day before the hurricane hit, that she had to flee New Orleans. The call alerted Miss Joanne to the gravity of the situation, which she then explained to her daughter in another frantic phone call: "If Shirley is leaving, then everybody should." Miss Joanne called other kin and friends in the city imploring them to "get out." Wendy wanted to get out, but she could not. She did not own a car, nor did she have money to pay anyone to get her out or even to help with the gas. "What my daughter was telling me was that she had no way out." So Miss Joanne offered to buy the gas for anyone who would help her daughter escape:

> Tell anybody, whoever it is, get whoever you could get it. Tell them I got money. I'll pay them on this side, I said, and tell the people, whoever's bringing you, that whoever they got and whoever they got behind them, bring everybody over. I'll take as much people as I can. I said if I even got to put y'all outside on my patio. . . . I said, "Well bring them because it's real bad." And I said, "I would hate to leave anyone back that I could have saved."

Wendy then moved quickly to set her network in motion. She contacted Rona, her friend Mr. Ellis, and some other relatives in the city. She gathered together those who had vehicles, and brought along as many relatives as she could find and fit in the cars. Bound to her own ethos of mutual assistance, Wendy's friend Rona would not leave without including her own family members who were stranded as well. Miss Joanne described the phone call she had with Rona at the time:

> Rona hesitated. [She said to me,] "But I got my children." I said, "Rona, bring your children." [Rona said,] "I got my sister-in-law." I said, "Bring her too and anybody else more." So [Mr. Ellis], he had like six people that was really sick that he had kept in his house with him. I said, "Bring those people too. They're very welcome to my house. Bring them. . . . You don't have time to argue with me. All you got is time enough to get out." I said, "That road [to Baton Rouge] is very heavy. I don't know if y'all gonna make it in time. But I'm praying that y'all make it."

I asked Wendy if she was surprised that her mother offered to open up her house to so many people. She responded by invoking her mother's deep religious faith:

> No, because I know my mother is a good person. She has God in her heart. She's just a sweet, kind person. . . . That's why she's big in her blessings, you know? Because she would help anybody out. She doesn't even have to know you. Some of the people I brought with me . . . she didn't know them. But she got to know them—she got to meet them. When I called her to see if it was okay, she said, "Bring them . . . if they don't have anywhere to go, bring them."

By early evening on August 28, the caravan left New Orleans. Although the evacuation group contained nearly equal numbers of men and women, it was organized entirely by women, with Wendy and Miss Joanne occupying the central roles. They chose whom to include, located them, and figured out how to coordinate everyone's needs and travel arrangements. These decisions and actions reveal the crucial role that women's communal care had for this network of evacuees. Although men's labor was crucial as well, directed as it was toward fixing technical problems, such as with the van that broke on the trip to Baton Rouge, it was not the driving force behind communal evacuation.

My respondents differentiated clearly between themselves, the beneficiaries of this network of help, and those others who had to leave their houses and go the Superdome and Convention Center for eventual evacuation. For Wendy, one of the horrors of the disaster was the experience of her family and friends who did not get out safely before the flood and were subsequently "shipped" by FEMA-sponsored buses or planes to places where they had no ties to others. She described it as "running loose" or being "on the loose," a random dispersal of people created by government decisions that completely disregarded former social ties:

> A lot of people were on the loose. A lot of people asking about their families. A lot of people were running loose . . . babies, fathers . . . I have friends and family in Atlanta, too. They weren't with us in the house. They couldn't get out at the same time. They didn't have nowhere to go and they were shipped to a different place. So many people shipped so far. It's hard, because sometimes you were shipped to places and you didn't want to be that far. You didn't know anybody. You don't know where you are. It's hard.

Being "shipped" is an evocative way to describe the process of "help" the government finally provided the survivors in the Convention Center and the Superdome. Shipping people evokes the transporting of cargo, and it struck a special chord for some evacuees who were reminded of the treatment of African Americans during slavery—purposefully separating kin from kin. In those few weeks of panic, Wendy's kin were sent mostly from the Superdome to Texas. "My family . . . my cousins. They went to Dallas, Texas . . . and San Antonio, Texas, too. But then they finally went to Houston because we had people to go to in Houston. . . . so they finally ended up in Houston. It almost looks like my whole family from my daddy's side is in Houston." The risks involved for those who were forcibly relocated were made worse, according to Wendy, because "you didn't know anybody." "Running loose" also conveys the significance of being socially unconnected.

In contrast to those who were "shipped" against their will, the fifty-four[6] people who made it to Miss Joanne's duplex on August 28 lived in a collective network in which care and interdependence represented core shared values. To survive, they had to draw on preexisting patterns of reciprocal assistance, although these also had to shift in this new context. New members were added and new demands were placed on scarce assets. But Miss Joanne expressed nothing but gratitude for her ability to assist individuals in their time of need:

Me and my husband slept in the hallway. We slept in the hallway. He had to work. He slept in the hallway. . . . I will wake up every morning or go during the night, come down the steps and check to make sure everyone is all right. We thought we would have to use the patio. Nobody, the whole fifty-four people never slept outside. Everybody slept inside. I looked down, somebody didn't have a cover. So I'm going to cover them up and make sure. See I got up early in the morning 'cuz I worked early, so I can't sleep late.

Miss Joanne also cooked and provided for everyone as much as she could:

But we cooked and we cooked for those people. And me and my husband know that was our money. And everybody kept saying, "We feel so bad for you, sleeping on the floor like that." I said, "I ain't got no problem with that." I said, "I was glad I was able to open my doors for y'all. . . . I'm so glad y'all made it through this. . . . I wish I coulda got more people than that. Don't worry about it, we'll make it." I cooked a big pot of grits, eggs, bacon, and . . . I would feed them in the evening time a big pot of food and have lunch for them too.

In describing this period, Wendy remarked that it was expensive to keep so many people in her mother's house for so long: "You using a lot of water, a lot of lights, washing." When I asked how her mother could afford that, she said, "Yeah, we [could] afford that because we all helped out. When everybody got their little money, they all pitched in." At least five people were working for wages: Miss Joanne, her husband, another person who "went out and did a little carpentry," and Wendy and Rona. Some received government assistance. Wendy explained how the expenses were managed in the house:

FEMA money. You know, when FEMA money [two thousand dollars] came through. They helped pay the light bill. They helped with the water. And we all pitched in for food. You know, everybody worked together. It really was a togetherness, you know. But everybody worked together.

Individuals contributed when they could, a situation made even more necessary because of the timing of the evacuation. According to Wendy, "The thing about it . . . it was the end of the month, if you didn't have [money] [that was okay] and when they got [money], they gave. We didn't make a big deal about who went to places [to purchase things]." When I asked whether a tally was kept and if they exchanged cash, she said:

No, they didn't really give us cash. Yeah, you might want to say they gave [my mother] cash. . . . She give us the bills and we go over there and pitch in for the bill. . . . Yeah, a bill would come in and we'd all pitch in. And when we needed groceries, I had food stamps, my sister-in-law had food stamps, [another individual] probably had food stamps, [Mr. Ellis] probably had food stamps, and we just went and everybody get meals at certain times, you know what I'm saying? You know everybody would go to the grocery store at the same time and get a couple of weeks of food. And then the next person would go with their food stamps and do it, you know. Everybody pitched in. Everybody helped.

Wendy then explained that, among more distant members of her extended network, this sort of exchange was not typical before the storm:

Well, I'm gonna say it's some of us. Not everybody. But some of us. If you need the help, some people would help, you know what I'm saying? But not everybody. So everybody wasn't friendly like everybody else, I'm not going to say that. But at that time, when everybody had a need, you do what you had to do. . . . Who's going to pay for all of that stuff? You'd be struggling.

Wendy points out that this special context gave rise to new norms of sharing and giving, even among those who had not done so in the past.

I was interested in exploring how Wendy defined doing "what you had to do" in this context, because it provides a window into the capacity of networks to respond to emergency events. Both Wendy and Miss Joanne and others I interviewed who lived in the house during that time insisted that they didn't have, nor did they want, anything close to a system for tracking and correcting differences in financial or other contributions. People were expected to give if they had the resources. The situation was especially fragile because, as Wendy explained, it was the end of the month and most people were low on cash. Government resources—especially FEMA money and food stamps—took the place of work income.[7] In these early days the resources were collectively shared to provide a safety net for the entire group in crisis.[8]

To some extent, the collectivizing of resources represented a departure from previous norms of exchange, because new members were added into the network. The ethos of covering those in need was carried over for some people and created anew for others from pre-Katrina days. Wendy explained the pre-Katrina expectations about exchange: "If [someone] was low on funds, and [they] need some change, money, call me and [I'll] help them out, or my mom will help them out. That is the kind of people we are, the person I am, how my heart operates. God keeps on blessing us by [allowing us] to give." While Wendy does appear to have a heart that operates in these terms, she developed it through a lifetime of immersion in networks of care in which interdependence is a core value. Unlike commercial transactions in which reciprocity is bought and sold based on standards set by the market, these forms of reciprocity were negotiated through assessments of the needs and the commitments of others to give something back—if not money, then companionship, childcare, and so forth.

At the same time, new networks of assistance developed beyond the household. Strangers and neighbors stepped in. And this implied a dispersal of help, a movement away from core networks to others who were not familiar, or sometimes not even known. Miss Joanne described how impressed she was with the many offers of help she received from strangers and others outside her personal networks:

> A girl came here, and she said, "I don't have no money, Miss." She said, "I got these food stamps," she said. And she said, "What you doing for those people . . . I can't do it, but I can give you something to help you. I got food stamps." She says, "Take these $120 food stamps and get some food for them people." I said, "Oh, no darling. I can't do that." She said, "No, ma'am, what you doing is wonderful." She said, "Now I don't have no money to give you. . . . But I do have this. . . . I got enough food in the house to last me until my next month." She says, "So I want you to take this and go get some food."

Miss Joanne was also struck by the generosity of people living in her housing complex:

> When I brought those people in, I didn't even know if those people [neighbors] was going to have me thrown out. Now, other people knew it that I had fifty-four people in my household, which I was not supposed to have that many people in my household. . . . All those people in that area know that I had those people there. I didn't have a key to the pool. They brought the key and said, "Let them swim, let the children swim. Let them children play in the park." Then they brought food for us. . . . That's a part of God coming back. Showing people to open their hearts. If you give, God give back more.

Part of this opening up involved the emergence of a new racial geography:

> It wasn't my color, my Black, only my Black [people who were helping]. They were White, Spanish, different races of people that lived in that complex that helped me out. People opened their hearts, which God wanted them to do. Open your heart. When you look at New Orleans, the thing God is trying to show us is that we need to get together with each other.

The racial diversity in her networks of assistance was a new experience. Indeed, before Katrina she had lived a racially segregated life. Her street was home, almost entirely, to African Americans, and while she had participated in the racially diverse workplace of Loyola University, she rarely exchanged personal or material resources with people of other races. The new, weakened racial boundaries around her household were surprising, yet not completely comfortable:

> I tell you the truth, there was never no disturbance in the house. That's probably why the people didn't report me or nothing. 'Cuz everybody saw them, White, Black, foreigner. What they were doing was giving me things for them. They were bringing big boxes of food. . . . The people over there at that complex never reported me to my landlord. My landlord didn't even know I had all those people in that house. They never made a complaint or nothing at the people here.

"FADING AWAY": LEAVING BATON ROUGE

The evacuation had been difficult, but as time went on, it was excruciating for residents of Miss Joanne's home to watch the thinning out of family and friends as they found alternate places to settle. Rona described witnessing this process of people leaving the house: "A lot of people scatter[ed] and they went where they had family . . . where they knew someone." Another member of Miss Joanne's household described it this way: "They were fading away day by day. . . . Everybody started to fade." Being "scattered," "fading," and "being shipped" were symbols of the rupture of community: while *being shipped* suggests being forcibly stranded, displaced, and isolated, *fading* and *scattering* suggest being separated from a web of connections. All represent images of being adrift.

The rupture of relationships, the disappearance of ties, and the lack of connections define this image of dispersal. In *Everything in Its Path*, Kai Erikson describes a deadly flood that virtually destroyed a coal mining town in Appalachia in 1972.[9] He found that the prolonged personal trauma experienced by survivors was rooted not only in the loss of life and property, but also in the loss of "communality"—the social interactions, the identification with others, the daily routines of exchange—that had tied self to community. If evacuation from New Orleans was celebrated by Wendy and Miss Joanne as creating new forms of interdependence, as well as cementing former ones, the displacement that began when people started leaving the Baton Rouge home in September 2005 represented yet new threats to survival, as well as identity.

By middle October 2005, most of those in Miss Joanne's Baton Rouge duplex were gone. Virtually all moved to be near other kin who had been relocated to other areas or who already lived there. Most moved to Texas and eventually reunited in Houston. One family unit moved to Kentucky to live with an adult child. Mr. Ellis opened up a new group home in another area in Baton Rouge. Miss Joanne described her feelings after their departure:

> Oh, Lord. But, you know, after they left, I felt so lonesome. I had too much time on my hands. . . . I didn't have nothing to do. With them, I had a lot to do. I felt so wanted with something to do. Then they go. I said, "Dawg." I said, "I wished more would come." I said, "I ain't dying yet." But, he [her husband] said, "Baby, the people got to go." I said, "But sure, but I sure miss them." . . . And [someone] called, and I said, "Dawg, I sure miss y'all." He said, "You miss us?" I said, "Boy, I miss y'all. I jump outa my bed, thinking I'm, I'm coming down to look for y'all down there." I said, "Oh, they gone. That's right, they're gone."

Wendy and Rona were the last to leave Miss Joanne's duplex, in middle October, when they moved north to Columbia, Missouri. Wendy moved with her three children and Rona's family of five. Wendy chose Columbia because of ties to an old friend who was currently living there:

> I had a friend's mom that stayed out here [in Columbia] for fourteen or fifteen years. About a year or two back, she asked me to move down this way with her. . . . When she first moved down here [to Columbia] with her husband, I used to tell her whenever she came to visit [New Orleans], "I'm coming, I'm coming." And I never came. So this was the opportunity. She called me again and said, "Come on out here. They are trying to help people, you need the help. Just come and give it a try here. You might like it." So my friend Linda brought me to Columbia. . . . If Linda wasn't here to tell us to come here, I wouldn't know where Columbia was. I didn't even know which way [direction] I was going, but I knew I was going.

Rona helped facilitate this move as a collective one by spending part of her two thousand dollars of emergency funds from FEMA on a van they used to drive to Columbia. She explained that she bought a van, rather than a small car, "so I could travel with people along with [us]."

But what did this move mean for Miss Joanne's value system of care? Miss Joanne explained that Wendy's departure was forced: "My daughter had to leave from here to go somewhere else" to get help. Miss Joanne speaks from the perspective of a mother who simply had no more to give:

> I was sad. Sad—I said my child has to go outa here. I can't help her. I don't have that kinda money. I know she know she gotta do it. Let her try

out there. But I was worried about her, 'cuz that was somewhere I didn't even know. So yes, 'cuz we was sad to look at the things falling down. . . . I said, darn, Wendy. God, I've been praying and I said I pray every night. I pray for the world. . . . And going somewhere I didn't even know, she didn't even know.

So Miss Joanne watched her daughter move out of that daily orbit, that center of gravity, that network of care, with fear and sorrow. "Things falling down," going "out so far," going "outa here." Displacement meant facing a new economy, a new set of strangers, and a different racial geography, all without the lifelong bonds of care.

Much to Miss Joanne's relief, Wendy's year in Missouri was, mostly, a good one. A local church gave Wendy access to a two-bedroom apartment, rent-free, for months. She began making rent payments when her housing voucher transferred from Louisiana. A local synagogue purchased a car and driving lessons for Wendy. Because of the lack of childcare, employment was more problematic. Wendy got job offers for overnight shifts, which were out of the question because she needed to be home, or for day shifts, which she also rejected because she did not have a place for her two-year-old daughter to stay during the day. But odd jobs, government assistance, and financial support early on to set up her household gave her a base upon which she created a comforting household for her children. Miss Joanne spoke of her gratitude for how well taken care of Wendy was:

Missouri people open their hearts to my child and my grandchildren. And when I seen that and heard Wendy say what they were doing, the relief, the grin . . . I said [to my husband], "We don't have to worry about Wendy. Wendy's doing better than what we doing." I said there are some beautiful people over there helping Wendy and caring for her, even that relative she had over there, too. I said, "Lord, thank you God. You opened my heart and you said that you would help me, and you did." That's through prayer. . . . But the people out there couldn't have been no better than if I was sitting right there holding her in my arms as a baby taking care of her.

Again, Miss Joanne emphasized the care that Wendy needed, not in a sense that Wendy was incapable, but because without "care" and "help," her well-being and safety would have been fundamentally threatened. Care and support were so webbed into daily life that Miss Joanne tied her daughter's happiness or well-being to their presence or absence. Wendy described her mother's concern:

It was hard for her [the move], but she is really grateful for the people, for the people that helped me and stuff. She was like, "They are amazing." She said, "It's good that you went somewhere where they help you . . ." She was hurt when I moved up here, but when she saw how well I was doing and I learned how to drive . . . she was amazed. She said, "You had to go that far to learn how to drive?" So she was happy for me.

CONCLUSION

The scattering, the spreading out, the fading away, and the leaving cracked the familiar and stable webs of connection and help that had become the backdrop of daily life, both in New Orleans and in Baton Rouge. In the story of Wendy's departure, we see that backdrop being dismantled. We see how two women interpreted the continuities and ruptures that displacement created. Traditionally, help was given and gained by reaching out to the known and the familiar. The movement out of New Orleans and from Baton Rouge to Missouri represented breaks not only in patterns of helping relationships but in the situated nature of women's networks. Help was found and given in new ways, in new places, among new people. Established patterns of help that had been rooted in long-standing proximity were transformed into a dispersal of help, a movement away from the original place where help made sense.

As we have seen, women, who had a long history of managing carework for kin, made the decision about when to evacuate. They knew how to locate people at a moment's notice, they organized the outreach to others, and they coordinated care among people with many different needs and priorities. Indeed, women's carework, rooted in informal systems of knowledge and practice, proved essential for the evacuation of the network I described. Government officials can use women's informal carework as a resource for locating and moving populations in grave danger. Isolation breeds danger, and as we have seen, displaced individuals will do what they can to reengage networks of care. Support by emergency programs should hasten the reengagement, and should certainly not impede it.

At the same time, evacuation planners must attend specifically to how economic, social, and racial differences among women figure into their evacuation practices. Remarkably little is understood about the significance of gender in disasters, particularly how patterns of women's work and gender inequality intersect with race and class inequalities to produce varied challenges and opportunities during crises. Women in different social positions used kin resources in varied ways. Collective ties and network exchange were what afforded protection among the vulnerable evacuees we met in this chapter. In many ways, this kin protection substituted for the formal resources that middle-class and more economically privileged women could access, such as credit cards, savings, job security, automobiles, and so forth.

I began the chapter by pointing out that the informal assistance provided by and among disaster survivors was not highlighted by the media investigating the disruption of Katrina. It is time now to ask why this perspective is important in untying the tangle of Hurricane Katrina. I argue that without attention to the essential labor that women perform in evacuations, public policy will continue to develop formal systems of assistance at the cost of infrastructures that could bolster the informal systems of care already in place. Clearly the women in my study organized evacuation and displacement. They needed and used formal assistance, but it was their informal and trusted practices of network assistance that galvanized people to move and provided the safety net to do so. They transformed formal resources into communal assets. It is this work that must rise to the surface in disaster relief policy.

NOTES

1. Barbara Ransby, "Katrina, Black Women, and the Deadly Discourse on Black Poverty in America," *Du Bois Review: Social Science Research on Race* 3, no. 1 (2006): 215–222.

2. Black women's economic and social vulnerability in New Orleans has been well documented by Barbara Gault, Heidi Hartmann, Avis A. Jones-DeWeever, Misha Werschkul, and Erica Williams (*The Women of New Orleans and the Gulf Coast: Multiple Disadvantages and Key Assets for Recovery Part I. Poverty, Race, Gender and Class* [Washington, DC: Institute for Women's Policy Research, 2005]). Other research into the trajectory of recovery for households headed by women documents extreme obstacles to recovery, in part because African American women's exploitation and vulnerability are so high during "normal" times. Structurally, the intersecting forces of gender, race, and class inequality made economic autonomy and independence impossible before, during, and after the storm.

3. Black women's economic and social vulnerability has given rise to intensive networks of resource exchange, as has been documented by decades of research. See, for example, Patricia Hill Collins, *Black Feminist Thought: Knowledge, Consciousness, and the Politics of Empowerment* (Cambridge, MA: Unwin Hyman, 1990); Kathryn Edin and Laura Lein, *Making Ends Meet: How Single Mothers Survive Welfare and Low Wage Work* (New York: Russell Sage Foundation, 1997); and

Carol B. Stack, *All Our Kin: Strategies for Survival in a Black Community* (New York: Basic Books, 1977). This chapter explores how the networks of exchange functioned in an emergency situation.

4. Chuck Adamson, "House Overflows with Family." *Columbia Daily Tribune*, September 7, 2005.

5. My forthcoming book, *Women of Katrina: Weaving Networks, Crossing Borders, Taking Care* (University of Texas Press), examines my fieldwork during this period and includes interviews I undertook with close to sixty evacuees from Wendy's network who had returned to New Orleans or who had resettled in Houston.

6. In addition to the twenty who were in Wendy's network, twenty-four others evacuated to Miss Joanne's through her different network connections, mostly through her husband's work and kin networks.

7. Research is now emerging to document differences in network support before, during, and after Katrina and the implications for postevacuation survival. In my own study, I found other networks where family disagreements arose with great force around the issue of sharing resources or residences and hindered evacuees' access to needed food and shelter. In a study of the swift return of the New Orleans East Vietnamese community, researchers document the significance of church leaders in organizing the community's return and recovery, as well as a legacy of displacement and culture oriented toward resettlement that the evacuees shared. Karen J. Leong, Christopher A. Airriess, Angela Wei Li, Chen Chia-Chen, and Verna M. Keith, "Resilient History and the Rebuilding of a Community: The Vietnamese American Community in New Orleans East," *Journal of American History* 94, no. 3 (2007): 770–779. Lein et al. (this volume) document another extreme. In their study of low-income families in Austin, Texas, who fell into destitution after the storm, they identify evacuees' detachment from their previous informal support networks as the major barrier to recovery, pushing them beneath the "basement of poverty." For an excellent analysis of the importance of network connections in emergency situations, see also Eric Klinenberg, *Heat Wave: A Social Autopsy of Disaster in Chicago* (Chicago: University of Chicago Press, 2003).

8. In a chapter in another book I argue that Rona's network eventually became so "flat"—it had lost its tie to Wendy's family and other sources of support—that it was stretched to the breaking point. Homelessness and hunger loomed as real possibilities at the time of my interview with her in 2009. Jacquelyn Litt, Althea Skinner, and Kelley Robinson, "The Katrina Difference: African American Women's Networks and Post-Katrina Poverty in New Orleans," in *The Women of Katrina: How Gender, Race, and Class Matter in an American Disaster*, ed. E. David and E. Enarson (Nashville: Vanderbilt University Press, 2012).

9. Kai T. Erikson, *Everything in Its Path: Destruction of Community in the Buffalo Creek Flood* (New York: Simon & Schuster, 1976).

11

THE WOMEN OF RENAISSANCE VILLAGE

FROM HOMES IN NEW ORLEANS TO A TRAILER PARK IN BAKER, LOUISIANA

This chapter introduces nine adult and aging African American women,[1] who, after working their way through various situations, ended up in the largest Federal Emergency Management Agency (FEMA) trailer park in Louisiana for displaced survivors of Hurricane Katrina. This park, located in Baker, came to be known as Renaissance Village, or just simply "the Park." Governor Kathleen Blanco initiated programs for those living in the Park through the Louisiana Family Recovery Corps (FRC). The intent of the programs was to coordinate housing, transportation, medical, and educational services for people displaced by Katrina and Rita and to provide case management plans that linked evacuees with employment and job training. The ultimate goal was for evacuees to become self-sufficient and to transition to permanent housing and begin their lives anew.[2]

As survivors of the largest forced migration of African Americans in US history, these women tell stories that highlight the people and social structures that helped them face dislocation and the harsh realities of daily life accompanying it. Even though those who experienced Hurricane Katrina will always be recovering, these conversations allow us to better understand the challenges women experienced in what became a continuing nightmare: the federal government's disaster process.

In December 2005, I interviewed nineteen African American women who had lived in and around New Orleans before Hurricane Katrina. We discussed how their new lives were unfolding as they came to grips with the loss of all that had been familiar to them. Two of the women had returned to New Orleans and were living in temporary housing, eight had settled in Baton Rouge immediately after fleeing the hurricane, and nine had moved from the Baton Rouge River Center, which housed over six thousand displaced persons from the hurricane, into Renaissance Village in Baker. The focus of this chapter is on the nine women living in the Park.

BEVERLY J. MASON

I found most of the nine interviewees by walking through the public areas of the Park and asking women if I could talk with them about their "Katrina experiences." Six of the interviews I conducted in the Park were in the women's individual trailers, two were in the trailer I had been assigned, and one was on the campgrounds near the community center. Women answered questions about what life was like after the storm, with a focus on their moves from shelters to the trailer park; what roles social networks played in their lives both before and after the disaster; what their plans for the future were; and how they navigated the government-led disaster programs.

The nine women were between the ages of fifty-one and ninety-seven; two were in their fifties, four in their sixties, and the remaining three were seventy-two, eighty-six, and ninety-seven years old. All of them had work histories in labor-intensive and low-paying jobs: nurses' assistants, cooks, bakers, housekeepers, and caregivers. All except one were parents and grandparents. The seven women aged sixty and older were officially retired, but all those with grandchildren provided intermittent or full-time care for them. Two of the women were unsure of the status of the jobs they had held before Katrina, but at the time of the interviews, they had no plans to return to them. While three women were recuperating from pre-Katrina surgeries, only one of the nine was visibly frail. Three women had owned their homes in New Orleans, and the remaining six had been renters. None of these nine women had post-Katrina housing options other than the Park—it was the trailer park or, as many said, "the street."

Before Katrina struck, women in New Orleans, like their counterparts in other urban areas, largely defined themselves by their families, neighborhoods, social clubs, churches, local schools, and a host of informal institutions. New Orleans was known as "home," the city that African Americans seldom left. And when they did leave, they returned often for visits and reintegration into their community. The city was a complex web of informal networks built on decades of interaction and grounded in extended families that actively participated in the well-being of their members. New Orleans may dedicate more days annually to revelry and celebration than any other American city, so weekend gatherings and holiday festivities often brought large families together.

The women in this study—Black adult and aging and working-class, armed with an undying love and responsibility for "their people," and grounded in devout, yet practical, religious beliefs—spent their lives building and maintaining social networks for themselves and their families. They were the broad-shouldered women on whom so much of New Orleans has always depended. Women's networks included blood relatives, fictive kin, and extended families created through their children's marriages and childbearing, the deaths of acquaintances, and neighbors that women had known for "donkey years" (generations).

The nine women in the study relied on networks to evacuate the city: six left with extended family members; two were airlifted, along with family and friends, out of the city to Baton Rouge; and one left with friends. All consulted family and friends about when to leave and where to go. With an eloquence and grace tempered by years of making life in New Orleans, these women spoke about leaving their homes and communities and struggling through weeks of life in mass disaster shelters where they lived with thousands of other devastated and distraught people. Their homes in the trailer park presented challenges unlike any they had ever experienced. The threads that run through all of these experiences, though, and in most cases were the differences that made the difference, were their social networks and the strength these women drew from them. Ms. Car and Ms. Trice are examples of the importance of familial networks.

Ms. Car, ninety-seven, had deep roots in New Orleans. Widowed in 1946, she had spent most of her life both caring for family members and working as a professional caregiver. Lifelong networks gave her the strength to care for her extended family:

> I went up to St. Joseph's and brought her [sister] back to New Orleans and kept her for three years until she passed. . . . I took care of all of my older people and my nieces. [Another] sister had one daughter and her daughter died while her children were all small. And I had to help her take care of the children. . . . She had six children. . . . So I helped my sister take care of all the children. We kept them until they got out of high school . . . and they all got good jobs.

Ms. Car described her contribution to her family with pride, not because of *what* she did for them, but because she could do it. Her involvement in her family network made a difference across three generations. Like that of many women in New Orleans, her life was characterized by commitment to family and friends and active involvement in her church.

When I met Ms. Car, she had just returned from visiting a local senior citizens' center in Baker. It was one of many trips organized by the Park's social workers. She was strolling through the camp checking on goods that had been distributed while she was away. She attended a local church twice weekly, and with new relationships and extended family close by, Ms. Car seemed to have adjusted to her new surroundings fairly well.

Before Katrina, Ms. Trice, fifty-one, had worked at a series of low-paying jobs, including the last as a prep chef at a Metairie country club. She also cared for a chronically ill son and a drug-addicted husband. Of the women interviewed, Ms. Trice had one of the most challenging movements out of New Orleans and into the Park. I met her while she was adjusting Christmas decorations around the frame of her trailer. Her immediate familial network appeared frayed; in fact, she described her family as having deserted her more than once. Six months before Katrina, she was in an accident that left her all but unable to walk. She suffered emotionally and physically when family members living close by did not bring her food for three days. When residents began to leave the city, her family left her to survive on her own. Her husband had disappeared well before the storm, and her son appeared to strike out on his own. Ms. Trice's landlord had agreed to rent a car for her on the Friday before Katrina struck, but he disappeared as well. Ms. Trice's life was saved by her daughter-in-law and extended family members, whom she did not know before the storm:

> So what I did was crawl around trying to get all kinds of means to get out. Couldn't get anyone; my daughter-in-law came by because she knew that I had had the surgery and that I was by myself. . . . She came to stay with me, she said, "I'm not going to leave you . . . because I know you're here by yourself and you don't have any way to get out. . . . So we're either going to get out or we're going to be here together."

Ms. Trice, with her daughter-in-law, spent the Saturday night before Katrina (August 27) praying for help. She was terribly anxious because she now also felt responsible for her daughter-in-law's safety. The next morning, after many telephone calls, an aunt who had a ride reached her daughter-in-law, who said: "Do you have enough room for my mother-in-law? Because if you don't, I'm not leaving." "They ended up saying, 'Yeah,' and that's how I got out," lamented Ms. Trice, "through people that I didn't even know."

Ms. Trice and her daughter-in-law ended up living next door to one another in the trailer park and spent hours together each day problem-solving and "seeing about the future." Her daughter-in-law brought Ms. Trice into her networks, many of whose members had transportation, something that proved valuable as she continued to struggle with mobility problems.

Ms. Trice and Ms. Car both came from a background where survival was made possible by the involvement and care of family and friends. Yet Ms. Car's networks—strong, extended, and reliable—provided her with confidence that helped her endure life in the Park. In contrast, Ms. Trice was plagued by feelings of insecurity brought on by the uncertainty in her new relationships with extended family and unreliable and demanding relationships with her immediate family.

THE SETTING

My conversations with the nine women took place in a dusty, graveled cow pasture. Some 1,696 evacuated Katrina survivors—most of them African American—were housed there in 588 new vacation trailers that were built to house four to six people each for summer vacations. At the time of the interviews, FEMA said that the occupants would be able to live in the trailers for eighteen months—this to people who had lost family members, all material possessions, and the comfort of the world they had created.

The trailers were unbelievably cramped, noisy, and cold during the winter and sweltering during the summer. They were theoretically presumed efficient but practically uninhabitable. Sounds were amplified from the inside out and the outside in. Separated from one another by three feet, the trailers contained dining and living areas, a bathroom, and bed spaces. The women complained of headaches and respiratory problems. Studies would later reveal that many trailers tested positive for formaldehyde, a carcinogen linked to various negative health outcomes.

Ms. Rose, eighty-six, had fourteen children and several grandchildren. Before Katrina, a daughter and six grandchildren lived with her in a large trailer in St. Bernard Parish. After the hurricane, the trailer was submerged under twenty feet of standing water. About a decade before the storm, because arthritis, hypertension, diabetes, and an ulcer had begun to take a toll on her strength, she relied on her daughters for running errands and other needs. During most of our Park interview, Ms. Rose literally screamed her answers, demonstrating a frightening level of frustration and fear. Two of her daughters were in the FEMA trailer during our interview, and they both expressed feelings of helplessness and anger.

Ms. Rose had bumped her feet several times while attempting to navigate around the small trailer. Her stress level remained high, as every day either brought new problems or signaled a lack of progress on old ones. For example, in order to receive assistance from FEMA for her trailer home in St. Bernard Parish, Ms. Rose had to verify its site—a task that was aggravated by the fact that the parish government offices had flooded. Her youngest daughter and husband had built a home close to Ms. Rose's and had planned to sign insurance forms on the Monday that Katrina struck; their entire investment was lost. Most of Ms. Rose's family who resided in the Park had been ill with coughing, wheezing, and headaches. One week before the interview, her baby granddaughter had been taken to the hospital with respiratory problems.[3]

While huge klieg lights surrounded the Park, many spaces on the grounds were dark and filled with shadows. And many residents felt vulnerable in their little trailers. Ms. Rose's daughters noted that the nights were frightening and dangerous, riddled with fights, underground economic exchanges, and unpredictable behavior by neighbors. Trailer fires brought home the precariousness of living so close to adjacent strangers. The thin trailer walls magnified every noise; people milling around outside or bumping into the trailer sounded like crushing aluminum and caused the entire trailer to shake. Having lived in a quiet, rural area before the hurricane, Ms. Rose found the confusion surrounding her trailer nightmarish. Her mobility was further curtailed by Park grounds, which were covered with gravel and dirt that turned to mud when it rained. Because of her mobility problems, she had to be carried across the grounds to leave the Park.

Ms. Rose's religion, family, and minister sustained her through these near-impossible times. She said she knew that God was taking care of her because on a trip back to the St. Bernard trailer site, one of her daughters found lying on the ground two of the angels Ms. Rose had collected over the years. Those battered angels were prominently displayed in her Park trailer, and everyone heralded the finding as miraculous.

Both in and outside of the trailers, the dust generated when cars and big trucks drove over the gravel made breathing and seeing a challenge. Noise from the main road running along the Park could be heard in the back of the camp; cars and trucks sounded as though they were entering the trailers, as they tore up and down nearby roads. Some of the interviewees feared going outside because of the lack of secure footing. Trailer window blinds remained partially closed during the day to provide privacy and a sense of security, but at the same time the dim light produced an eerie, shadowy reality, filled with strange noises and muffled voices. The Park had only one entrance and exit and was several miles down a two-lane road with ditches running along both sides and no sidewalks. For-sale signs were beginning to dot the lawns of nearby homes leading up to and past the Park. The trailers were parked in neat rows of nine and eighteen per row with three feet separating each trailer, and a six-foot gravel road between each row so that residents could drive through the Park. One wide two-lane road ran from the entrance to the rear of the Park. In the center at the rear end of the camp was a large, unheated, orange open-air tent where meetings among residents and between service providers and residents were often held. Residents elected a council that proved to be ineffectual. And many complained that only large protests attracting media attention brought action. Consequently, media access to the camp was later curtailed.

Three meals a day were served in the orange tent, and it was also the place where some giveaways were distributed. These donations that arrived at the Park several times a day from across the country were important because they brought many residents out of their trailers, allowing them to meet and commiserate with one another as they shared survival stories and information. And, of course, the giveaways allowed residents to accumulate material goods: large and small food packages, small pieces of furniture, bicycles, cell phones, and cheap plastic toys that were often broken before children returned to their trailers. One drawback was that the freebies, often impractical at best, were large and occupied valued space in the tiny trailers. Once the giveaways ended, a major question was: What would bring residents out of their trailers to interact with neighbors?

Along the rear of the Park, FRC social workers interviewed residents in converted vacation campers. FRC's on-site coordinator, Ms. Peace, with whom I had extensive conversations, worked with community groups and government agencies to organize health services, which were located adjacent to her trailer. Tractor trailer trucks, converted into dental and surgery facilities (for minor operations), were staffed by dentists, physicians, and other medical professionals from local universities and public health offices. Medical services were available to residents three times a week and sometimes more often. One truck had been converted into a hair salon that was open once or twice a week.

The Park manager's office, in one of the administrative trailers in the front of the camp, also housed a social worker and clerical staff. People streamed in and out of the trailer, some reporting the delivery of goods and others attempting to secure services. Having honed his managerial skills in "waste management," the Park manager was effective at addressing the physical problems of the massive facility. The material and psychosocial needs of the residents were often addressed by social workers and their co-ordinator, who were dependent, in large part, on resources donated by public and private organizations and institutions. For example, the Red Cross, National Football League and National Basketball Association, Rosey's Kids, the Soros Foundation, and hundreds of churches and schools, national and local, made valued contributions.

The Park was designated, not designed, exclusively for "older residents" (those age fifty years and older) and families with young children. Officially, 1,696 people were said to live in the trailers, but it became clear that many more people, especially young, technically homeless adults were living with family and friends throughout the Park. This combination of populations presented another disaster as time passed. Trailer-bound aging residents, some alone and unsure of themselves, felt even more confused and vulnerable when a few young men engaged in fights and illegal drug activities. Parts of the camp were taken over at night by rowdy, bored young people, who, many of the interviewees said, forced them to lock themselves in their trailers before dark and hide in fear. After the original security company was accused of corruption and indifference to the residents, a second firm was hired, yet residents said they felt no more secure.

In Baker, Governor Blanco's on-site coordinator organized the storm survivors into four distinct parks governed by demographics like age, health status, gender, and family structure. There was a park for aging people and families with children; a park for adult unmarried males; one for people with medical crises; and a small park for those who did not comfortably fit into the other three. These artificial groupings separated dependents and loved ones and mixed strangers with different values and cultures. To confirm residents' legitimate claims to meals, social services, giveaways, and the trailers, each person was required to wear a picture identification badge at all times. Not wearing one was supposed to invite being stopped and queried by security. Residents were also expected to "police" the park and report unauthorized persons to the administration. Yet I saw residents not wearing badges and badgeless people not being stopped. Residents tended not to report others in part because they never knew if they would have to shelter a friend or family member; some, no doubt, feared retaliation against informers by fellow park residents.

FEMA's policies—contradictory, draconian, and inefficient—felt more like an attack on the survivors of Hurricane Katrina than strategies to assist them. When I arrived at the camp, the expectation that residents would live in the park for eighteen months and then go off into brave new lives was being reinforced in newspapers and throughout the camp's administration.

Residents were already beginning to ask: "Go where? Live how? Work at what jobs? And meet basic needs how?"

The drumbeat had begun to add undue stress to the residents' lives. They had just won a struggle against FEMA, which initially required them to pay for expensive heating and cooking gas, a requirement rescinded when it became obvious that many living in the Park had not received any funds since leaving New Orleans in August. While a few of the women had begun receiving stipend checks and/or Social Security checks routed from their homes, some were waiting for the first FEMA contributions. At first, FEMA would not provide emergency funds for those without proper documentation—an obvious problem for most survivors. FEMA later reversed this requirement, but only after creating havoc in the lives of survivors.

People in the Park, many retired, had worked in a variety of occupations, from service workers (housekeepers, cooks, maids, bricklayers, and carpenters) to professionals (doctors, college professors, lawyers, and teachers). A third of the residents from the latter group had the means to live elsewhere, but chose to reside in the Park in order to remain close to their homes under repair in New Orleans. Some chose to live in the Park because they maintained their prestorm jobs, but could find no housing in New Orleans. They rose early each morning and returned late in the evening after traveling the 140-mile round-trip journey on a Park-operated bus.

Many Park residents, aging and alone, physically and/or mentally exhausted or ill, and economically stressed, presented distinct problems for administrators. The FRC coordinator spent hours organizing programs for and providing assistance to these groups. Social workers visited residents in their trailers and ushered them to on-site and off-site medical and psychological appointments. The American Association for Retired Persons (AARP) provided assistance to residents, as did varied volunteers from Baton Rouge and Baker, yet the assistance was piecemeal and inadequate to address residents' comprehensive needs.

For example, women who had been far more active while living in New Orleans often felt confined to their trailers and spoke of being tired, with sleep often bringing them more distress. Ms. Ander, sixty-two years old and the mother of four adult children, retired in 2000 after working for the Orleans Parish's school board as a cook and baker. She and her husband, a double amputee, had just finished remodeling their home when Katrina struck. Despite knowing that life in the Park was temporary, she was distressed about her lack of energy and overall health status: "Well, when I walk now, I can't go too far. I get out of breath."

She rode a bicycle around the perimeter of the Park, an exercise replacement for the treadmill she worked out on in her New Orleans home. While their parents worked, she sent her grandchildren to school in the mornings and looked after them in the afternoons. She struggled with the idea of returning to New Orleans and began having recurring nightmares about the flood and the damage it did. In the dreams, she would see herself running about the house looking for lost items and packing up moldy goods. When the weekend arrived and the family journeyed to New Orleans to clean, repair, and restore their home, she was too exhausted to help very much. She longed for the stability of her old life, the old pace:

The main thing is getting your life back together. You know, our own place; like you were before. . . . There are a lot of adjustments you have to do, you know. . . . A lot. It's just being surrounded with so many people. That's number one. And like I say, I'm not doing anything. There are a lot of activities going on. They're giving a lot of things away. I guess I miss out on them because I'm not coming out, you know, so I miss that. But it's just too much to deal with right now.

Also struggling with feeling overwhelmed and depressed, Ms. Guess, seventy-two, a widow and mother of four, was a retired kindergarten teacher and recuperating from breast cancer surgery when Katrina hit. In the interview she expressed concern that her arm had recently begun to swell. When asked if she thought the swelling was related to stress and exhaustion, Ms. Guess said "yes." She then admitted that she was depressed:

I think you really don't know how hard this has hit you unless you go and find out, really. . . . There may be something deep down within that I haven't explored yet. I've cried. And that helped me. But in front of the kids, I'm strong. . . . But I break down when I'm alone, you know.

Ms. Guess would not allow herself to engage in what she described as "self pity" or to acknowledge the psychological devastation she experienced. This denial of feelings seemed to have several sources: a lack of appreciation of or sense of entitlement to one's own pain and an inability to identify the appropriate response in a wholly surreal situation.

Ms. Guess had worked hard to find all of her family and many of her friends. Her son, who had recently joined her in the Park, had been stranded in New Orleans immediately following Katrina. He slept on Veterans Boulevard for four nights with little food or water. She was thankful that her networks were "doing fine," but her problem, the problem of so many survivors, was what to do next: return to New Orleans and live in a repaired house with the possibility of another storm or find a new city and a new home for her and the family. Everyone, she said, looked to her to find their futures.

GODLY FRIENDS FOUND IN AN UNGODLY DISASTER

As women moved through their various stages of dislocation—leaving New Orleans, seeking refuge in disaster shelters, and arriving at the Park—they developed new relationships at each stage that proved to be practically useful and spiritually uplifting. From across Louisiana and beyond, legions of women and men visited the River Center in Baton Rouge to distribute material aid and give emotional support. The Park women spoke with love and gratitude as they described the strangers who came into their lives, appreciating the spiritual and psychological support and the time they spent talking with the women and their families. Ms. Ander, for example, was overwhelmed with the goodness she experienced from people she met during her arduous journey. With little to do at the shelter in Baton Rouge, she and her family visited local churches, and in turn many from those congregations began visiting the River Center. They volunteered their time and labor and helped Ms. Ander to become involved in Baton Rouge. Ms. Ander said:

> They came to us and they took our clothes to their homes. They washed our clothes, folded them, and brought them back to us. Different ones, you know, cooked the meals. We had different meals from different churches. . . . some would bring the food and some would cook it right there at the shelter. They really took good care of us. . . . We met two couples from one of the churches we visited. . . . Since we've been here [in the Park], they have brought blankets to make sure we are warm. . . . And they're just friends for life now.

The networks that developed were different from anything they had previously experienced. Ms. Ander and others described their new networks as the practical application of divine intervention. All of the Park women I met were sustained during their ordeals by their religious beliefs. They viewed the hurricane as "God's plan" and saw the loving response from strangers as God's "work in action."

As they settled into the Park, the women continued friendships they made at the River Center and began new ones with fellow survivors. Before

Katrina, Ms. Poole, sixty-seven, was a renter, had no children, and lived with a housemate and two dogs. She arrived at the River Center by way of a coast guard helicopter, a plane, and then a bus, traumatized after spending several days trapped by floodwaters. People she met at the River Center, two of whom lived in the Park, often visited each other in the central tent, reviewing their experiences before and after Katrina. She called them "friends forever."

Various occasions brought women together; the most common one, of course, was standing in lines. As they waited to meet with social services or for their grandchildren to be delivered by school buses at the Park's front gate, the women shared information, which relieved some of their feelings of remoteness and longing for home.

Health issues also brought women together. Many had experienced nightmares, anger, stress, increased heart rates, disbelief, feelings of being lost, and depression—all symptoms of post-traumatic stress disorder (PTSD). None of the women was being treated for PTSD, but six described the symptoms and identified women they spoke with in the Park with similar problems. Ms. Ander assumed the role of quasi-psychologist by listening to people, hugging them, and empathizing with their pain.

REINVENTION

To personalize their trailer homes, many residents decorated them with Christmas lights and placed artificial Christmas trees in the small yards in front of the trailers. Later, several residents decorated their trailers with gold and purple to acknowledge the coming of Mardi Gras. They were all trying to make a home for themselves and their families.

The devastation and daily reality of dislocation forced many women to reinvent themselves. They tried to keep busy with new activities, including ones that women would never have engaged in had there not been a Hurricane Katrina: attending AARP meetings and activities, visiting senior citizen centers, participating in church activities in Baker and Baton Rouge, and seeking out other women in the Park to give and receive support.

Ms. John, fifty-three, was married and had worked at a New Orleans hospital for twenty-five years as a certified nurse's aid. She had left her position before Katrina after becoming disabled with heart disease complicated by hypertension and diabetes. After settling in the Park and assuming before- and after-school care responsibilities for her grandchildren, she became bored and volunteered a few days a week at a school attended by her grandchildren and at a local senior citizen's facility. She valued the networks she developed at both institutions, especially those at the senior facility, where she reconnected with two women she had met at the River Center. The isolation of the Park forced her to reach out and find activities in the greater community, even though mobility problems caused her concern as she navigated the graveled roads and dangerous streets.

Before Katrina, Ms. Wego, sixty-one, mother of two children, had worked as a housecleaner in motels and restaurants. She too reinvented herself after Katrina. At the River Center and the Park, she became a goodwill ambassador by assuming many informal, yet public, responsibilities: talking with and comforting other people and spreading the news about goods being handed out at the Park. While she worried about her daughter who had seen a physician for panic attacks, she pressed on, caring for her grandchildren and spreading her philosophy of group survival:

> A lot of them were crying . . . saying what all they had been through and stuff. I had been through some, but mine wasn't as worse as theirs. . . . So I just talked with them and hugged them and told them, "Just pray and, you know, that's all we can do is pray. We are all in this thing together." . . . Some, some are worse. All we can do is talk to each other, hug each other, pray.

Challenges for the women included one very important decision about the future: whether or not to return to New Orleans. Plans for returning were impractical for some and impossible for others. Despite many bureaucratic traps and empty promises of government assistance, most homeowners were working to repair their homes so as to at least provide themselves the option of returning. The renters, Ms. Trice, Ms. Car, and Ms. Wego, lost all of their material possessions in the flooding, and even though landlords promised to restore their living spaces, it was hard to believe that the apartments would be made available to them once they were repaired, especially at the pre-Katrina rent prices. All of the women except Ms. Will had family living in the Park, and although she had a brother within ten miles whom she planned to live with, they had not arranged her move. But even as the women were confronted with daunting challenges, most were thinking of ways to re-create their lives and were actively making plans for life after that in the Park.

CONCLUSION

What does a disaster such as Hurricane Katrina look like through the eyes of African American, working-class adult and aging women? For the women I interviewed, New Orleans was a disaster before Hurricane Katrina struck. They worked long hours in low-paying jobs and had to contend with various forms of discrimination. So the women experienced the posthurricane response by the government as a continuation of a frontal attack.

While social service providers did the best they could to provide assistance to Park residents, their best could not meet the overwhelming need. The Park's Black poor and working-class aging women struggled to meet their own needs, while at the same time trying to provide for their loved ones, to hold their families together, to learn the rules of their new environments, and to protect grandchildren from internal and external assaults in their new community.

Leaving New Orleans or moving through disaster centers or settling into life in the Park, women relied on their social and familial networks. As they made new friends among those who assisted them in the receiving communities, many of the women were surprised by and appreciated strangers' kindness and giving. They also were renewed by their religious beliefs—relying on their beliefs to undergird their strength and determination to reestablish their lives. When asked how a disaster like Katrina and the levee breaks could have happened, not one woman blamed any governmental entity. They chose to explain their fate through their religion—"God's will"—and to look for salvation in the same place.

As the women settled in Renaissance Village, they found new challenges constantly testing their spirit and energy. When I interviewed them in December 2005, they did not complain about the disaster they had recently experienced. The precariousness of their existence, however, was evident: limited funds, concerns about access to food, safety inside and outside of their trailers, living spaces that were environmentally challenged, fear for their grandchildren who were undergoing attacks from White schoolchildren, and concern about help with employment and training that residents prayed would elevate them above their pre-Katrina experiences.

Yet they continued remaking themselves. Whether it was riding a bike for physical and mental therapy or assuming the mantle of informal psychologists, women engaged in acts of reinvention. They sought out volunteer efforts and engaged in nonfamily activities that they would not have experienced otherwise.

ACKNOWLEDGMENTS

During the months following Hurricane Katrina, I lived on a generous grant from the Howard Hughes Medical Institute. I proposed to the Institute that I interview women who had evacuated the New Orleans area about their experiences and their plans for rebuilding their lives. The grant allowed me to conduct nineteen interviews in December 2005 and to transcribe the recordings. I am eternally grateful to the Institute, as its funding allowed me to make contact with the people of that region, whom I came to love and respect unconditionally. Words cannot express my appreciation to the women I had the pleasure of speaking with about their Katrina experiences. They were all gracious as they allowed me to delve into their pain. This chapter and all subsequent publications are dedicated to the Women of the Storm. My undying appreciation to those who helped bring my research to you: Richard Turner, Debbie Berry, Elizabeth Rhodes, Amy Hite, Renaissance Park administrators, "June," Lori Peek, Lynn Weber, Kai Erikson, and the members of the SSRC Research Network.

NOTES

1. Adult women are those from eighteen through sixty-five; aging women are sixty-six and older.

2. Agnes Peace, on-site coordinator for FRC, interview with author, 2005, Renaissance Village, Baker, Louisiana.

3. Trailer occupants complained of nosebleeds, sinus infections, wheezing, coughing, asthma attacks, and eye, lung, and nose irritation. The elderly and children were made the most ill by problems caused by formaldehyde.

12

TWICE REMOVED

NEW ORLEANS GARIFUNA IN THE WAKE OF HURRICANE KATRINA

In the days immediately following Hurricane Katrina, journalists, social service providers, academics, and religious leaders urgently began collecting data on evacuees, their whereabouts, and their needs. These studies painted a picture of a New Orleans sharply divided along Black and White racial lines, a system that neglected its poor, and entire communities fallen prey to an utter lack of disaster preparedness and planning.[1] Evacuees' experiences would later complicate the narrative of racial division and community destruction, challenging assumptions and premature conclusions.

This chapter tells a story that was excluded from official narratives and data collection efforts. It is the story of Garifuna immigrants, Afro-Caribbeans who have contributed to the cultural landscape of New Orleans since the Standard and United Fruit Companies' reign over the Gulf Coast began in the early twentieth century. This group, once settled in Houston after the storm, would become a more cohesive community linked by their migration to, evacuation from, and memories of New Orleans.

The Garifuna of New Orleans, as a historically mobile and transnational community, challenged the exhausted political dichotomies that prevailed in New Orleans before and after Katrina. As a prestorm community, the Garifuna were both locals and foreigners. Many moved back and forth between their hometowns in Honduras and their adopted home city of New Orleans. Their presence in New Orleans contributed to a thriving, albeit small, pre-Katrina Latino population, and as a community, they participated in local unions, African American churches, and Spanish- and Garifuna-speaking community organizations.

The Garifuna in this study revealed that movement across physical and cultural borders is both a familiar and intricate endeavor. The New Orleans Garifuna negotiated various identities and societal locations, but because of their mobility and migration status, they were also part of the larger vac-

CYNTHIA M. GARZA

uum left by the race, class, and gender cleavages that rendered them vulnerable to the neglect and chaos of evacuation and resettlement. I argue here that it is this same unique history of the Garifuna—as New Orleanians, African Americans, Latinos, Caribbeans, evacuees, residents, border-crossers, locals, foreigners, hurricane survivors (Mitch and then Katrina)—that also sometimes allowed the men and women in this study to turn a catastrophic situation into a manageable resettlement process. Given this background, their story is important because it allows us to learn what individual and communal resources were helpful to those who made a success of the forced evacuation following Hurricane Katrina, and which factors were a hindrance to recovery and resettlement.

WHO ARE THE GARIFUNA?

The Garifuna are descendants of Carib, Arawak, and West African peoples who settled primarily along the coasts of Belize, Guatemala, Nicaragua, and Honduras.[2] The history of the Garifuna is one of constant migration, survival, and diaspora that began on the eastern Caribbean island of St. Vincent. The island, home to Arawak Indians, received migration from Africa when, in the year 1635, two Spanish ships carrying Nigerian slaves shipwrecked off the coast. Modern accounts of the Black Carib culture that developed there during the Colonial period depict an indigenous society that fought fiercely in defense of its culture and territory during a number of European wars. The greatest battle took place in the Carib War of 1795–1796 and ended when the Caribs, and the French who supported them, surrendered to the British. Black Caribs who refused to surrender were hunted down and imprisoned, their crops and homes destroyed.[3]

In 1797, the British, fearing retaliation and perhaps successful slave rebellions like those occurring in Haiti, deported the surviving Garifuna to Roatan Island off the coast of Honduras. Movement of the Garifuna throughout Central America began when the community of about 2,500 settlers petitioned the Spanish government for permission to settle on the mainland, where they would have access to more fertile land and greater opportunity for employment.[4] Garifuna were employed as Spanish soldiers until Central American independence in 1821, and, in the early 1800s, they joined British woodcutters in Belize and moved contraband along the coasts of Honduras, Belize, and Nicaragua. Those who remained in Honduras worked mostly on banana plantations.

Although the Garifuna had always been a mobile community, the late nineteenth and early twentieth centuries brought about new waves of transnational migration, and it was in this period when the Garifuna first arrived in New Orleans. While census data have never documented what percentage of Hondurans migrating to the United States was Garifuna and how exactly they arrived in New Orleans, a steady flow of migration began as early as the nineteenth century when the Standard Fruit Company carried cargo and workers from Honduras through the port city. Anthropologist Nancie Gonzalez, in *Sojourners of the Caribbean*, also notes that in the twentieth century, Garifuna men joined the British and US merchant marines after the building of the Panama Canal and during World War II, beginning a pattern of back and forth migration and settlement in US port cities such as New York and New Orleans.[5] In 1997, it was estimated that there were between 2,000 and 4,000 Garifuna living in New Orleans.[6]

THE STUDY

As a Katrina migrant myself, I came to study Honduran Garifuna evacuees from New Orleans when a former colleague initiated a project called "The Saddest Days" at the Benjamin Hooks Institute for Social Justice at the University of Memphis. The project was created for the purpose of collecting oral histories of African American evacuees in cities across the United States, and I was living temporarily in Houston.

It took much persistence on my part to convince the project directors that Garifuna immigrants should be included in the project as "African Americans." Despite the long history of the Garifuna in New Orleans, the Latino population, and especially the African-descendant Latino community, has been virtually invisible save for a few academic inquiries. Upon receiving consent from the directors to include these individuals, I collected nineteen oral histories with six men and thirteen women, all between the ages of fourteen and seventy-eight. The interviews were conducted primarily in Spanish, although some respondents slipped into English occasionally.[7] I met families through church fairs, donation drives, the Urban League of Houston, and Honduran restaurants in October of 2005. These meetings led me to a larger community of over a hundred Garifuna from New Orleans living in one location in the southeast suburbs of Houston.

Within the greater cultural and societal landscape of New Orleans before Katrina, Garifuna respondents were both undocumented day laborers and legal residents with long-standing careers in the oil and shipping industries. Five of the nineteen respondents in this study were insured home-owners, and the rest lived with family or divided up rent and shared small apartments with friends or other families. Nine were legal residents who had access to post-Katrina government programs—such as student loans, food stamps, and FEMA vouchers—while the rest were undocumented and relied on donations from local churches to make ends meet.

MOVEMENT AND ADAPTATION

The New Orleans Garifuna are members of a transnational community whose coastal villages throughout Central America have been threatened in recent decades by economic development, political neglect, and natural disasters.[8] Movement and adaptation, themes persistent throughout Garifuna history, also shaped the stories told by respondents in this study. Past experiences of migration from Honduras to New Orleans and other cities in the United States were described as both hindering and aiding processes of evacuation and resettlement during and after Katrina. For example, for some participants who had moved back and forth between New Orleans and Honduras for many years, adapting to life in Houston was less of a shock. For others, however, more experience with movement meant fewer roots in New Orleans, and therefore, fewer social network ties and financial resources that might have otherwise eased the transition period following the storm.

Despite so much movement and transition among the Garifuna, little has been written about this population in general. There is no source that isolates Garifuna migration trends from overall Central American or Honduran migration. The stories below help to fill this void.

Born in Colon, Honduras, in 1967, Ana talked about adapting to a new life in New Orleans. After what she described as a "pleasant" childhood in Honduras, she migrated at the age of nineteen to Los Angeles and then to New York. Following the death of her mother in 2000, Ana moved to New Orleans and found life there to be challenging, but manageable:

> Before the hurricane [life was] a bit difficult, but then I adapted to the system because when one moves to a new place, it's all about passing through a period of many decisions. At first, I didn't have a job and then I found one, and I said to myself, "From here on out, this is just the way it's going to be," and that's how it went.

In the face of the risky and life-altering process of international migration, adaptability was a necessity for Ana, as for many other respondents in this study, and change a fact of life. For Luisa, a thirty–year resident of New Orleans before the storm, movement and change were also simply part of her reality as a daughter and then a wife:

> I was young and single when my father brought me to New York from Honduras. . . . So I got married there. I had two daughters, and we moved to New Orleans, and in New Orleans I had two more children.

Like Luisa, Diana explains in the excerpt below that she followed a family member to the United States. Her father, who was recruited to work on banana cargo ships traveling to New Orleans, stayed in the city and established himself as a longshoreman before bringing his family over.

> [My childhood] was perfect. I was with only my mother because my father was over here working. But it was perfect. I had finished high school when I went to the United States. . . . My father brought us over.

For others, movement from Honduras to New Orleans was prompted by natural disaster. After having endured the joblessness and persistent poverty exacerbated by Hurricane Mitch[9] in Colon, Honduras, Laura left the town where she had spent the first forty-five years of her life and made the trip to New Orleans alone. Once there, she married another Garifuna immigrant:

> I arrived the ninth of January in 2001 [three years after Mitch], and I stayed with my brother. I only worked cleaning [houses] then. Well, I sometimes cleaned and my sister sometimes supported me [financially]. Then I got together with a man, but when I found out that he was already married, I had to leave. So then I met my current husband, Ricardo. I've been with him for three years. We got together, looked for a room, and found one there on Martin Luther King Boulevard. We moved in there and have stayed there since.

With Katrina came another wave of evacuation and migration that proved powerful enough to uproot the Garifuna community once again. For Ana, who had migrated from Honduras to Los Angeles to New York and then to New Orleans, movement and transition were not uncommon themes in her life. But when the moment came to move once again, this time via forced evacuation from the city she now called home, things were different. Upon receiving the news about the magnitude of Hurricane Katrina, Ana decided to leave, but was convinced by her brother-in-law that the news reports were exaggerated—that the storm would pass through with minimal damage like all of the others in recent years. Ana and her children went to New Orleans East to wait out the storm with extended family, and the ensuing traumatic five-day evacuation eventually landed her family in Houston:

> But after the hurricane everything changed . . . a lot. I was in the East . . . my brother-in-law took me because I don't know that part of town very much. I was on my way to Houston, but he told me, "Don't leave, nothing is going to happen," and I thought about how last year [with Hurricane Ivan] they had said the same things and nothing happened. And the truth is that I was also short on money. . . . Later, I honestly thought that we were the only ones who had stayed because I didn't see anyone else. Then, I guess people were hiding away in their homes, and those that perhaps couldn't leave, stayed there. There was a young girl who was pregnant that ended up getting in the water and lost her baby. We saw it happen. . . .
>
> We were near I-10, and when it wasn't raining yet, I saw a current of water coming, but since I'm not familiar with the area, I told my brother-in-law, "There's some water coming, but it's not raining. There's only wind. Where is this water coming from?" And then I said, "Let's go. We've got to get out of here." First of all, I don't know how to swim. I'm from the coast with a big open sea, but I don't know how to swim.

Also explaining why her family didn't leave, Isabel, a twenty-year-old university student, emphasized the role that her father played in the decision.[10] She stated:

> My dad didn't want to. He didn't think that it was gonna be serious. Since they always say, "A big hurricane is coming," and nothing ever happened. He thought it was gonna be the same this time.

When the family did finally make it out of New Orleans, it was only after Isabel, her father, and her sister Sonya swam through neck-high water for hours to find help. Sonya suffered a seizure while swimming through the water, and the family was separated after many days of being stranded first on the Causeway, then at the University of New Orleans, and then at the airport. According to Valentina, Isabel's mother, her husband was so consumed with guilt about the bad decision he had made for his family that he not only refused to participate in this study, but also would not talk about the hurricane at all with anyone.

In contrast to women who deferred to their male family members' decisions to stay in New Orleans, Laura, whose husband refused to leave, decided to look after herself. Because she did not have transportation, she and her neighbor took the bus to her neighbor's employer's house in Uptown. They knew that the employer had already evacuated, and believed that her house would be safer. They both remained there until two days after the storm, when "there wasn't any more drinking water."

Despite the fact that her father and sister stayed, Cristina, a young single mother of two, and her mother decided to leave New Orleans before the storm hit:

> [My mother and I] drove [to Houston] in my car and decided to leave at the last minute. We had heard that the hurricane was coming and went back and forth, "Should we stay, should we go?" So we finally decided to evacuate . . . for what we thought would be about three days. . . . look, that was the first time . . . I had never been through an experience like that. My mother had been through Camille, but I was too little to remember it. It was a sixteen-hour trip, what would normally be a five-hour trip. We have family here, so we went directly to their house. When we got here, we slept only about an hour because I have a sister who stayed [in New Orleans], and my mother came with me. My father stayed with my sister.

Norma, Cristina's mother, explained that although she had stayed through "so many other hurricanes," she knew this one was different:

> Well, we decided to evacuate because we didn't want to be there when it hit because they were saying on the radio and on TV that this one was gonna be a strong hit. That's why we decided to leave, but I never imagined that it was gonna hit like it did . . . such a big flood.

Because the New Orleans Garifuna are a transnational community with the Gulf of Mexico as their hub, several respondents had previous experience with hurricanes and hurricane evacuation both in Honduras and in New Orleans. As was the case with Norma's husband who refused to leave, however, the magnitude of Hurricanes Camille, Betsy, and Mitch weighed less in the minds of most in this community than the prospect of a costly evacuation in response to a false alarm or the fear of male family members losing their jobs. After all, just the year before, the thousands of New Orleanians that fled the city before Hurricane Ivan returned to an unscathed city, and many had lost their jobs for not showing up to work.

While ten of the nineteen Garifuna I interviewed stayed in New Orleans through the storm, by October 2005 they all were living in the same community in Houston. And while this community that formed around a Garifuna identity and language was initially crucial in aiding evacuees in their search for housing, the absence of other networks impeded the resettlement process for the Garifuna of New Orleans.

THE ROLE OF NETWORKS

In pre-Katrina New Orleans as in other immigrant receiving communities in the Diaspora, Garifuna cultural associations and festivals thrived.[11] Geographically, however, New Orleans Garifunas were not settled centrally in one neighborhood, parish, or part of town. Before the storm, respondents lived in the Gentilly, Midcity, Riverbend, Metairie, New Orleans East, and Uptown neighborhoods that vary drastically in terms of population demographics, economic status, and physical location. Furthermore, having arrived at different times, under widely varying conditions, and living under different statuses of "legality" and documentation, respondents led very different lives based on social class and access to resources. As evidenced by the examples above, different class positions created varied experiences during evacuation from Katrina.

Once the Garifuna were in Houston after Katrina, however, important networks arose from the Diaspora that many non-Garifuna evacuees born and raised in New Orleans did not have following the storm. Connections to family members and friends, employment networks, and a specific Garifuna faith-based community distinguished post-Katrina Garifuna experiences from those of African American evacuees whose networks extended no further than the family members who evacuated with them.

One very important connection was Pastor Erik, the cousin of one of the women I interviewed, who brought together a community united by migration and evacuation. Erik Castro, a Honduran Garifuna, moved south from New York City in 2002 and opened a small church in Houston that same year. He got his mission off the ground when, one summer day, a stranger offered to donate a small building and some church pews. Pastor Erik knew that God had sent this stranger to him. So when he heard that a large community of Garifuna had been evacuated to the Houston Astrodome after

Hurricane Katrina in 2005, he felt it was his duty to repay God's generosity by assisting those who were forced from their homes in New Orleans:

> I wrote a message in Garifuna on a cardboard sign with a black marker. My wife and I walked straight into the Astrodome with it. No one asked us any questions. It didn't take long to find my community, and then word spread that I was offering help.

Pastor Erik would eventually relocate over a hundred Honduran Garifuna evacuees to three apartment complexes in the southeastern suburbs of Houston. He facilitated the FEMA application process for those whose residency status made them eligible and found housing and clothing donations for those undocumented respondents who did not qualify for government assistance. The pastor offered weekly post-Katrina therapy sessions, masses delivered in Garifuna, and various other services in Spanish and Garifuna. Evacuees also knew that it was safe to discuss documentation status with the pastor and his wife.

The Houston Garifuna evacuee community offered a safe haven for respondents and a supportive network of mutual assistance. Yet in the immediate aftermath of the storm it became clear that Erik's assistance would only go so far for those that were undocumented. As is apparent in the narratives below, documentation status continued to play a role in shaping the experiences of the respondents.

DOCUMENTATION STATUS AND EMPLOYMENT

While Pastor Erik offered an extraordinary opportunity and social network ties based on Garifuna identity, this community was often not strong enough to overcome the hindrances to resettlement posed by the lack of legal documentation—joblessness, broken employment network ties, and even fear. Those who were legal residents had long-standing careers and, therefore, transferable employment following the storm. Undocumented men who worked as day laborers were able to support their families in New Orleans, but found themselves stranded in Houston after Katrina, worried about their families' welfare and afraid to look for work in a new city for fear of being reported to *la migra*.

Augustin's immediate and extended family, for example, were well-equipped to reestablish themselves after Katrina as a result of his three-decades-long career as a seaman, which provided them with home owners' insurance, health insurance, US residency, and a savings account. At the time of his interview in November 2005, Augustin was traveling back and forth between Louisiana and Texas to continue his position as a leader for the local chapter of the seamen's union, and this leadership position gave him contacts in Houston that aided his family with their job and apartment search following Katrina:

> [In New Orleans] I worked with a union that has offices all over the United States—New York, Philadelphia, Baltimore, Jacksonville, [Houston]. So I can work anywhere. . . . [I worked] at sea. And before the hurricane, I did a lot of work in Houston. So, yes, I will work here.

Augustin's work connections also provided housing for him and his entire family. In early September, after having been separated from his family and sent to the Astrodome during evacuation, he found housing through a friend from work. Even his estranged wife was provided temporary housing through a work-related acquaintance.

Other male heads of household were not as fortunate. Oscar went to New Orleans after Hurricane Mitch and found a job as a carpenter, as did his three male cousins and his brother, Moises. They all moved to Metairie, a suburb of New Orleans, between one and four years before Katrina struck. Oscar and Moises, both in their early twenties, brought their partners and children over after securing jobs. While these jobs were enough to provide for each family's basic necessities, they were noncontractual and temporary, rendering the men and their households vulnerable both before and especially after the hurricane.

In the days following Katrina, while Augustin's status as legal resident allowed him to apply for food stamps and other types of government assistance, Oscar and his family pieced together donations from local churches. Moreover, while Augustin was able to go back to work almost immediately, Oscar was timid about searching for construction work, fearing he would be deported.

Naín and Rafael, Oscar's cousins, had been working for a year and four years, respectively, as day laborers in New Orleans before the storm. In a group interview with the men, Naín described his experience in Houston after the storm, and as the others weighed in, the importance of documentation became painfully clear.

> NAÍN: I applied for FEMA [assistance] but couldn't get a voucher because I don't have residency or a social security number.

RAFAEL: Then we heard about a place that was giving help to "illegals," so we went there. But when we got there, they started asking all these questions about where we were from, our names. They wanted to see identification. So we left.

MOISES: I have a Social Security number, so I got a FEMA voucher and an apartment.

NAÍN: [laughing] So we're all living with him. All of us and the kids are sharing this apartment and the one next door.

OSCAR: What we need the most is work!

MOISES: We're not asking for anything. We don't want amnesty or citizenship or any of that stuff. What we want is work and documents so we can have our identity back . . . and get ourselves out of this situation.

RAFAEL: Yeah, there's gonna be a moment when all of this help ends and we need work to pay the rent. Some people have kids to take care of. I believe that everything is possible, as they say . . . but only if we have work.

Because men were the primary source of income in most families in this study, their employment and documentation status was a deciding factor in how soon the recovery process would begin after the hurricane. For those families headed by undocumented males, there was a double burden of not being able to apply for government assistance, such as FEMA and food stamps, and not being able to find work. In fact, in December 2005, the only respondents in the study who were back at work were those who were documented and had contractual work before the storm.

Women also had wide-ranging experiences with resettlement based on documentation status. Cristina, a second-generation Garifuna born in New Orleans, held a high school diploma, an associate's degree, and a job with a major oil corporation that paid her overtime after the storm because of the company's desperate need for a bilingual administrative assistant. This allowed her to take care of extended family as well:

I got [this apartment] right away because I work with an oil company. They started calling me right away because they needed me to work. So when my sister arrived with my father, I paid for two rooms in a hotel for a week until they found out that the Red Cross would pay for things like that. So that was a big relief to my pocketbook because I was paying for everyone. And then I had to travel between Dallas and Houston because I was working in Dallas. My company was paying for an apartment for me in Dallas. Later, I found out that the Red Cross aid was going to end, so I applied for an apartment and paid the deposit . . . to take them all out of the hotel.

In contrast, before the storm other women I interviewed tended to work in noncontractual jobs as babysitters, housekeepers, and even costume makers. Moreover, many women had previously depended on their husbands, fathers, or other family members for connections to employment and community. When left to their own devices in Houston, these women were uncertain of how to find work on their own. Laura, whose husband had recently returned to Louisiana to work, described post-Katrina life in Houston without her husband:

> [Houston] has been difficult. Since we didn't have a way around [when we arrived], we would go out with our neighbors and come back at ten at night because we would get lost. Then my husband arrived and bought a car. But as luck would have it, my husband flipped the car in an accident on the interstate, and then everything reversed again. At least he wasn't killed. . . . Now, if there's any work, my sister comes to let me know because my husband is working in Houma, [Louisiana]. . . . If not, I would just sit here.

Having no ties to the greater Latino community in Houston also hindered the formation of employment networks like those that they had been a part of in New Orleans before the storm. Julio, a carpenter and drywaller who moved to New Orleans in 2002, expressed a concern for ever being able to find work in Houston because of a lack of ties to other day laborers there:

> I lived in Metairie, which is not too close to where my jobs were in New Orleans. But I could still ride my bike and take the bus to get around. . . . We always had work. I lived with my cousins and some friends, and whenever one of them found work, they would let everyone else know. There was never a lack of work. . . . But now, we're all out of work and stranded in . . . I don't even know where we are or how I would catch a bus if I wanted to go look for work. But I'm afraid to go look [for work] because people say that *la migra* is always busting people here.

While lack of employment networks created a certain longing to return to the routine of life in New Orleans, many respondents also longed for the communities they had left behind. Diana remembered her life in the River-bend neighborhood of Uptown, where, although far from family members, she felt accepted and respected:

> I got along well with everyone in my neighborhood. In that respect, I never had problems. Everyone was "good people." All of my neighbors were older—I was the only young person there. There were a lot of older women who owned houses, women in their fifties. And there I was in my thirties. I was the young one, and they had a lot of love for us because of the way we lived our lives—buying homes and working to help our children move forward in life.

Sonya longed for the small-town feeling of New Orleans. At a loss for words when asked to describe what she liked most about her previous life in New Orleans, she found it easier to contrast it with her new life in Houston:

> It was nice. [pauses and thinks] I had a lot of friends. It was better than over here because you know everyone . . . you know where to go, and when you're bored you can just go outside or go by a friend's house. Here, you can just easily get lost because Texas is big! . . . The [neighborhood] we lived in before Katrina, it was nice. It was quiet. It was better for us, more quiet, more peaceful.

These displaced Garifuna articulated a desperate need for New Orleans. Although a large network of Garifuna existed in this suburban Houston neighborhood, it was isolated from the city, public transportation, jobs, and other Spanish-speakers. Respondents expressed nostalgia for community, routine, and a former way of life that was shaped by the ease of moving about New Orleans. Yet, when pressed to answer questions about return, respondents—especially those who suffered a post-storm, days-long evacuation—were not as steadfast about the New Orleans they remembered, because they feared it would never be the same.

RESETTLEMENT, RETURN, AND POSITIONALITY IN NEW ORLEANS

As Pastor Erik started to find more and more Garifuna families that had evacuated from New Orleans to Houston, he located housing for them in three apartment complexes in the suburbs of Houston. Ten of the nineteen respondents lived in a complex that was occupied almost entirely by New Orleans Garifuna families after Katrina. This became a central location for the pastor's furniture donation distribution and FEMA voucher application assistance. The other evacuees lived in complexes nearby.

Although some interviews were conducted at the Urban League and food stamp offices, I visited this central location for several initial and follow-up meetings. Each time I arrived, I heard people speaking across balconies in both Garifuna and Spanish, and I almost always found members of many different families congregating in each other's apartments—sharing meals, childcare, and advice. Once while waiting to conduct an interview, I listened to two neighbors planning a caravan trip to New Orleans for three families that were going to clean up their homes.

While stories of mutual assistance such as these were common among evacuees after Katrina, Pastor Erik's intervention played a role in creating a community based on Garifuna identity. If respondents did not maintain contact with other Garifuna—either spatially or culturally—while in New Orleans, the pastor's housing arrangements, therapy sessions, and Garifuna-language masses created this cohesion in Houston.

When I met with Pastor Erik and his wife in November of 2005, I asked why they felt it was important to establish therapy sessions in Garifuna and exclusive to this Garifuna community. Pastor Erik responded:

When I started talking to my cousin and her family, and other Garifuna evacuees from New Orleans, I realized that they had similar stories. Many of them felt discriminated against during their journey to Houston, and they were even afraid because of their skin color and their language. . . . Some of them felt like they were being mistreated because of who they were. I thought that was an important topic to continue to discuss, so I started the therapy sessions . . . to talk about these experiences, but also other ones as well.

Throughout the interviews, the sentiment that Pastor Erik mentioned was palpable. For example, Augustin, a sixty-year-old evacuee, expressed surprise at how he was treated by local authorities during the evacuation process in New Orleans:

Police officers should not use derogatory language, ugly words, words that are out of line. And that's what they did. Now, when we met up with police officers from other places, they seemed more educated. Not the local police. They were acting really poorly. I don't know if it was because they were overworked, but they did not behave well. . . . A bad experience.

Augustin later stated that he was hesitant to let these same authorities hear him speaking Spanish for fear that this would move him and his fellow Garifuna even further out of favor and further back in the line to evacuate. Victor and his uncle decided they would avoid authorities entirely as they left New Orleans three days after the storm:

We decided we were gonna walk to Texas. We didn't want to see the police because we were afraid they'd hit us. Because maybe they'd think we were doing something bad. You know how they think bad things about us sometimes. So we just started walking.

Interestingly, in the example above, while Victor admitted that his fear was based on his undocumented status, his uncle, who is a United States citizen, also chose to walk out of the city rather than seek help for fear of being mistreated. This fear was not unfounded. In her essay "Katrina's Latinos," sociologist Nicole Trujillo-Pagán argues that Latinos in New Orleans were grossly underrepresented in census data reports.[12] This led to the broad presumption in the media and among aid workers that post-Katrina Latinos in New Orleans were "imported workers," and as a consequence, Latinos were "systematically excluded from many relief services"[13] and racially profiled at shelters.

Garifuna residents of New Orleans, who represented a cross-section of several racial, ethnic, and class-based minority groups in the city before Katrina, experienced discrimination on various levels throughout the evacuation process. Stranded in New Orleans after the storm, Laura, who had already survived the after-effects of Mitch, knew she had to get out by any means possible. At first, however, she was afraid to call 9-1-1 for fear of being deported or misunderstood. Yet her poor English was not the biggest deterrent to leaving New Orleans. She explained:

At first I thought I didn't understand well because my English isn't very good . . . but when we called 9-1-1, they said, "We can't do anything for you now. You were told to leave and you didn't. Now you just have to wait." But no other number worked when I tried to call out. Just 9-1-1!

Many respondents related stories of undocumented Latinos being lured back to New Orleans by job prospects only to find themselves entrapped by border enforcement officials. Rafael brought up these stories during our interview:

> You know, they say that they're arresting illegals back in New Orleans for trying to work. . . . Why don't they leave us alone? Us Hispanics are doing all the cleanup, all the dirty work, and those of us that are still here need the work also. Gringos and, you know, Americans are sickened by that type of work. Hispanics aren't because we're in so much need. . . . Just like we work like donkeys everywhere else, we're giving our backs to re-build the city and make it more beautiful. . . . All we're doing is working! . . . And the people that are stealing and doing bad things are going about their business while we're getting hassled by the police and *migración*.

Cristina, a daughter of Garifuna parents born in New Orleans who iden-tified herself as New Orleanian in an earlier question, began tearing up when speaking of the treatment of Latinos in post-Katrina New Orleans:

> CRISTINA: The only problem I have right now is related to the immi-grants that are working in New Orleans. . . . You hear a lot of em-ployers telling workers that they can go work in New Orleans without worrying about Social Security, and then a lot of people go to work. And then who arrives? Homeland Security to detain them and take them out of there. . . . And for the mayor of New Orleans to say that he doesn't want Mexicans in the city . . .
> GARZA: Where did you hear about the poor treatment of Latinos work-ing in New Orleans?
> CRISTINA: I hear about it a lot. Like I told you, when Black Americans talk to me, they have a certain trust [Cristina used the word *confianza*, which means confidence, trust, and also a way of speaking without formality]; they think that because I'm Black, that I'm like them. . . . So lots of times, I've had people tell me that we don't pay taxes. And I say, "What? We pay taxes." I fight with them. And they say, "Yeah. Latinos, Chinese, all of those people don't pay taxes, and they come here to take away our jobs," and all that. But a lot of Latinos have humble jobs. The majority of Latinos have humble jobs. If they [US citizens] won't work in housekeeping, how can they say that Latinos are taking away their jobs? It would be different if someone came here and took away an executive job—[switches to English] an administra-tor or something like that—[back to Spanish] but we're talking about

humble jobs. Cleaning—anyone can get a job cleaning—color, race, and all that stuff doesn't matter.

As a second-generation Garifuna in New Orleans who grew up among and identified with African American peers, Cristina explained that she suddenly felt like an outsider (*alguién de afuera*), even though New Orleans was her hometown.

As Sonya pointed out, while this Spanish-speaking immigrant community was susceptible to specific vulnerabilities before the storm, the color of their skin lumped them into one category in the eyes of some rescue workers, from whom she sensed another type of hostility:

> In San Antonio, we slept under a tree. They was treating dogs more better than us. . . . Because the dogs had vets and everything and we were like out there on the streets. The dogs had their own little cages and their own little food and everything. They got treated good. And we were just sleeping on the floor. Like regular nothings. And the people that were trying to help us, they were scared to touch us like we got germs or something. They think that we got some kind of infection or something. Like when we was getting on the airplane to go to San Antonio, we had to pass through [security], and the guy said, "I don't want to touch them Black people. Just let them go, let them go, I don't want to touch them."

Despite a long history of migration and adaptation, the Garifuna of New Orleans experienced many challenges to resettlement in Houston. While Pastor Erik provided for the immediate needs of the community, he was unable to address the structural obstacles to recovery—such as discrimination (based on ethnicity, language, skin color, and/or documentation status)— that many felt prevented them from getting back on their feet.

As a result, as these displaced Garifuna dealt with starting over and being outsiders in a new city, they expressed feelings of helplessness and fatalism. After Ana evacuated New Orleans and then dealt with the burglary of her Houston apartment, neither she nor her sister had the resources to make another evacuation decision when she heard that Hurricane Rita was headed toward Houston. Ana explained:

> When I left that week, to see if I could find work back in New Orleans, they broke in and took everything I had, the television, everything. And I was left with nothing again. In my house in New Orleans, they stole everything, too. The air conditioner that I had just bought, the kids' toys.

I couldn't bring anything back from there. [she sighs deeply, holding back tears, and continues with a broken voice] So here I am again in the run-around . . . and I'm leaving it all up to God because he is the only one that decides if things will change. Us humans sometimes are so useless that we have to leave it up to God.

NEW ORLEANS GARIFUNA THROUGH THE LENS OF DISASTER

Toward the end of my stay in Houston, I interviewed Pastor Erik at the Garifuna Mercy of God Christian Church, which he and his wife founded in 2002. The church is housed in a two-story building that would other-wise be suitable for a low-income rental and sits at the end of a long street of humble row houses in a neighborhood situated beneath the intersection of Interstate 10 and Southwest Freeway 59. The deafening sounds of traffic and trains, the street's oaks and palms, and the neighbors' conversations in Spanish reminded me of Houston's participation in many worlds: the Texas-Mexico borderlands, the Caribbean, and the Gulf Coast South. Just as I was contemplating the road that led me to this place, Pastor Erik approached me with a warm smile and a hug.

Following our half-hour interview, the couple's children joined us for a longer prayer session, and Pastor Erik's wife translated for me, occasionally switching from Spanish to Garifuna. Erik had no doubt about how I had ended up there. He thanked God for sending me to the Garifuna evacuee community to be the "voice of the voiceless" and a "herald of the Garifuna plight." He also thanked God for helping his people to be strong and coura-geous despite the ongoing hardships in the community. While I felt an over-whelming sense of destiny in the experience myself, I also remembered that the post-Katrina experiences of New Orleans Garifuna were profoundly shaped by class, race, gender, and citizenship status.

Because the Garifuna are a population with a heritage of movement and adaptation, the mass evacuation after the hurricane was both a familiar and a jarring experience. This latest Garifuna dislocation revealed a community that was both unified by country of origin, language, and a history of mi-gration and heterogeneous in ways that led to new questions regarding how the Garifuna fit into New Orleans society. With media often portraying the Latino community as a new workforce "invading" New Orleans following the hurricane to replace African American workers and to reshape the city's culture,[14] the Garifuna I met found themselves standing astride the dis-courses that alienated Latino migrants from African American residents.

Many Garifuna had contacts in Houston that proved to be a valuable source of support during the months after Katrina. Pastor Erik was also a key figure in the lives of many respondents, because he stepped in with housing, clothing, and other assistance for those who were not eligible for government aid. His work also reinforced a specific Garifuna evacuee identity through physical proximity, therapy sessions, and church services conducted in the Garifuna language.

In the end—despite the networks that provided immediate assistance to the Garifuna of New Orleans after arriving in Houston, through previous work connections in New Orleans or via Pastor Erik's community in Houston—evacuation, resettlement, and return were hindered by the fact that many were undocumented, Spanish-speaking, and newly arriving migrants. Moreover, the Garifuna of New Orleans were an often disregarded people overlooked by census data even before Hurricane Katrina magnified the vulnerability of a community living in the spaces between African American and Latino, local and foreigner, migrant and New Orleans native. This same position of vulnerability, however, pressed this group to draw on past experiences of migration and displacement, as well as cultural resources such as language, to cope with one of the worst disasters in the history of the United States.

NOTES

1. Sheldon Danziger and Sandra K. Danziger, "Poverty, Race, and Antipoverty Policy before and after Hurricane Katrina," *Du Bois Review: Social Science Research on Race* 3, no. 1 (2006): 23–36; Chester Hartman and Gregory D. Squires, eds., *There Is No Such Thing as a Natural Disaster: Race, Class, and Hurricane Katrina* (New York: Routledge, 2006); Ismail K. White, Tasha S. Philpot, Kristin Wylie, and Ernest McGowen, "Feeling the Pain of My People: Hurricane Katrina, Racial Inequality, and the Psyche of Black America," *Journal of Black Studies* 37, no. 4 (2007): 523–538.

2. The word *Garinagu* refers to a community of people that speak Garifuna. Because the Garinagu are now commonly known as Garifuna and because participants referred to themselves as Garifuna (when speaking about the community, themselves as individuals, their language, and their culture), this is the term I use throughout the chapter.

3. Nancie Gonzalez, *Sojourners of the Caribbean* (Urbana and Chicago: University of Illinois Press, 1988), p. 21.

4. Ibid., pp. 38–49.

5. Ibid.

6. Hayes Ferguson, "Many Garifuna Families Moving to New Orleans," *New Orleans Times Picayune*, April 6, 1997.

7. The questionnaire used in this study was originally written for a specific community—New Orleans–born African Americans. Though the survey was later altered, early interviews did not include questions regarding residency status, migration patterns, language use, cultural associations, etc. Despite this, several common themes prevailed throughout the interview process.

8. Hayes Ferguson, "Black Hondurans Try to Preserve Culture," *New Orleans Times Picayune*, April 6, 1997.

9. Two nonfiction films—*Garifunas Holding Ground (Lucha Garífuna)* and *Cuando el Río y el Mar se Unieron*—document the struggles of the Honduran Garifuna as a politically and economically marginalized community that faced further devastation in the deadly wake of Hurricane Mitch in 1998. *Cuando el Río y el Mar se Unieron* (Comité de Emergencia Garífuna de Honduras and WITNESS, 2004), videocassette; *Garifunas Holding Ground (Lucha Garífuna)* (Comité de Emergencia Garífuna de Honduras and WITNESS, 2002), videocassette.

10. Prior research on gender, disaster, and evacuation has shown that women tend to be more risk-averse than men. This may help explain why the women in my sample wanted to evacuate, while the men in their families tended to downplay the risks associated with staying behind in New Orleans. See Elaine Enarson, Alice Fothergill, and Lori Peek, "Gender and Disaster: Foundations and Directions," in *Handbook of Disaster Research*, ed. H. Rodriguez, E. L. Quarantelli, and R. R. Dynes (New York: Springer, 2006), pp. 130–146.

11. Christine Bordelon, "New Twist to Salsa Beat, Group Dances to Honor Heritage," *New Orleans Times Picayune*, September 14, 2003; Gina Cortez, "Garinagu Celebrate with Mass," *New Orleans Times Picayune*, December 28, 1995; Ana Gershanik, "Music Sheds Light on Garifuna Roots," *New Orleans Times Picayune*, September 7, 2000; Sheila Stroup, "Preserving Culture Is Fun," *New Orleans Times Picayune*, April 8, 1999.

12. Nicole Trujillo-Pagán, "Katrina's Latinos: Vulnerability and Disasters in Relief and Recovery," in *Through the Eye of Katrina: Social Justice in the United States*, ed. K. A. Bates and R. S. Swan (Durham, NC: Carolina Academic Press, 2007), pp. 147–168.

13. Ibid., p. 155.

14. Nicole Trujillo-Pagán, "From 'Gateway to the Americas' to the 'Chocolate City': The Racialization of Latinos in New Orleans," in *Racing the Storm: Racial Implications and Lessons Learned from Hurricane Katrina*, ed. H. Potter (Lanham, MD: Lexington Books, 2007), pp. 95–113.

AFTER THE FLOOD
FAITH IN THE DIASPORA

*It's like, nobody could have told me to leave New Orleans
when the hurricane came, and I stayed because the spirit of
the Lord didn't tell me to leave. So I stayed there, and I was
comforted that nothing, there would be no harm, no matter
what happened that I would survive.*

*I said, well, as long as the Lord gives me health and
strength you know, we're going to survive.*

On this Wednesday night in April 2008, there are thirty people at the prayer service in Baton Rouge. It is nearly three years after Hurricane Katrina, and this congregation is one of several formed during the displacement of people from New Orleans. About half the people at the evening prayer service are Katrina survivors from New Orleans. The others are from Baton Rouge.

In the days following the evacuation, local congregations found that many of their members had scattered to nearby cities: Dallas, Houston, Baton Rouge, Atlanta, and Jackson. Some of these congregations created on-site worship opportunities in those cities, and by 2008, approximately fifteen had become permanent. The congregation that I observed is one—a congregation founded in New Orleans but re-formed in Baton Rouge.

The prayer group is located at a new satellite congregation in Baton Rouge that is in a mixed-race suburb with occupied homes and open businesses on the clean streets. The home church in New Orleans, a turn-of-the-century building, is in the Central City neighborhood several blocks away from the tree-lined streets and antebellum homes on St. Charles Avenue. It is now surrounded by "urban prairie"—empty buildings and over-

PAMELA JENKINS

grown lots. The house falling down across the street still has the hash marks from Hurricane Katrina and the hand-painted sign reading "Please rescue" on the front.

The congregation is part of the long tradition of the Black church, which for generations has served to support families facing crises and to promote social change.[1] Congregations were so integral to the lives of the former residents of New Orleans that the church and the members found each other wherever they landed. The ability of the Black church to sustain the community in crisis and collectively organize the community for action forms a backdrop for understanding the narratives of the displaced presented in this chapter.[2]

This study explores how displaced members of divergent Black congregations survived the storm and the subsequent displacement through reliance on their faith, their church, and their community. In this sense, a church is not a building or a place that people have to leave behind when they are forced to flee. It is a way of gathering, a context, a social form, a pattern of life that people take with them as they leave for distant places. My aim in this research is to understand this broader meaning of "church" in the lives of African American Katrina survivors.

New Orleans is often portrayed as a place where the "good times roll," but at its center it is a religious community. According to some reports, more than eight hundred separate congregations existed in Orleans Parish before Katrina.[3] Nationally, the Black Christian church, like many other denominations, is moving toward "megacongregations" that attract thousands of worshippers each week. Yet in New Orleans, the older tradition of small neighborhood congregations remains strong. In pre-Katrina New Orleans, congregations shared pastors and even buildings. A small congregation would set up worship in the church building of a large congregation until it grew enough to move into its own church building. Churches were everywhere—in the middle of residential blocks, in homes, in tents, on street corners.

After Katrina, as churches and congregations struggled with their own recovery, the pattern of sharing space became even more pronounced. For example, more than three years after the hurricane, one church in the Upper Ninth Ward had four different congregations meeting in its space every Sunday. Local observers began to refer to these other congregations as "invisible churches." They are not usually listed in telephone directories or on building signs, and no sign on the church indicates their existence. At the same time, larger congregations with more resources were tracking down their congregants in evacuee cities, sometimes serving them in already established congregations and sometimes opening "satellite" congregations in the host cities.

THE STUDY

The information in this chapter is drawn from a larger and still ongoing study. In the early aftermath of Hurricane Katrina, our research team[4] contacted ministers and other members of satellite congregations in Baton Rouge, as well as ministers and congregants of already established Baton Rouge congregations. Through these contacts and the review of websites, newspapers, and other secondary data, we identified fifteen congregations that had, at that time, permanent satellite congregations in seven host cities (Baton Rouge, Atlanta, Houston, Dallas, Shreveport, Jackson, and the smaller community of Amite, Louisiana). Initial contact with ministers and church elders led us to additional contacts in each city. In Baton Rouge, we interviewed members of one satellite congregation and new members, displaced by Katrina, of one already established congregation.

This chapter focuses on the former Orleans Parish residents now living in Baton Rouge. Baton Rouge, the capital of Louisiana, is only sixty-six miles from New Orleans and shares a common Louisiana heritage, but the communities are very different. Baton Rouge is more conservative and more prosperous than the larger and more diverse and Democratic city to the south. Yet Baton Rouge became one of the major evacuee centers after Katrina.

Because the interviews we conducted were open-ended and intended to facilitate storytelling, I refer to the interviewees as narrators and their stories as narratives.[5] No matter where we started the interview, the narrators began with the day they left the city and continued to the present.[6] Of the thirty narrators I draw on in this chapter, twelve were men and eighteen were women.[7] They ranged in age from twenty to sixty-nine, and all were African American. Their class positions ranged from working poor to middle class. The interviews were conducted in the church after Wednesday night prayer service, in the narrators' homes, at restaurants, or in coffee shops. We did not directly ask participants about their faith or belief in God, although these themes emerged repeatedly in each interview.

FAITH AND EVACUATION

The connection of the displaced to New Orleans is a pattern of long-distance relationships still in process. Congregations are integral to the fabric of evacuees' current lives. They provide support, help in decision-making about returning, and a connection to parts of the former, pre-Katrina lives of those displaced. The narrators had traveled similar paths—from New Orleans to Baton Rouge—even though their thinking about the choices they faced was not the same. A young single woman described her feelings in this way: "Well, I feel pretty much settled here, but this isn't really the place I want to be at—I'm not settled here." Another young woman with two small children disclosed a similar uncertainty:

> [God] brought me through a lot of this because when I first came here I wanted to go back to New Orleans and then I didn't want to go back. I always was miserable. I just was drained, so I finally just submitted and went right back to work so that helped me a lot.

This uncertainty is found throughout the narratives but is countered, as these young women described, with faith. A young mother of four, who had been stranded with thirty other people on the second story of a public housing project, remembered the water coming up to the first floor of her apartment. She described the prayers on the Tuesday after the storm, as the levees were breached and overtopped:

> Yeah, that Tuesday we got on the porch all the neighbors, we decided, and by this time, we are seeing helicopters flying everywhere. So we holler for help, we begging for help, we got white towels doing all kind of stuff just to get people's attention. So my neighbor, her son was a minister, so he's over there with her, he's like, "Man, we need to pray, we need to pray, we need to get together." Well we were already on one accord cause we were trying to figure out how we were going to get out, we was like, "We need God in this one now, we need God in this one." So we are praying, sitting on the porch praying. "God you got to get us out of this, something got to give, you got to, I know you not gonna let us die like this."

This group decided to act by walking to the Crescent City Connection (the bridge to Jefferson Parish above New Orleans), where they were turned back by police. They then walked toward the Superdome, commandeered automobiles, and drove to Baton Rouge. "Reasoning through prayer" contributed to their successful evacuation as they walked together through high waters filled with floating bodies. So the phrase "we need to pray, we need to get together" is more than a call for God's help, but a way that they acted as a group with "his help."

An older man said about the morning after the storm: "Yes the same day, the same morning, the sun was out. It reminded me, actually, of . . . Noah's Ark . . . when the dove came back and brought this olive branch." He continued:

> But my faith sustained, having trust and faith in God, and that's the thing that covers me, I was covered in the blood of Jesus when the hurricane hit. I stayed because I was not directed by God to leave. A lot of friends and family members were calling upon me but I stayed. And as I stayed I guess it materialized into a testimony, so that someone else can testify that there is a God, that there are miracles, and that there is some record what has happened and in every situation in history and in life there's always been survivors, someone to record what has happened.

These narratives reveal a strong reliance on prayer. But more than that, they also highlight the connection between prayer and action and the ways that prayer resonates throughout everyday life.[8] Similarly, Davis[9] notes that prayer for African Americans is "not an escape that leads to passivity but cooperation with God to act against evil and oppression."

THE SEARCH FOR HOME

People ended up in Baton Rouge for a variety of reasons. As individuals and families tried to find their way, these stops and starts in searching for home could last anywhere from weeks to years. Several narrators mentioned their journey to Houston first, to Atlanta next, and finally to Baton Rouge. These journeys sometimes involved a number of moves within a host city, for example, from a shelter to an apartment to a house. One young woman traveled first to Houston with her brother, sister-in-law, mother, and niece. Once there and with Hurricane Rita approaching, she took her mother to Atlanta, where they lived with twenty-five other family members. Assured that her mother was safe, she then traveled to Baton Rouge, where she decided to stay. She said, "I wanted to come home to Louisiana, but did not want to come to New Orleans. Baton Rouge was close enough."

The difficulty of this kind of travel appears in all the interviews. Each move involved negotiating where to stay and figuring out how to obtain basic necessities. And each one seemed more difficult than the one before. A single woman in her fifties who eventually stayed in Baton Rouge said:

It was very difficult because you were looking at the fact that you are dealing with what has happened and you are trying to make a decision that you can live with, too. So I felt like I was in this little card game or something. Like I'm in Houston, now you in Atlanta, now you are going to go back to Louisiana.

Within this decision-making process, people always questioned whether they had made the right decision. For the narrators in this study, the answer often rested with their faith, their family, and their job. A fifty-two-year-old African American man talks about how his decision to be in Baton Rouge was influenced:

I trust in God, you know, and I believe in God. And I believe that . . . he was going to provide for us and deliver us out of what we had experienced. After we done lost everything and the only thing that you had was just the two or three outfits that we took with us. You know and I told her [his wife], I said, "I believe that the Lord going to deliver us, everything will be okay."

A single woman with four children, who had spent much of her adult life living in the housing projects in New Orleans, also talked about how her decision-making process was based on her faith and trust in God:

Oh God, God has blessed [us] tremendously. When we first moved to Baton Rouge, we lived on, well we lived in what they call Dime City on Calais, which was like another [housing] project. I was like, "Now Lord, I know you didn't take me out the projects to put me back into the projects, no I know you didn't do that to me, no, this is not going to happen."

Through the help of her family, she was able to find a Section 8 house in a much safer community. Her housing search was time-consuming and at times stressful. Yet she framed this decision as based on her faith. She continued:

It's funny though. I think about just before Katrina happened, I always prayed that God would take me out of there so my kids could have a better life. So I came back and said to God, "You didn't have to do it that drastic."

Years after the storm, people are still in the process of rebuilding their lives—finding schools for their children, securing jobs and housing, and replacing losses. Many were on the highway more and more between New Orleans and Baton Rouge. Ministers and other staff from New Orleans drove several times a week to Baton Rouge. Evacuees from Baton Rouge traveled regularly to New Orleans to be with family, to attend church, to go to work, to take their children to school, and to work on their homes.

As part of their recovery, they also looked for a congregation to attend, no matter how temporary. Some joined new congregations in Baton Rouge, while others found the satellite congregations that opened there. But changing congregations was difficult for all. For example, according to a middle-aged woman who began attending a satellite congregation in Baton Rouge:

> [S]ome people really, really give up. The things that I'm mentioning every person had to deal with it. If they weren't in church that's even worse, but the people that were in church had to deal with changing churches and looking for the love they have felt . . . what they call home.

It was not just about finding a place to worship, but about finding a church home. A young woman from New Orleans carefully detailed the centrality and importance of a church home during times of crisis:

> I really did depend on the church as a young girl. I was alone and the church was what got me through the death of my mother. So I highly depended on the church in New Orleans. I depended on the church so much that I was pretty much there every day, whenever they had something going on. Looking for that same thing in another church—you don't always get it all the time.

Thompson and McRae credit the Black church with developing a way for members to create a sense of belonging with others.[10] This belonging appears to have been more important after the events of Katrina and the flooding of New Orleans. Another woman described her search in choosing where to worship:

> Well I'd say that it was like a puzzle piece. . . . It was a necessity for me to join a church because I never went without going to church. But I had not

made a decision of joining my home church, [which] is still active in New Orleans. They haven't taken me off their roll, and they probably won't. But I definitely needed a place for my spirit to feel at home, because my spirit home was destroyed in New Orleans—you know as it relates to church. Once I joined here, that final puzzle piece was put in place, and I believe I felt in my spirit God was pleased, I was more at ease, and time to move on to the next thing.

As satellite congregations opened, people who had been members of churches in New Orleans reunited with their old church families in Baton Rouge. Again, a single mother of four described what many accounts reveal—the surprise, the joy, and the sense of being home:

We were going to church here, and it was okay, mind you, it was okay but it wasn't my home church. I worship and praise God wherever I am even in my car, but it just wasn't like being around family . . . so you don't know what I went through, you don't know what happened, so you can't really share my pain, you can console me but you can't really share in what I went through. What happened was I ran into one of my other church members, Felicia, in Wal-Mart, and she said, "You know, Pastor's gonna come to the church, coming to Baton Rouge." And when I made it there, I saw faces up there who recognized me. That was it for me, I must say that's when I broke down, that's when I broke down. Church family was what I needed to see, and to hear my pastor was enough for me. And that was a Sunday that I'll never forget.

The accounts of those who joined satellite congregations differ from those who searched for new church homes among established Baton Rouge congregations. For the latter, the search meant visiting many congregations, evaluating the minister, the music, and the members of the congregations. A young single mom with several children talked about joining a local Baton Rouge congregation. While her report is mostly positive, she acknowledged the unevenness of her reception in Baton Rouge:

But once I came here for the first time, I knew this is where I needed to be while I was in Baton Rouge. Having a place for my kids to be rooted and grounded and shaped and helped, because they were from babies always in a teaching church. The church is again a huge refuge, a place of refuge which the church is supposed to be. Mind you, I have felt vibes that weren't good since I've been here, but I am thankful that God has grown me to an area in my life that caused me to not let anyone deter me from serving him and trusting in him and so therefore the negative did not outweigh the good.

Even those who found a new church home where they felt comfortable and at peace often spoke of missing their old congregations. The Baton Rouge faith experience for most involved larger congregations, not the smaller churches they were part of in New Orleans. A middle-aged married woman talked about both her new and old congregations:

Even though I have never really talked to him [the pastor] in person, because the church is so huge, I'm not used to this. At home, our pastor sit at the front door even though they got five hundred people there, he knows everybody in that church. He knew my daughter, he knew me, he knew my husband, he knew everybody.

Another woman and her family had integral roles in their smaller congregation in New Orleans, and they were not used to the more passive role in the new, much larger congregation in Baton Rouge:

I have Sunday school teachers that are retired teachers from East Baton Rouge School Parish. There are a couple and they are historians. I feel like after Sunday school I've had my sermon because they are so good and they make it so real. And then my pastor is very dynamic as is the choir. I've always enjoyed Baptist singing and Baptist preaching, so it makes me feel a little more at home. But the congregation is so large, so I feel like I'm just this one little dot that's kind of lost in the sheep. So I find myself, actually all three of us, we find ourselves going into the line after worship to make sure we shake the pastor's hand and tell him how we were blessed by the message so he knows who we are. We realize that they didn't have to open the doors for us but they did.

While this woman's faith remained strong, her actual lived experience in Baton Rouge was a challenge:

When I was in New Orleans I was very active, very outgoing, always busy, teaching at my church, working at the church. I was a deaconess. I go to church every Sunday. Sometimes I go to Bible study on Wednesday. I'm more isolated unfortunately. I'm trying to work through that in my mind. I have this home. But sometimes I just stay in the home and my husband will come home and he'll see the newspaper outside in the yard and he'll say, "Why did you leave the newspaper outside?" I don't know. I just couldn't find my way to walk out the door. I haven't found my place yet and I don't know if that sounds really bad.

When I began these interviews, I expected that the respondents would refer to the material aid they received from their congregations.[11] But hardly anyone mentioned it. As one man said, "I did not ask them or anything, I did not tell them I was from New Orleans." Joining these congregations was not about material things, it was, for evacuees, about attaching to traditions and reestablishing a faith community.

CONCLUSION

Baton Rouge presents a unique setting for those displaced by Hurricane Katrina. For the narrators in this study, it is the short distance to home (New Orleans) *and* the relationships that are maintained that are most central to their possible return. At the same time, displaced congregations are making permanent plans, and individuals are putting down roots. The congregations are not just about worship on Sunday or even prayer group on Wednesday; they are about building faith and community in New Orleans and the host cities.

The narrators in this study worked and lived in two places, New Orleans and Baton Rouge. The most startling quality of this liminal life was how this transitional phase became normal. The people we interviewed are surviving, where many displaced are failing. They are buying homes, getting new jobs, yet still experiencing the trauma, the loss, and the anger from the event. Years later, they still recall the experience of the storm as if it were yesterday. They are grieving the separation and loss of their parents, grandparents, and friends.

The role of the Black church after Katrina is much like its role in the civil rights era: the religious themes and biblical references helped to frame the experience, and the churches played a key role in the mobilization of aid to their members.[12] Billingsley and Motes[13] state that the ability of the African American church to promote resilience post-Katrina is an important resource for future disasters, mostly through its capacity to organize communities and provide service. Yet in this study, it was not these types of services that members sought; it was the more spiritual function that seemed to matter most to the displaced. Those who found their new congregation in an already established Baton Rouge congregation expressed gratitude for their new church home, but those who stumbled onto a satellite congregation from New Orleans thought they had actually found "home."

The narrators' accounts reveal that church and faith were crucial in terms of the ability of the displaced to survive and even to thrive. For exiles, finding a home was not easy; it involved translating their loss into something manageable. The Black church and their deep faith helped these narrators manage their loss and prepare for their new life. The men and women in these congregations tell both an ancient and modern tale of survival and faith.

ACKNOWLEDGMENTS

Reverend Marshall Truehill was a doctoral student in planning and urban studies at the University of New Orleans. He was also senior pastor of First United Baptist Church in New Orleans (a church and parsonage totally destroyed in the flood). I was chair of his dissertation committee; he was my entrée into the communities under study and my friend for nearly two decades. On December 19, 2008, he was awarded his doctoral degree writing about the Black church since Katrina. On Christmas evening six days later, he died. This research would not have been possible without his work and faith.

NOTES

1. W. E. B. Du Bois, *The Philadelphia Negro* (Philadelphia: University of Pennsylvania, 1899); W. E. B. DuBois, *The Souls of Black Folk: Essays and Sketches* (New York: Modern Library, 1903); Curtis Evans, "W. E. B. Du Bois: Interpreting Religion and the Problem of the Negro Church," *Journal of the American Academy of Religion* 75, no. 2 (June 2007): 268–297; C. Eric Lincoln and Lawrence H. Mamiya, *The Black Church in the African American Experience* (Durham, NC: Duke University Press 1990).

2. Scott T. Fitzgerald and Ryan E. Spohn, "Pulpits and Platforms: The Role of the Church in Determining Protest among Black Americans," *Social Forces* 84, no. 2 (December 2005): 1015–1048.

3. Operation Brother's Keepers, "Report on Status of New Orleans Congregations" (unpublished report, Center for Hazards, Response and Technology, Milneburg Hall, University of New Orleans, 2004).

4. The research team was composed of the late Reverend Marshall Truehill, who made initial contacts and conducted interviews, Barbara Davidson and Nancy Freeman, who interviewed a number of the respondents, and me, as project director.

5. Irving Seidman, *Interviewing as Qualitative Research: A Guide for Researchers in Education and Social Science* (New York: Teachers College Press, 1998).

6. Kevin Fox Gotham and William G. Staples, "Narrative Analysis and the New Historical Sociology," *Sociological Quarterly* 37, no. 3 (1996): 481–501; Jaber F. Gubrium and James A. Holstein, "Narrative Practice and the Coherence of Personal Stories," *Sociological Quarterly* 39, no. 1 (1998): 163–187.

7. Another component of this study involves interviews with ministers of congregations in Baton Rouge, Houston, and New Orleans (none of those interviews are used here).

8. Timothy J. Nelson, *Every Time I Feel the Spirit: Religious Experience and Ritual in an African American Church* (New York: New York University Press 2005).

9. Reginald F. Davis, "African-American Interpretation of Scripture," *Journal of Religious Thought* 57/58 (2005): 93–105, quotation from p. 104.

10. Delores A. Thompson and Mary B. McRae, "The Need to Belong: A Theory of the Therapeutic Function of the Black Church Tradition," *Counseling and Values* 46, no. 1 (October 2001): 40–53.

11. Brenda Phillips and Pamela Jenkins, "The Roles of Faith-Based Organizations After Hurricane Katrina," in *Helping Families and Communities Recover from Disaster: Lessons Learned from Hurricane Katrina and Its Aftermath*, ed. R. P. Kilmer, V. Gil-Rivas, R. G. Tedeschi, and L. G. Calhoun (Washington, DC: American Psychological Association, 2010), pp. 215–238.

12. Fitzgerald and Spohn, "Pulpits and Platforms."

13. Andrew Billingsley and Patricia Stone Motes, "Hurricane Katrina: The Role of the African-American Church in Promoting Post-Catastrophe Resilience. Brief Report," in *Coastal Resilience Information Systems Initiative for the Southeast: Showcasing University of South Carolina Hurricane Katrina Research Projects* (Columbia: Office of Research and Health Sciences, University of South Carolina, 2006).

CHARTING A PATH FORWARD
SECTION INTRODUCTION

The studies in this volume tell an important story about the practices, policies, and structures of systemic inequality that impeded resettlement and recovery for Katrina's displaced. The previous chapters chronicle the experiences of socially vulnerable groups during disaster, as well as many obstacles to an effective and humane response—one that works for all of the people, not just the wealthy, White, and well connected.

Many who have written about Katrina, and the disasters that came before it, have argued that poor, disadvantaged, socially vulnerable populations must have a voice in the mitigation, response, and recovery processes if disasters are to do more than replicate and increase existing inequalities. Yet few have addressed how to involve these populations. This final chapter underscores the importance of challenging social inequalities in order to diminish the disparate impact of disasters in the future.

Driving the research network's collaboration from the beginning was a commitment to contribute to knowledge that supports a more humane, more just, more effective disaster response and recovery. We are well aware that naming and describing the obstacles to such a response are a necessary but in no way sufficient part of making social change for justice. So we choose to end this volume with this contribution from Rachel E. Luft. Her research on community activism for social justice in New Orleans before and after Katrina helps us to see the continuing efforts of some groups to challenge the organization of power and the distribution of resources in the United States. In a careful study of the People's Hurricane Relief Fund, she reveals the challenges to social movement organizing with a population dispersed by disaster, the conflicting demands of meeting basic needs versus working for social change, and the raced and gendered ways that activists approach their work. In addition to describing these processes, she suggests ways to improve activist strategies by integrating political organizing with

LYNN WEBER

service provision—a solution that emerged from a gendered analysis of the movement.

Luft's work is a fitting ending to this volume because, like the other studies presented here, she explores the impact of the disaster through the experiences of those living through it. However, the group whose words, actions, and visions her work explores is unique—people working for social justice in the midst of disaster recovery. And because the movement group she examines sees disaster as a microcosm of larger failures in the social contract, Luft's insights connect the specifics of Hurricane Katrina with the broader conditions of race, class, and gender oppression in the United States.

14

COMMUNITY ORGANIZING IN THE KATRINA DIASPORA

RACE, GENDER, AND THE CASE OF THE PEOPLE'S HURRICANE RELIEF FUND

Within hours of Hurricane Katrina's landfall, social justice organizers joined millions of Americans in responding to the humanitarian crisis precipitated by the storm. In addition to mobilizing to meet basic needs, however, organizers sought to cultivate a collective, political response to what they framed as government malfeasance before, during, and after the hurricane. With an early analysis of the social origins of the disaster, grassroots leaders hoped to organize survivors and sympathetic allies into a movement that would fight not only *for* the immediate well-being of the victims, but also *against* the broader social conditions that had turned the hurricane into a disaster. They believed Katrina could be a politicizing and galvanizing experience for hurricane survivors and other Americans. Kali Akuno,[1] executive director of the People's Hurricane Relief Fund (PHRF), characterized the perspective shared by leaders of the Black Liberation Movement: "The catastrophe—the suffering, the displacement, the broad visualization of it domestically and internationally—was going to reignite resistance; it would be a spark to bringing the Black Liberation Movement. A lot of us had had that premise." During the three years following the storm, movement organizers accomplished extraordinary mobilization in the midst of grim and often overwhelming conditions. But organizing a dispersed population consumed with survival needs and channeling those needs into political demands also proved difficult.

This chapter examines the challenge of movement-building in the context of disaster and displacement. In particular, it explores the relationship between grassroots organizing and the great demand for meeting basic needs in the aftermath of Hurricane Katrina. Toward this end, I juxtapose the development of political strategy among Black Liberation leaders with the experience of Katrina evacuees who encountered their mobilization

RACHEL E. LUFT

efforts. A gendered analysis of the tension between political mobilization and service provision not only contributes to our understanding of the gendered nature of social change efforts among disaster survivors, but also offers broader insights into movement-building in the current national context of economic instability and shrinking state services.

This discussion is based on a case study of PHRF, a movement coalition that emerged after the storm. Headquartered in New Orleans, PHRF's primary constituency was poor, Black New Orleanians, both those who remained displaced from the city following the mandatory evacuation of August 28, 2005, and those who returned. The study suggests that evacuees in the PHRF orbit found the movement organization's political critique appealing, and some of them underwent significant consciousness-raising and activation. Most, however, were consumed by their daily survival needs, which they framed as being in tension with participation in movement activity. Their experience raises tactical questions about community organizing during displacement and, in turn, about the role of relief work in community organizing.

THE STUDY

I am a sociologist at the University of New Orleans with research interests in race, gender, and social movements, and a White woman activist in local movements for racial and gender justice. I became involved in grassroots political responses to Katrina immediately after the storm. In September 2005, while still in evacuation myself, I was invited to join a national conference call with organizers who were forming PHRF. When I returned to New Orleans in January 2006, I began participant-observation in PHRF and several other grassroots reconstruction efforts in the city.[2]

At the end of 2007, when PHRF was formally dissolving, I conducted in-depth interviews with two PHRF leaders, Kali Akuno and Malcolm Suber, and three paid staff organizers in diasporic cities with large evacuee populations: Addis Ababa in Atlanta, Georgia; Gina Martin in Houston, Texas; and Wilma Taylor in Jackson, Mississippi. I also interviewed four activists in Atlanta and Jackson who supported PHRF work and, in some cases, such as Chokwe Lumumba of Jackson, who were instrumental contributors to PHRF strategy. Together these nine political figures constitute the organizer interviews for this study. All of them were Black, with varying degrees of political experience, and two were women.

Interviews with evacuees also took place between January and April 2008, in Atlanta, Houston, and Jackson. PHRF activity in the diaspora focused on organizing displaced New Orleanians, and my sample was composed of people from New Orleans or a surrounding parish. Participants in the study were evacuees who had come into contact with PHRF activity in the previous two and a half years. The local PHRF organizer set up the interviews and introduced me to each respondent, whom I paid fifty dollars. Each evacuee interview lasted between forty-five minutes and two hours. I conducted twenty-seven of those evacuee interviews, and closely supervised two Black graduate students who conducted an additional seventeen. Two PHRF organizers also interviewed five evacuees, for a total of forty-nine evacuee interviews. All of the organizer and evacuee interviews were audio-recorded and transcribed.

The vast majority of evacuee participants in the study did not consider themselves "political" or "activist," though some had participated in civic, neighborhood, non-profit, or church activities before the storm. While a few participants had owned homes and held lower-middle-class jobs before the storm, most were working class or members of the underclass. For example, during the interviews a number of participants mentioned impending threats to their current housing status either because they had just received another round of Disaster Housing Assistance Program (DHAP, the Department of Housing and Urban Development's disaster housing program[3]) expiration notices or for some other reason that reflected the instability of their living conditions. Twenty of the evacuee participants were male, and twenty-nine were female. The oldest respondent was sixty-seven years old, and the youngest was twenty-one. All participants were Black.

While all research that traverses racial, economic, and gender lines involves complex negotiations, participant-observation among social movement groups expressly oriented to these issues often makes these negotiations explicit. I made methodological decisions that were designed to value and incorporate organizer input into the project, from creating the interview schedule together to paying the diaspora staff organizers as logistical coordinators to set up the evacuee interviews. In addition to remunerating them for their time, this arrangement allowed organizers to authorize me — or not — to the evacuees, who were weary of speaking with anyone who appeared to be an official. Despite these and other efforts to pursue accountable scholarship, race, class, gender, and other power differences between the research participants and me inevitably limited both what they were willing to say and what I was able to hear.

PHRF was formed out of a loose network of racial and economic justice organizers and organizations that existed in New Orleans before the storm. Within weeks of the hurricane, longtime Black organizer Curtis Muhammad, together with dozens of local far Left Black leaders and with the support of national Black nationalist and revolutionary organizations, formed PHRF.

Much of the senior leadership of PHRF was composed of Black male baby boomers, all lifelong organizers with political roots in revolutionary, nationalist, and/or communist movements. There were also local and nonlocal Black, feminist women organizers who were very active in the first four months after the storm, such as Shana griffin of INCITE! Women of Color Against Violence, Mayaba Liebenthal, and Margaret Prescod of Global Women's Strike. An Interim Coordinating Committee (ICC) was formed, which also consisted of local and nonlocal Black men and women. In the spring of 2006, in a public split, Curtis Muhammad left PHRF to form the People's Organizing Committee, and Kali Akuno, a thirty-two-year-old Californian with national organizing credentials, from the Malcolm X Grassroots Movement and involved in PHRF since September 2005, became its executive director.

While PHRF began as a coalition that included the strong presence of feminists and a Women's Caucus, by spring 2006, its organizational and gender composition had changed. Many of the key women left to work in other social justice organizations. PHRF had become less a coalition and more a political organization. It was led by Akuno and Suber and the ICC and supported by a rotating pool of additional staff, such as the organizers in diaspora cities and volunteers. When I refer to PHRF leadership in this chapter, I mean the key ideological and organizational shapers: Muhammad, Akuno, Suber, Lumumba, and members of the ICC, among others. Despite the early participation of female leaders, the input of ICC women, and the role played by two female organizers (Gina Martin and Wilma Taylor), the lasting ideological and organizational activity of PHRF was driven by men.

While there were a variety of political orientations among PHRF leaders, three central political principles emerged in the early months. The first was that the hurricane reconstruction should be directed by those most affected by the disaster, in what Muhammad called a "bottom-up" organizing strategy of the "poorest and Blackest." The vehicle for this grassroots leadership would be Survivor Councils, community meetings of poor, Black hurricane survivors in New Orleans and throughout the diaspora.

During the first seven months after Katrina, PHRF organizers created dozens of Survivor Councils across the United States. They were to be the primary tactic for base-building, political education, and decision-making among evacuees, whom PHRF leaders called "survivors" until adopting the term "internally displaced persons" in alignment with the United Nations Guiding Principles on Internal Displacement. Organizers and supporters, including allies from preexisting movement networks and displaced activists from New Orleans, contacted evacuees in large shelters, at service centers set up by FEMA and the American Red Cross, in FEMA trailer parks, at community centers and events, and in hotels and housing complexes where evacuees were placed by federal and state governments. Survivor Councils helped design the agenda for several PHRF Reconstruction Work Groups and participated in a variety of political events.

The second predominant political principle of PHRF was that displaced people had the "right of return," language carefully crafted to invoke international human rights principles and nationalist struggles and which quickly became a PHRF rallying cry.

The third principle moved beyond the immediate domain of hurricane relief and justice toward a more sweeping vision of national movement-building. Built on a white paper produced by Saladin Muhammad, chairperson of Black Workers for Justice, and called "Hurricane Katrina: The Black Nation's 9/11!,"[4] this position understood the disaster to be a political opportunity for regalvanizing a broad-based justice movement, led by low-income Blacks. Amid other competing political and strategic tendencies, these three foci formed the backbone of PHRF political work.

POLITICAL MOBILIZATION VERSUS SERVICE PROVISION

From the beginning, PHRF leadership made a key strategic distinction between political mobilization and relief work or service provision. This political distinction was gendered not only through the sex of its proponents (male leadership as opposed to female staff organizers), but also in the meaning and implications of the position itself, a dynamic I explore in the second half of this chapter. Certainly everyone involved during the early days of emergency response contributed to some relief activities. Akuno describes his own involvement in the Bay Area in September 2005:

I was . . . even there [in Oakland] getting into it full time you know, help-ing with survivors in Oakland and San Francisco and Palo Alto: doing interviews, helping people get settled, helping them find resources, things of that nature, *and* trying to build a united front in Oakland and the Bay Area.

But PHRF leadership was clear that neither their political aim nor pri-mary tactic was the disbursement of aid. Instead they focused on politi-cization, self-determination, and the political organization of poor, Black hurricane survivors. Saladin Muhammad was the first to publicly articulate this orientation in the position paper mentioned above:

> The response to this human tragedy must be more than a humanitarian response in order to deal with the magnitude and complexity of issues, international political ramifications, the legal aspects, and the various levels of local, regional, national, and international coalition and network building and mobilizing that must take place to build a powerful move-ment for social justice.[5]

PHRF leaders, as part of the broader Black Liberation Movement, explic-itly resisted a service-based response to the crisis, which they perceived to be a threat to their objectives. Their substantive critique of service provision was based on a historical assessment of the role of the service industry and the "non-profit industrial complex" in the United States since the 1960s.[6] They had four primary concerns with a relief-centered response to disaster.

The first was rooted in the desire to foster political and institutional au-tonomy. Chokwe Lumumba, a major figure in Black nationalist politics and a core supporter of PHRF, put it this way:

> [If the goal is] developing independence, then the people take responsi-bility in the building. We are not a welfare group. To the extent we say we are doing this *for* you, that's betraying the revolution. . . . [Instead] it's getting into the street.

Despite the discourse of self-reliance, Lumumba's position is far from a culture of poverty argument. His call for autonomy links the traditional community organizing principle of self-determination to a Black nation-alist platform.

The second concern stemmed from a material analysis of resources and a political assessment of the government's role in a capitalist economy. Akuno explained this point:

> The issue is not that there aren't enough services. The issue is who is doing them, how are they being done, with what resources. The only institution [government] that has the resources that can do the services that are needed, we have to fight in order to [have access to] those resources. But we have to have the political power to fight for those resources so they are distributed in an equitable fashion. It's the chicken and egg then. Do you have to provide services in order to build a base? I say no. It doesn't hurt. But doesn't have to be.

While some forms of Black nationalism may seek complete independence, Akuno makes it clear that in the current economic system, the state is still the most important gatekeeper of resources. Building mass power in movements is, from his perspective, necessary to leverage these resources.

A third concern came out of a growing critique of the social service industry and what activists call the "non-profit industrial complex." The non-profit industrial complex "manages and controls dissent by incorporating it into the state apparatus, functioning as a 'shadow state' constituted by a network of institutions that do much of what government agencies are supposed to do with tax money in the areas of education and social services."[7] In the following lengthy interview excerpt, Akuno argues that service and non-profit industries siphon off political energy, while institutionalizing an unequal balance of power and capacity. The provision of relief is, he argues, by nature a pacifying and temporary solution to much more endemic problems, and in the long run it exacerbates those problems:

> Our movement, the Black Liberation Movement, had a clear position. . . . we've been very clear that on the whole, the poverty programs that got up in the '60s, administered through the 1970s, that set up the whole non-profit industrial complex, played a very negative role in undermining the whole political impetus of the movement. It's the "poverty pimps" analysis. . . . All the services that were being provided, in the '60s and '70s . . . that didn't bolster the social movement in any way . . .
>
> And I'm saying for us to create this whole service infrastructure [with] no political focus to it . . . it's not going to change that at all. The only reason that service infrastructure was created was because of the mass movement [of the 1960s], the pressure the mass movement put on the

federal government anyway. [Today] [w]e don't have that. . . . So the only way we are going to get any of those resources right now is philanthropic capital, which is reactionary as hell. So if we are going to [be] depending on the private resources, we know we are not going to get that from the Black community first and foremost, which is hurting. So it's going to come from that source. But its political orientation is not where most of us want to go. So how do we deal with that?

The federal government is the only institution that has the capacity to make people whole, to bring them home. And the reason [the disaster] happened in the first place is because we didn't have power. So we are trying to build power in order to move the government. If we use the resources to relief, it goes in a week. [We want to] use the resources to build power, to organize.

According to PHRF leadership, trying to meet the basic needs of poor Black communities is not only an exercise in futility, it is at cross purposes with a political agenda devoted to increased Black autonomy, governmental accountability, and community mobilization.

Fourth, and finally, the strategic objective of linking Katrina, the specific disaster, to ongoing social policy and inequality depended on framing the hurricane fallout as a crisis of degree, not of kind. In other words, Hurricane Katrina was understood to be both exceptional *and* representative of ongoing conditions in the United States. From the perspective of Black Liberation leaders, while Katrina magnified the survival needs of hundreds of thousands of people, it did not alter the context of service provision, race and class inequality, power relations, or the struggle for resistance in the United States. For this reason, PHRF leaders framed Katrina as a presenting symptom of a much larger, systemic problem. The political target was power relations and the distribution of resources, not a lack of disaster services.

ORGANIZING IN THE EARLY MONTHS AFTER KATRINA: SURVIVOR COUNCILS

In the winter months of 2005–2006, PHRF began to pay staff organizers to continue the work of organizing Survivor Councils. Social justice movement networks and national speaking tours by PHRF leadership raised the necessary funds. During different periods in 2006–2007, the Survivor Councils in Atlanta, Houston, and Jackson met every two weeks. Council meeting attendance ranged from five to twenty-five participants, with some of the members coming consistently and some evacuees appearing at one or a few meetings and not returning. Special events such as those described below brought out larger numbers.

While Addis Ababa, the Atlanta organizer and former Black Liberation Movement activist, was not a hurricane survivor, Gina Martin in Houston and Wilma Taylor in Jackson were evacuees from New Orleans. The three of them ran Survivor Council meetings in their respective cities, organized local protests against FEMA, the Department of Housing and Urban Development (HUD), and the American Red Cross, and brought vanloads of people to Washington, DC, Baton Rouge, and New Orleans for demonstrations, meetings with government officials, and other activities. The objectives were political education, the cultivation of a survivor-led movement agenda, base-building, public mobilization, and pressuring government and relief organizations.

Each local group emphasized the issues that reflected the needs and interests of the lead organizer. The Atlanta Survivor Council, led by Ababa, who had been involved with the nationalist Republic of New Africa in the 1970s and who had the support of the Atlanta-based U.S. Human Rights Network, brought survivors to Washington, DC, to protest FEMA and organized an Atlanta Human Rights Tribunal in conjunction with the larger Tribunal PHRF put on in New Orleans in August 2007. Gina Martin, herself an evacuee engaged in a protracted struggle with FEMA and HUD over housing vouchers, focused on this issue in Houston. In Jackson, Wilma Taylor spearheaded an effort to pressure an evasive American Red Cross to disburse funds earmarked for Katrina survivors.

THE DIASPORA: SURVIVING THE RECOVERY

As others in this volume have documented,[8] in the weeks and months after the storm, evacuee need was often absolute. Housing, clothing, food, transportation, medical care, and children's needs had to be filled from scratch. In addition to lacking financial resources and material goods, most displaced people had also lost the social networks that supplemented their resources and sustained them.[9] In September 2005, evacuees who landed in other cities were met by a flurry of FEMA officials, social service providers, relief organization representatives, church members, national and local non-profit staff, and good-hearted individuals all proffering promises. When it actually came through, organizational assistance—whether public, private, or non-profit—arrived with many bureaucratic rules and conditions. The majority of the displaced would spend the next years navigating among systems, opportunities, constraints, and dead ends. Approximately two and a half years after the storm, most of the participants in this study were still living in unstable conditions, uncertain about how long they could stay in their current accommodations, deciding whether they would be moving back to New Orleans, and facing employment challenges, medical problems, and ongoing family separation.

Second only to the need for material support, according to respondent narratives, was the need for information about how to get that support. An evacuee trying to extend a housing voucher or move back to New Orleans encountered a dizzying array of organizations and stacks of incomplete and often contradictory guidelines and applications for getting assistance. Accurate and comprehensible information was a rare and desperately needed lifeline. Martin, the Houston organizer, described the difficulty of trying to get coherent information even from the primary disaster relief organizations:

> First of all we was like pulling teeth to get information. Now when you finally got a chance to go down to the FEMA center itself, you had things set up there, different agencies set up there that were supposed to help you. Well, you kinda got a little information there, but once the FEMA center closed . . . it was, if you went to Red Cross, you had to be cousins with your case manager for service, literally, for real. You had to really know people really well.

Because it represented the apparent lack of commitment behind institutional offers of assistance, the elusiveness of caseworkers was a particularly frustrating problem. A thirty-year-old female evacuee in Houston spoke about trying to reach her DHAP (HUD) caseworker: "[When I have questions] I try to ask my counselor, I tried to call. . . . I have a caseworker [and I can] never get in contact with him. I don't even know who is my caseworker. . . . I have never talked to him on the phone. They say he have an assistant. I called for his assistant. Never returned my phone calls."

In this context of protracted survival management, PHRF sought to reframe needs as the product of injustice and collective action as the only reliable solution. Organizers tried to recruit evacuees to meetings and demonstrations and to build a community of survivors who would make the links between the struggles they faced after the disaster with those they had experienced before it. For PHRF organizers, Hurricane Katrina had opened a political opportunity for leveraging federal and public support. They believed that turning disaster grievances into collective action could be the beginning of a groundswell.

For the evacuees, however, the struggle to meet basic needs was paramount. In most cases, it was the need for information that brought them to the Survivor Councils in the first place. And when they stopped feeling that they were getting the information that made the meetings worthwhile, they stopped going. For example, there was a sixty-four-year-old man who had been involved in a relatively high level of civic activity in New Orleans before the storm, such as visiting inmates in Orleans Parish prison. When I asked why he had attended Survivor Council meetings in Houston, he replied:

> Oh, searching for help. And so the most reason why I went, I was enthusiastic so I can come back and pass this on to my fellow brothers here in the [apartment] complex. Whoever else I would run across, inviting them all, if they from New Orleans, I can have information to pass on to.

A fifty-four-year-old divorced mother, avid churchgoer, and substitute teacher who was living in Jackson gave a similar account of why people came to Survivor Council meetings and to the Red Cross protests:

> Well, they wanted help. People aren't doing real well here, they wanted to see what kind of assistance we could get to help us, you know. Some people probably needed jobs, some people probably still need counseling, vehicles, whatever kind of assistance they could have gotten.

A sixty-seven-year-old evacuee who was caring for her elderly mother, with whom she had evacuated, became highly involved in the Atlanta Survivor Council. A gentle, soft-spoken woman, she had been to three PHRF demonstrations and testified at the Atlanta Human Rights Tribunal. During 2007 she made regular calls to bring people out to the Survivor Council meetings, and she too was aware that the pull for many was information. She explained:

> I'm sorry [PHRF] went down, because I found that they was the only ones giving out lots of information. I would help here in Atlanta, because that's where I live, help give out information. Addis would have it, Addis would have all the information. And all of us would come to the meeting and take some. Information about how you can get help from different

organizations. Information about Red Cross, information on the human rights, information just on a lot of things. How you can get help to get the mold out your house. I know he got some information because he got stacks and stacks. I had some at my house.

Finally, a former resident of the St. Bernard housing project described her relationship to the Survivor Council. She was explicit about her instrumentalist connection to the group:

Only way I'll go to a meeting down there now is if they saying we having a meeting to discuss "where you guys want to move at," and "we gonna have some funds for y'all to move wherever y'all want to move," you know. Or maybe if we giving out cards or we giving out some free something, you know, that's the only way I would want to go.

While these participants were conscious that their own or others' primary motive for being involved in the Survivor Councils was getting immediate help and vital information, others did not say so directly, but the desperation of their situation communicated something similar. For some, participation in any organized activity became too much. A forty-nine-year-old man who was bused from the New Orleans Superdome to Texas initially participated in PHRF events and had been enthusiastic about bringing people from New Orleans together. A veteran and former felon, he had stopped using drugs and was holding down an industrial job before the storm. He had gone with the Survivor Council van to New Orleans for the second anniversary of the storm and attended the PHRF commemorative march. "I heard about [PHRF meetings], and I got in touch with Ms. Martin, and she turned me, she put me in a new way. I went on a trip to New Orleans. It was very inspirational. They were speaking about all the laws that were violated by the United States, and trying to help people get back home you know, giving you insight on what's going on with that now." He also attended a Red Cross protest in Houston, and helped bring people to the meetings.

But over his two and a half years in Houston, he had had "forty or fifty job interviews," and no one would hire an ex-felon. He was living in a converted single-occupancy hotel, washing dishes in the bathtub, and had started using drugs again. By December 2007, he said, "I just bottomed out." His mother had died in a hospital in New Orleans during the storm, and her death haunted him. The difficulty he had in getting a job and finding a stable place to live was overwhelming:

Katrina is something all of us from New Orleans, a lot of us, never come to recognize it. It flipped our lives and it flipped our minds, our brains, our feelings. Wiped us out. . . . Right now I'm [getting] psychiatric care. I just gotta deal with it, you know. I would love to go home . . . but I don't have the finances to really start over. FEMA feel like they gave us ten thousand dollars and that was enough.

Later during the same interview when I asked about the issue he had found inspirational at the march—the pursuit of the human rights case against the United States government—it was apparent that he was in a different place: "I think it's a waste. I don't see it happening." When I wondered what he thought *would* be useful, he was clear:

Helping those who wanna move back home, you know what I'm saying, cheaper rent, letting [those] who wanna go home [go home], you know? Rent's so high down there. Like I said, at the present time today, I'm stressed out. What would I support? Basically nothing right now. You know, I got to think about me. See what fits in. I don't have too long. The first two and a half years I was here, you know, I was out there. Now I don't even wanna go out there. Like I said, it's been stressful on me. It's very long, very long. I dunno. I just want peace right now. . . . It . . . seem like . . . it's like it's over with. . . . Everyone else is movin' on. I just wish I could go home. I really do.

If the prospect of getting support was the primary incentive for attending meetings or demonstrations, then the sense of having even more pressing needs was a significant disincentive. Because most participants had no prior personal exposure to social movement activity, they had little reason to believe in collective efficacy. If their pre-Katrina experience of the government was of intransigence, they had no reference point for collective power. When filtered through a lifetime of state and agency encounters, their post-Katrina experience only confirmed the negative aspects of these encounters. In Jackson, the churchgoing woman who used to call people to come to the Survivor Council noted:

[T]he meetings got smaller and smaller. And I really believe it's because people weren't getting their needs met and they just felt like, why am I coming here? I'm not gonna sit here for a couple of hours and listen to somebody [officials, in this case from the Red Cross, brought in by the Council] lie to us, . . . People are looking for results. Nobody wants to hear somebody lie to them and that's all they did. . . . Finally [the Red Cross] got a couple of social workers and then they started working with us, like I said on the vehicles [that Red Cross had said it would make available], but people just felt like it was just a bunch of talk and that's really what it wound up being.

For the majority of participants, mistrust of government agencies became cynicism that any official or organizational representative could be trustworthy or efficacious. Their perspective on social services bled into an outlook on all groups—including grassroots movement groups—promising support or change. For many participants, PHRF was indistinguishable from a blurry spectrum of other kinds of organizations—federal, faith-based, and non-profit—from HUD, to ACORN, to local church groups.

PROVIDING SERVICES, MEETING NEEDS

Wilma Taylor and Gina Martin, the two women staff organizers of PHRF working, respectively, out of Jackson and Houston, were very clear about the degree of ongoing need faced by their constituency. They were moved to respond to it individually and collectively. Before having had any exposure to Black Liberation Movement politics, Taylor had her own reaction to the activities offered by movement and service organizations at an event for displaced people in Jackson in 2006. A friend had received an invitation to attend the event, and Taylor accompanied her. She described her experience:

And so we went to see what it was about and I think at the time [one of the organizers of the event] is more into [a] vegetarian [diet]. And so they had a vegetarian thing for us and some people just wasn't for that. I think she wanted to deal with our health issue, which she had very good intentions about, but we weren't studying health issues. We were more on survival mode. So her timing was off. . . . See, they lost them when you're trying to get people to worry about their high blood pressure and they don't have a roof over their head. And I just think our timing was off 'cause a lot of people just didn't want to hear that and so they just didn't go back.

Taylor's sense of the gap between what was being offered—no matter how well meant—and what was needed was part of what inspired her to get involved in collective action.

Both Taylor and Martin organized around issues that, if successful, would provide immediate material benefits. Unlike Ababa and some of the senior PHRF leadership, they were hurricane evacuees like the people they were working with, and their perspective was filtered through this experience. Indeed, the Katrina displacement brought them to political activity, which neither had participated in before. For example, Martin was struggling herself to get the Houston Housing Authority to transfer its voucher to New Orleans so that she could return. She subsequently organized events exposing the Housing Authority's stonewalling and worked on other issues having to do with public and affordable housing in New Orleans. Similarly, Taylor's work revolved around pressuring the Red Cross to release its funds, and she contended that the campaign was instrumental in winning financial awards for eighty-five evacuees in Jackson.

Martin and Taylor shared the view that needs should be prioritized. To Martin, it made no sense to focus on political activity when people were barely hanging on. It was a position based on her own experience of displacement and her gendered attention to daily needs. She noted the reasons that many people contacted PHRF:

[B]ecause they didn't have lights. And they didn't have food. A lot of it was just, a lot of people was not mentally capable, and I'm [not] saying they had a mental illness, but after a natural disaster, they just had to shut down. You know, I was to that point. But that is a lot of it, because they didn't have their basic needs, so they couldn't focus on nothing else.

Martin's response was to help the evacuees she encountered in any way she could. She made house calls, gave rides, and supported persons displaced by the storm in a variety of additional ways, though in some situations she was hardly better off. For her this was part of what it meant to be an organizer, as well as being the right thing to do. But she knew this position was not shared by PHRF leadership:

They just didn't want you to focus on social service. You were not a social service agency. "We don't provide rides, we don't provide food," or whatever. They will tell you [that] if you know of a place that provides food, or provides transportation, [if] you know, [then] you tell them, but you don't research it, that was the part, you don't research to go and give people that kind of information. "We're a political organization."

When I asked her what being a "political organization" meant, she laughed:

> I had no idea. . . . They really wanted to, they just wanted to just educate, showing the rights, you know, how they really shouldn't depend on government agencies and that sort of stuff, and what leadership we had years ago that failed, what kind of leadership we should be looking towards now, or no leadership at all, that kind of stuff. Just, you know, that's the kind of stuff they talked about politically.

While Martin and Taylor were the two female PHRF paid organizers, I include Nefesh Funmilayo in this discussion as well. Funmilayo was a long-time community organizer from New Orleans who prefers to be identified as "African" rather than "African American." Together with her mother, Miss Oyo, she had run a community center before the storm.[10] After evacuating to Houston, she helped get PHRF off the ground, but eventually split off because of some of the strategic differences described here, and continued doing her own form of community-building. She and Martin had become friends, and as someone with more political and organizing experience, she had become a mentor to Martin. Funmilayo did not accept the distinction between political mobilization and basic human support:

> People's Hurricane Relief Fund, I'm a part of that, and we actually started the Houston Katrina Survivor Council from that, but when People's Hurricane Relief Fund, when they thought that, basically, that helping people, it wasn't political, it wasn't making a statement that you were organizing the community . . . Because you have to have the people. You nothing without the people.

Martin characterized Funmilayo and Miss Oyo's approach: "They were already in the community doing everything. And I don't know, they was with no specific group or anything, that's just in their nature, that's what they do." Though Funmilayo and Miss Oyo were living out of a van for months after the hurricane, they soon created a small non-profit organization for Katrina survivors, called Safe Return: "People want to go home, you help them with the moving, first month, last month's rent, and stuff like that, and then help people who [are] here who needed assistance." Funmilayo elaborated on their activity:

> Well, what I've been doing is if the need is rent or utilities or food, I usually call up the place [e.g., social service agency or church group], and

I give them the name of the evacuee, and you get a faster reaction from the people. "Okay send 'em over, give me their names." . . . I intervene and I call, "Look, this person is coming over, I need to make sure this is real resources, I'm not going to have them on the bus or taxi to come to nothing. Let me know if you can help them or if they can come get help." And I reassure them that, if I'm getting something, you have it.

Martin revealed a similar orientation in her own efforts:

[PHRF leadership] told us, you know, you can't do that, you can't be a social service agency. Addis would fuss about that all the time, and I would just hang up from the two-hour phone call and go over to somebody's house, you know, go over somebody's house who I know needs. [Pause] There are people who couldn't get to the meetings, there was this older woman [in a neighboring community] . . . she couldn't get to the meetings, she was way on the south side, she couldn't even get to her doctor's appointments. I would go and take her to her doctor's appointment, because she couldn't get to them, you know. But of course I didn't tell [PHRF leadership] that's what I did.

Martin, Funmilayo, Miss Oyo, and Taylor were driven by a variety of motives, not the least of which was their own displacement experience. It was apparent in the language that the women used, however, that a gendered imperative to caretaking work was central to their activity. Indeed, they had an explicit gender analysis of PHRF leadership and strategy. Martin explained:

You know, because men wanted only to be political, and it's not just, you can't mobilize people with just politics, you have to address basic needs, especially in the aftermath of a disaster. And women [are] willing to address needs *and* mobilize politically, and that's where the difference is.

While Martin reserved the word "political" for a narrow range of activity consistent with normative masculinity in accord with classical models of politics,[11] she believed that caretaking could also achieve movement aims. The evacuee whom Martin took to the doctor, for example, was a retired teacher. Martin described their relationship:

[S]he was so fiery and she had all these good ideas, you know, and she couldn't get to the meetings and I just would go and sit down and talk to her about the things we talked about in the meetings, and she would have great ideas. And she can't get to her doctor. I just take her to her doctor too, even though we weren't supposed to do that, that's what I did. I needed her.

In movement terms, Martin received "mentorship"[12] from her support work with an elder. She remained convinced that service provision was a worthy component of movement-building and that it would ultimately strengthen the constituency:

> I believe that had we kind of focused on getting some kind of, I don't know, grants or whatever, money to assist people with their needs, or even partner with some kind of agencies that did that, that you know, if people's needs were met then they would have the means to come out.

REFRAMING NEED

Feminist movement scholars have criticized narrow, gendered conceptions of the "political" that reduce movement motives and outcomes to lofty, abstract, rational elements.[13] For Martin, personal needs and political frames were not mutually incompatible; neither were they limited to political instrumentalism. In the early months after the storm, while moving between relatives and hotels and facing the loss of her father, despite having never participated in social movement activity, she had begun to gravitate to political analyses of the disaster. Later she described the process by which her expressive and emotional needs were being met through political activity. She explained that getting involved in political organizing was initially for "sanity":

> I felt a need to do this. . . . I was just doing that for therapy. . . . I was sitting in front of the TV in the beginning and trying to figure out what to do. I just knew that if I didn't do something, if I didn't volunteer, if I didn't get a job, if I couldn't go home and get a job helping with the rebuilding process, then I literally was going to lose my mind. Because, you know, I felt like I was going to be in the state I saw other people in. A depressed state. And just not come out of it. I just felt like I had a little piece to do. Like I believed every single person who was from New Orleans had a little piece to do and I needed to do my little, little piece. It wasn't much but I can sleep at night saying my city was totally destroyed but I did this to help.

Applying these insights to the survivors she saw around her, Martin linked a lack of political involvement to increased post-traumatic stress. The reciprocal was true as well; she concluded that trauma and rage not channeled into collective action were partly responsible for the absence of a political groundswell: "And it's the reason why the mobilization didn't happen, you know, people stayed angry to themselves . . . and we could have used that anger to turn into action the way it did for me."

Human needs are not only material, but have the potential to be filled by "political" activity in the way PHRF leadership had hoped. Conversely, political activity when linked to basic needs can help to politicize those needs. By directing a broader range of expression than appeared in most PHRF discourse—including psychological distress and a gendered awareness of the importance of daily maintenance—into resistance, Martin herself achieved the PHRF aim of developing a political consciousness and becoming politically active, and sought to do that for others.

SOCIAL CHANGE LESSONS FROM THE KATRINA DIASPORA

Feminist social movement scholars have noted that women's movement participation often emerges out of traditional gender roles.[14] They agree that many of the responsibilities and skills that constitute "women's work"—such as organizing the food, shelter, and care necessary for daily survival (reproductive labor); maintaining ties (networking); and emotional labor (solidarity work)—are central to community organizing and other forms of movement-building. However, "only recently has women's social-reproduction labor in the community, often essential for survival in lower-income communities, been recognized as a type of resistance or political activity."[15] Feminist reframing has helped scholars and activists recognize women as social change agents and movement leaders, and broadened their conception of what counts as "political" activity.[16] In light of the great threat to human survival in the prolonged displacement of Katrina, the role of community maintenance should not be underestimated. At the same time, while survival is the first step of resistance, it is not in and of itself social change. For incisive political reasons, the male leadership of PHRF was concerned that the effort to meet basic needs would consume all activist energy. Their objective was to build mass power as the necessary ingredient for *change*, beyond sheer survival.

Because of the ongoing crisis of basic needs in the United States today, the Katrina disaster is in many ways a microcosm of the broader political landscape. Changing economic conditions, growing privatization, a national housing crisis, and a shrinking welfare state have swelled the ranks of people struggling to survive, an increasing number of whom are also facing displacement—whether by disaster or at the hands of the state.

Feminist scholars have identified how the very framing of "needs" in the early-twentieth-century founding of the welfare state was feminized.[17] Caring for needs is also deprecated as women's work.[18] Since the expansion of the social service industry in the 1960s, the professional class of service providers is also overwhelmingly female. So much about needs—having them, filling them, providing or denying services for them—has been gendered female. Further, women of color are overassociated with the ranks of the "needy" and disproportionately represented in the ranks of social service providers. A political critique of the service complex must carefully walk a fine line between uncovering its repressive and mystifying dimensions while not further targeting the people caught in its web, whether they are those who need, receive, or provide services. To reject the current social service industry accountably, we must do so without pathologizing or further impoverishing the people who are associated with it, who, whether female or male, are often pathologized through feminization. The experience of Katrina evacuees further underscores the need for intersectional analysis, strategy, and tactics that take into account the interaction of race, class, gender, and the state. Recent work by feminist scholars and activists of color has elucidated these convergences through pathbreaking work on the social service and non-profit industries.[19]

As the leaders of PHRF were aware, "The problem is not with providing social services. Many radical groups, such as the Black Panthers and the Zapatistas, have provided social services as a tool for organizing. The problem comes when *all* our time and energy is diverted toward social services to the detriment of long-term social change."[20] The Black Panther Party is perhaps the best US example of the successful synthesis of service provision and movement-building. The Panthers tied humanitarian interventions to strategic mobilization and called them "survival programs pending revolution."[21] In the current era of a shrinking welfare state and significant macro constraints on social movements, an important question for movement organizers today is how providing community care and meeting basic needs can be a tactic for movement-building. As Gina Martin, Nefesh Funmilayo, Miss Oyo, and Wilma Taylor discovered, there is no political base if people cannot survive, for "you have nothing without the people." While great impoverishment has precipitated mobilization in other countries, it has rarely done so in the United States.[22] After three years of trying to mobilize, PHRF leadership came to some of the same conclusions. Lumumba reflected on the lessons learned and the struggle for new models linking relief work and movement-building:

> There was no way to organize without dealing with the people's need to survive. This was a failing on our part. We were faced with an overwhelming problem we weren't ready for. People being more concerned with their immediate need, and some pimping that need. And we on the ground trying to go in a totally different direction. Going total organizing, we didn't stop addressing needs, but it wasn't a priority. That's a problem. Political organizing is part of that, service and survival, meeting the needs of the people. It is easier said than done. The secret becomes, how do you organize something for the people that also organizes them politically? We didn't have modern-day models. We had the Panthers.

To argue that community caretaking work is an important part of movement-building does not mean that it is always already in the service of social change, but rather that it can be when tied to other dimensions of political activity. Ideally, "the realm of community which women create through their everyday activities becomes 'the third element' that mediates between the public and private spheres and provides the base for a new politics."[23] The challenge for social justice movements in a time of increased suffering and shrinking public services is how to maintain and nurture this "third element" in a politically galvanizing way.

It is too soon to evaluate comprehensively the movement-building tactics of early Katrina organizers, because both disaster and struggle are ongoing. Additionally, the seeds that the Katrina resistance movement sowed are still gestating. They were planted in the individual consciousnesses of its constituency and also in the lessons learned by movement groups. What is apparent, however, is that the challenges Katrina raises for organizers about political resistance in the context of ongoing basic needs crises are already applicable to the broader, non-disaster-specific context of the United States in the twenty-first century.

ACKNOWLEDGMENTS

This study was inspired by the visionary efforts of PHRF leaders and organizers after Katrina, and also by the will to survive displayed by those displaced by the disaster. I am grateful to Kali Akuno, Malcolm Suber, Chokwe Lumumba, Gina Martin,

Wilma Taylor, and Addis Ababa for their tireless organizing and their support of this project. Additionally, I appreciate the collegiality and friendship of the Social Science Research Council (SSRC) Research Network on Persons Displaced by Hurricane Katrina. Lori Peek and Lynn Weber in particular provided invaluable feedback on earlier drafts of this chapter, as did Sharon Martinas. Finally, I am indebted to Kai Erikson, the SSRC, the Rockefeller Foundation, and the Ford Foundation, without whom this and so many other Katrina stories would not have been recorded.

NOTES

1. In this chapter I use the actual names of the PHRF organizers, because this information is in the public domain.

2. Rachel E. Luft, "Beyond Disaster Exceptionalism: Social Movement Developments in New Orleans after Hurricane Katrina," *American Quarterly* 61, no. 3 (September 2009): 499–528.

3. See Pardee, this volume.

4. Saladin Muhammad, "Hurricane Katrina: The Black Nation's 9/11!," 2005, http://www.greens.org/s-r/39/39-05.html, accessed February 24, 2011.

5. Ibid.

6. INCITE! Women of Color Against Violence, ed., *The Revolution Will Not Be Funded: Beyond the Non-Profit Industrial Complex* (Cambridge, MA: South End Press, 2007).

7. Andrea Smith, "Introduction: The Revolution Will Not Be Funded," in *The Revolution Will Not Be Funded: Beyond the Non-Profit Industrial Complex*, ed. INCITE! Women of Color Against Violence (Cambridge, MA: South End Press, 2007), pp. 1–18, quotation from pp. 8–9.

8. Lein et al., this volume; Peek, this volume.

9. Fussell, this volume; Litt, this volume; Mason, this volume.

10. Nefesh Funmilayo and Miss Oyo are pseudonyms.

11. Sandra Morgen and Ann Bookman, "Rethinking Women and Politics: An Introductory Essay," in *Women and the Politics of Empowerment*, ed. A. Bookman and S. Morgen (Philadelphia: Temple University Press, 1988), pp. 3–29.

12. Thanks to Rowan Shafer for this insight.

13. For instance, Martha A. Ackelsberg, "Communities, Resistance, and Women's Activism: Some Implications for a Democratic Polity," in *Women and the Politics of Empowerment*, ed. A. Bookman and S. Morgen (Philadelphia: Temple University Press, 1988), pp. 297–313.

14. Ann Bookman and Sandra Morgen, eds., *Women and the Politics of Empowerment* (Philadelphia: Temple University Press, 1988); Nancy A. Naples, ed., *Community Activism and Feminist Politics: Organizing across Race, Class, and Gender* (New York: Routledge, 1998); Mary Pardo, "Mexican American Women Grassroots Community Activists: 'Mothers of East Los Angeles,'" *Frontiers: A Journal of Women*

Studies 11, no. 1 (1990): 1–7; Belinda Robnett, "African-American Women in the Civil Rights Movement, 1954–1965: Gender, Leadership, and Micromobilization," *American Journal of Sociology* 101, no. 6 (1996): 1661–1693.

15. Roberta M. Feldman, Susan Stall, and Patricia A. Wright, "'The Community Needs to Be Built by Us': Women Organizing in Chicago Public Housing," in *Community Activism and Feminist Politics: Organizing across Race, Class, and Gender*, ed. N. A. Naples (New York: Routledge, 1998), pp. 257–274, quotation from p. 260.

16. Bookman and Morgen, *Women and the Politics of Empowerment*.

17. Nancy Fraser and Linda Gordon, "A Genealogy of 'Dependency': Tracing a Keyword of the U.S. Welfare State," in *Justice Interruptus: Critical Reflections on the "Postsocialist" Condition*, ed. N. Fraser (New York: Routledge, 1997), pp. 121–149.

18. Marjorie L. DeVault, *Feeding the Family: The Social Organization of Caring as Gendered Work* (Chicago: University of Chicago Press, 1994).

19. INCITE! Women of Color Against Violence, *The Revolution Will Not Be Funded*.

20. Paul Kivel, "Social Service or Social Change?," in *The Revolution Will Not Be Funded: Beyond the Non-Profit Industrial Complex*, ed. INCITE! Women of Color Against Violence (Cambridge, MA: South End Press, 2007), pp. 129–149, quotation from p. 143 (italics in the original).

21. JoNina M. Abron, "'Serving the People': The Survival Programs of the Black Panther Party," in *The Black Panther Party [Reconsidered]*, ed. C. E. Jones (Baltimore: Black Classic Press, 1998), pp. 177–192, quotation from p. 179.

22. Frances Fox Piven and Richard A. Cloward, *Poor People's Movements: Why They Succeed, How They Fail* (New York: Vintage Books, 1979).

23. Feldman, Stall, and Wright, "'The Community Needs to Be Built by Us,'" p. 261.

AUTHOR BIOS

ALICE FOTHERGILL, associate professor of sociology at the University of Vermont, had a background in disaster research before Hurricane Katrina struck. As a researcher at the Natural Hazards Center at the University of Colorado, she studied women's experiences in the 1997 Grand Forks, North Dakota, flood, and volunteerism in New York City following the 9/11 terrorist attacks. Most of Professor Fothergill's work has centered on inequality and vulnerability in all stages of a disaster and has examined the ways in which gender, race, ethnicity, and class affect outcomes. In the early months of 2005, Professor Fothergill and Professor Lori Peek had discussed the possibility of doing research together on children in disasters, a critically important but understudied topic. When Katrina hit, they were both busy assistant professors at universities far from the Gulf Coast, yet they knew with certainty that they needed to document the experiences of children and youth and their families in Katrina and its aftermath. Thus, they began a six-year qualitative study of children's experiences in one of the worst disasters in the history of the United States. Currently, they are finishing their book on this study, *Children of Katrina*.

ELIZABETH FUSSELL, now an associate professor of sociology at Washington State University, was an assistant professor at Tulane University when Hurricane Katrina struck New Orleans. She came to this work as a migration and life-course scholar who participated in the largest disaster-driven evacuation since the Dust Bowl of the 1930s. As an evacuee, she was both a participant in and an observer of the multiple migrations produced by Hurricane Katrina and its aftermath. These migrations included the short- and long-term displaced residents of New Orleans and those who returned, as well as the new Latino migrants who participated in the rebuilding of the city. Her research on these migrants uses both qualitative and quantitative methods to reveal the scope and the multidimensional effects of this unprecedented urban disaster.

CYNTHIA M. GARZA, a PhD candidate in Latin American studies at Tulane University, had just completed dissertation research in Lima, Peru, when Hurricane Katrina struck the Gulf Coast. While her doctoral work deals primarily with the Peruvian Creole community and its responses to recent shifts in Lima's urban landscape, her training in urban anthropology and ethnographic methods led her to Houston to interview New Orleanian Garifuna evacuees of Honduran descent. Since the United and Standard Fruit Companies' reign over the Gulf Coast in the early twentieth century, the Afro-Caribbean Garifuna population has contributed to New Orleans' cultural landscape. For the Garifuna, the forced evacuation after Katrina was just another of many migrations in a long history of disaster, resettlement, and resilience that has spanned two continents and multiple generations.

PAMELA JENKINS, professor of sociology and women's studies at the University of New Orleans (UNO), is a founding and associate member of UNO's Center for Hazard Assessment, Response and Technology. She became involved in documenting the effects of Hurricane Katrina almost immediately after the storm. As with nearly all the residents of New Orleans, her life and work were altered dramatically, as she participated in the recovery on both personal and professional levels. Before Katrina, her research interests included how to evaluate collaborative groups involved in social change, how domestic violence programs operate to provide greater safety for women, and how coastal communities understand risk and preparedness. After the storm, what she studies remains the same, but the lens has broadened to include recovery in urban areas. She has published on the experiences of Katrina's first responders and the experiences of the elderly during and after Katrina. Her chapter in this book focuses on faith-based communities' response to the storm.

LAURA LEIN, now dean and Katherine Reebel Collegiate Professor of Social Work at the University of Michigan, was professor of social work and anthropology at the University of Texas at Austin when Katrina made landfall. *Ronald Angel* is professor of sociology at the University of Texas at Austin. *Holly Bell* is a research associate at the Center for Social Work Research at the University of Texas at Austin. *Julie Beausoleil* was also a research associate at the Center at the time of the Katrina project, but is now in Geneva, Switzerland.

When Hurricane Katrina hit, all four authors were working together on several projects that drew on mixed methodologies to study the ways in which poverty policies, including those involving healthcare, welfare, housing, and food, affect vulnerable populations. In the week after the hurricane, the research team was involved with hurricane evacuees. The city received over twelve thousand evacuees from the Gulf Coast, and some members of the team worked in the Austin Convention Center shelter or with organizations in other locales. The team also worked with the City of Austin as city workers tried to identify and track Katrina evacuees. In those first weeks, the team began to realize that the evacuees, many of whom arrived with little preparation and few possessions, would not be able to return home anytime soon. To give their experiences voice and to explore the weaknesses and strengths of the emergency programs and longer-term poverty policies affecting the evacuees, the research effort represented in this volume was launched to identify and track a panel of evacuees during the ensuing year and a half.

JACQUELYN LITT, now dean of Douglass Residential College and Douglass Campus and professor of women's and gender studies at Rutgers University, New Brunswick, began her research on Hurricane Katrina while living in Columbia, Missouri, which received over five hundred evacuees, largely low-income African American women. Although before Katrina she had explored mothers' carework—the everyday practices that women undertake in support of their family, kin, and community—the women evacuees she met in Missouri taught her that motherhood and kin care were central features of women's evacuation experiences and, indeed, that this work saved lives. The chapter in this volume is drawn from ethnographic research undertaken between 2005 and 2009, in which she examined the shifting terrain of carework as women evacuees moved from place to place—many back to New Orleans and many to Houston—in search of renewed safety and stability. Her work highlights not only the centrality of women's carework, but also the social and economic conditions under which women's carework can function effectively to buffer the effects of displacement.

RACHEL E. LUFT, who came to New Orleans a year before Katrina struck, is associate professor of sociology at the University of New Orleans, with research specialization in race, gender, and social movements. After the hurricane she was displaced until January 2006, when she returned to the city to be housed in a FEMA trailer park built for university faculty and staff. In the months that followed the storm, her relief and research efforts were mediated by emergent social movement groups that were organizing a political response to the ongoing events. As a member of various collectives, she participated in the Movement for a Just Reconstruction. She documented these efforts and sought to build collaborative research projects with grassroots leaders. Her objective was to record the movement activity in a way that would be useful to the movement itself, as well as contribute to critical scholarship on post-hurricane activism and recovery efforts. In her chapter in this book, she uses an intersectional framework to identify racialized and gendered dimensions of the experience of the disaster, as well as of the social movement activity that arose in response to it.

BEVERLY J. MASON, associate professor in the social science division at Allen University, taught at Xavier University of Louisiana for nine years and was chairperson of the Sociology Department before Hurricane Katrina struck. Dr. Mason, a displaced person herself, left New Orleans at 10:30 a.m. on Sunday, August 28, 2005. One of her volunteer efforts before the storm with a political organization of workers, activists, students, and professors led her to work with working-class and poor women. In early December 2005, she began interviewing African American women who had fled before the hurricane and some who left after the levees broke. At the time of the interviews, the women were living in New Orleans, Baton Rouge, and Baker, Louisiana. Her chapter in this book grew out of her interviews with adult and elderly women that centered on how they left the city, what strategies they engaged in during their journeys, and, most importantly, how they saw themselves rebuilding their lives.

LEE M. MILLER, associate professor of sociology at Sam Houston State University, had just started her new faculty position in August 2005 when Hurricane Katrina devastated New Orleans and the Gulf Coast, sending large numbers of evacuees into East Texas. Then, with Katrina evacuees still in the area, Hurricane Rita frightened millions of residents of the Texas Gulf Coast to evacuate inland and northward. Thousands arrived in Huntsville, temporarily increasing the population by 50 percent. Reflecting a fascination with the dynamics of the disasters and the community responses to them, her research is focused on helping understand how small cities and towns with limited resources deal with disasters. Why did Huntsville, undamaged by either natural event, respond as it did? How were local resources mobilized? Did the way people are interconnected help explain the response? Is sheltering different when evacuees are outsiders? Is generosity a time-limited phenomenon? These are some of the questions that have guided her research over the past five years, and are engaged in her chapter in this book.

JESSICA W. PARDEE, assistant professor of sociology at the Rochester Institute of Technology, came to New Orleans as an undergraduate at Tulane University. Interested in issues of poverty, housing policy, and urban development, she remained in New Orleans for graduate school. When Hurricane Katrina hit, Jessica had lived in New Orleans for ten years and was preparing to study the relocation experiences of women due to HOPE VI from two public housing sites for her doctoral dissertation. But because of the massive flooding of both the city and one of her research communities, Jessica reorganized her work to examine the post-disaster survival strategies of these same women. Her interests centered on how women with limited incomes rebuilt their lives and reestablished housing and survival security following the storm. Her chapter in this book examines how post-Katrina housing policies shaped the experiences of women displaced by the storm.

LORI PEEK, associate professor of sociology and codirector of the Center for Disaster and Risk Analysis at Colorado State University, has studied the social consequences of disasters for more than a decade. When Hurricane Katrina made landfall, she began work on two separate research projects. The first study focused on the resettlement experiences of families with children who were displaced to Denver, Colorado, after Katrina. The second study, a collaborative project with Professor Alice Fothergill, is a longitudinal project on children's recovery trajectories in Louisiana. While these studies, and her chapters in this volume, focus on different contexts, the core research questions have common threads related to understanding the challenges that children and families face in post-disaster settings and the ways in which members of these communities cope with both acute and chronic crises.

LYNN WEBER, professor of psychology and women's and gender studies at the University of South Carolina, is a pioneer in the developing field of intersectionality, the study of the ways in which race, class, gender, sexuality, and other dimensions of socially constructed inequality are interwoven in our lives. As cofounder and director of the Center for Research on Women at the University of Memphis, and later as director of the Women's and Gender Studies Program at the University of South Carolina, she promoted intersectional research and practice through engagement with local communities. In 2002, she spearheaded the Women's Well-Being Initiative—an interdisciplinary, collaborative, community-based participatory action research project aimed at improving the lives of women and girls in West Columbia, South Carolina, a low-income and working-class, racially diverse community across the river from Columbia. When Katrina struck in 2005, over ten thousand evacuees arrived in Columbia, South Carolina, many of them settling in apartments in West Columbia. Since she was already involved in community-engaged research and action there, Weber was drawn to understand how the displaced would be received in West Columbia. At the same time, she joined an interdisciplinary team studying inequalities in the recovery process along the Mississippi Gulf Coast. She sees this work as defining her career for years to come—trying to learn what this ongoing disaster can tell us about the social construction of inequalities and looking for ways to prevent having "natural" disasters become contexts for the construction of new and more virulent forms of oppression.

INDEX

Page numbers in italics refer to figures and tables.

AARP. *See* American Association for Retired Persons

Ababa, Addis, 234, 241, 243, 247, 254

Adversity and Resilience Study, 153, 165

African Americans: largest forced migration of, 183; in West Columbia, SC, 81, 83

Akuno, Kali, 233, 234, 236, 237–238, 239–240, 253

Alabama, 18n5, 79

American Association for Retired Persons (AARP), 191

American Community Survey, 19n9

American Recovery and Reinvestment Act of 2009, 87

American Red Cross: difficulties with, 242, 245–246; mentioned, 68, 151, 160, 190, 208, 209, 237, 244, 247; protests against, 241, 243

Angel, Ron, 27

Astrodome and Reliant Center (Houston), 105, 113

Atlanta, GA: characteristics of, *6–7, 8–9. See also* receiving communities

Atlanta Human Rights Tribunal, 241, 243

Austin, TX, 27; characteristics of, *6–7, 8–9,* 18n9, 51; numbers relocated to, 51; problems faced by displaced in, 52–61; research in, 48–49; shortage of low-cost housing in, 56. *See also* receiving communities; Texas

Baker, LA, 147, 190; characteristics of, *6–7, 8–9. See also* Louisiana; receiving communities

Barton, A. H., 112

basement of poverty, 13, 27, 48, 49, 61; defined, 47

basic needs: and bureaucratic rules and conditions, 241–242; feminization of,

252; and motivation for participation in Survivor Councils, 243–245; and political activity, 231–232, 233, 234, 250–251, 252–253

Baton Rouge, LA, *3;* characteristics of, *6–7, 8–9;* compared to New Orleans, 220; congregation in, 218–219, 224–227; evacuees traveling back to New Orleans from, 224; journey to, 222–223. *See also* Louisiana; receiving communities

Baton Rouge River Center, 183, 193

Beausoleil, Julie, 27

Bell, Holly, 27

Benjamin Hooks Institute for Social Justice, 200

Billingsley, Andrew, 228

Black Liberation Movement, 233, 238, 239, 240, 241, 246

Black nationalism, 238, 239

Black Panther Party, 252, 253

Black Workers for Justice, 237

Blanco, Kathleen, 130, 183, 190

Bosick, Stacey, 152, 164–165

Buffalo Creek, WV, 164

bullying, 41–42, 43, 44, 126–128, 138

Bush, George W., 129, 130

Castro, Pastor Erik, 205–206, 210, 211, 214, 215, 216

Catholic Charities (Denver), 33, 34, 35

Central Midlands Regional Transit Authority. *See* CMRTA

children, displaced: affected by parents' reactions, 125–126; bullying experienced by, 41–42, 43, 44, 126–128, 138; crime in New Orleans discussed by, 136–138; and the criminal justice system, 59–60; discrimination experienced by, 41–44, 126–127, 128, 139;

evacuation experiences of, 123–125, 128–129, 154–155; experiences of, shaped by race, region, and/or class, 41–44, 128, 138–139; friendship, 129; health hazards experienced by, 42, 123; housing situations, post-Katrina, 133–134; impact of disasters on, 136, 139; losses suffered by, 123–124, 125, 132, 137–138, 142n21; missing, 119; numbers evacuated, 119; numbers remaining displaced, 119; permanent temporariness of, 121, 131–134, 138, 139–140; positive experiences of, 128–129, 132–134; in poverty, 61, 119–120, *120*; powerlessness and invisibility of, 139; problems faced by, 29, 41–44, 49, 53–54, 124, 125, 126, 127, 132; racial and political awareness of, 129–130; research on, 121–122, 141–142n17, 141n16, 142nn18–21; returned to home state or communities, 119, 134–138; voices of, 120–121. *See also* schools

churches: Black Christian, 219, 224, 227; in disaster response, 221, 224; invisible, 219; satellite, 219, 225

City Council (New Orleans), 63, 64

Clyburn, James, 83

CMRTA (Central Midlands Regional Transit Authority), 90–91

Coble, Bob, 83

collective trauma, 150, 163–164

Colorado, 31, 36–44. *See also* Denver, CO

Columbia, MO: characteristics of, *6–7*, 8–9; research in, 168, 182n5. *See also* receiving communities

Columbia, SC: characteristics of, 6–7 table 1.1, 8–9, 80, 81, 82 table 6.1; compared to New Orleans, 86, 87; housing crisis in, 87–90, 98; migration of new populations to, 28; and the needs of the local poor, 98–99; numbers relocated to, 83; political climate in, 86–87; population change data, 81, 83, 101n7, 82 table 6.1; public transportation in, 98; reception of displaced persons in, 83–84, 98–100

compassion fatigue, defined, 33

congregations: in Baton Rouge, 218–219, 224–227; community sustained and organized, 219; and evacuees, 218, 219–220, 221, 227; in New Orleans, pre-Katrina, 219; satellite, from New Orleans, 228; sharing space, 219. *See also* churches

context of reception, 15, 27, 32–34, 107–110

Convention Center (New Orleans), 2, 11, 14, 124, 149, 173

criminal justice system, 55

Dallas, TX: characteristics of, *6–7, 8–9*. *See also* receiving communities; Texas

Davidson, Barbara, 228n4

Davis, Reginald F., 222

death count, 1

Delgado Community College, 146, 152

Denver, CO: changing context of reception in, 27, 32–34; characteristics of, 5, *6–7, 8–9*, 31; compared to New Orleans, 31; and displaced persons' choice, 26; and Katrina fatigue, 27, 33–35; numbers relocated to, 31. *See also* Colorado; receiving communities

DHAP (Disaster Housing Assistance Program), *65*, 65–66, 234

diaspora, locations of, 2, *3*

disaster: and assumptions about return to stability, 116; and children, 136, 139; literature, 110, 150; planning, 17, 20n17, 29, 117, 231; vulnerability to, 150, 231. *See also* children, displaced

Disaster Housing Assistance Program. *See* DHAP

Disaster Voucher Program. *See* DVP

discrimination: African American, 15, 16–17, 17, 20n27, 40, 64; against displaced persons, 32, 35–39, 40, 41–44, 45, 71; in employment, 39–41, 45; experienced by displaced children, 41–44, 126–127, 128, 139; experienced by Garifuna community, 211–212; in housing, 37–39, 45; obscured after

Katrina, 44–45; overt in Louisiana, 40; in schools, 41–44, 45; and survival, 124. *See also* harassment; racism; stereotypes

displaced persons: and destitution-level poverty, 47; locations of, 2, *3*; multiple relocations, 4, 13–14, 154–156; number of, 1, 2; permanent temporariness of, 131, 134; returning to New Orleans, 16–17, 134–138; terms for, 2. *See also* children, displaced; resettlement; women, displaced

DVP (Disaster Voucher Program), 66

Dynes, Russell R., 110

economic losses, 1

employment: and the criminal justice system, 59–60; and discrimination against displaced persons, 39–41; and documentation, 13, 26, 58, 68; problems faced by displaced in Austin, TX, 51, 58–60; and public transportation, 51, 93; and refugee status, 39–40, 58–59; and single mothers, 60

environmental migrants. *See* displaced persons

Erikson, Kai, 22, 45, 140, 150, 164, 177, 197, 254

evacuation, 1; experiences of children, 123–125, 128–129; and faith, 221–222; forced, 2, 10–11, 18n5, 25, 32, 172–173, 183; and networks of care, 171–177, 180, 182n6; planning for future, 180; prior to Katrina striking, and subsequent choices, 11, 157–158; resources of, and control over, 125, 128, 158–159; and separation of family members, 10–11, 29, 132, 158–159; and social networks, 150–152, 154–158, 185, 196; social ties ignored in government decisions and policies, 172–173

evacuees. *See* displaced persons

Everything in Its Path (Erikson), 177

exiles. *See* displaced persons

faith, 221–222, 223, 228

Family Independence Program. *See* FIP

Federal Emergency Management Agency. *See* FEMA

FEMA (Federal Emergency Management Agency), 65; and Columbia, SC displaced, 83; difficulties with, 242; and housing assistance eligibility, 89; and housing discrimination, 71; locations of applications for aid, *3*; mentioned, 31, 90, 151, 155, 160, 237; protests against, 241; trailer parks, 131, 133, 134, 147; typical benefit package, 68; vouchers rescinded by, 69, 74; Welcome Home Center, 122, 142n20. *See also* DHAP; IHP; Park, The

feminist scholars, 23, 250, 251, 252

FIP (Family Independence Program), 93

Florida, 18n5

Ford Foundation, 254

formal networks, 10, 146, 148–150, 181

Fothergill, Alice, 5, 22, 26, 29, 257

FRC. *See* Louisiana Family Recovery Corps

Freeman, Nancy, 228n4

Fritz, C. E., 112

Funmilayo, Nefesh, 248–249, 252

Fussell, Elizabeth, 5, 22, 146, 165, 257

Garifuna community: challenges to gender order, 148; community of, created in Houston, 210–211, 216; in evacuation process, 145–146, 204, 211–212; history of, 199–200, 216n2; living in liminal spaces, 212, 215, 216; migration and adaptation, prior to Katrina, 198–199, 201–205, 215; networks unique to, 205; New Orleans viewed by, 209–210; numbers of, in New Orleans, 200; obstacles experienced by, post-Katrina, 206–210, 214–215, 216; in pre-Katrina New Orleans, 198, 205; research on, 198–199, 200–201, 217n7

Garifunas Holding Ground, 217n9

Garza, Cynthia, 22, 146, 148, 257; research site of, *4*

gender, 79; and analysis of PHRF leadership and strategy, 249; and formal networks, 148; and risk-aversion, 217n10;

significance of, in disasters, 180; and social movement participation, 231, 251; and social service, 252

Global Women's Strike, 236

Gonzalez, Nancie, 200

Griffin, Shana, 236

Habitat for Humanity, 89, 133

HANO (Housing Authority of New Orleans), 63; and the demolition of public housing, 64, 76, 77, 135

harassment, 36–37, 43. *See also* discrimination; racism; stereotypes

Hispanics. *See* Latinos

homophily, 146, 150

HOPE VI, 64, *65*, 77, 77–78n7; mentioned, 66, 67

housing: barriers created by assistance programs, 73–77; children's experiences, 133–34; demolition of public, 64, 77, 87, 135; destroyed by Katrina, 63; disaster-related programs, *65*, 65–66, 70; and disaster response professionals, 38–39; discrimination in, 17, 37–39, 70–72; and documentation, 56, 57; and evictions and displacement in post-Katrina New Orleans, 63, 76; and failure to adjust voucher values, 75–76; federal program, *65*, 66; and FEMA's typical benefit package, 68; and multiple displacements, 69; and private rental actors, 69–73; problems faced by displaced in Austin, TX, 56–58; problems for displaced African American women, 27; and the removal of vouchers, 73, 74; and rent increases, 63, 69, 73, 75; research on low-income women in, 66–68; and returning to New Orleans, 28, 70; and Section 8, 57; shortage of, in New Orleans, 119; shortage of, in receiving communities, 26, 87–90, 99–100; trends in policy, 77. *See also* DHAP; HOPE VI; IHP; KDHAP; Section 8

Houston, TX, *3*, 215; characteristics of, *6–7*, 8–9. *See also* receiving communities

Howard Hughes Medical Institute, 197

HUD (Department of Housing and Urban Development), *65*, 73–75, 76, 241; mentioned, 89, 234, 236

Human Rights Network, 241

Huntsville, TX, 5; characteristics of, *6–7*, 8–9, 107, 111; compared to New Orleans, 108; context of reception, 107–110; differences between volunteers and displaced persons in, 108–109, 114, 117; displaced persons viewed in, 111–112, 114–115; established immigrants in, 108; evacuees to, 104–105, 109; perceptions of emergency response managers, 105–106, 114–116; and public transportation, 108; readiness to receive displaced persons, 109–110; reception of displaced persons in, 104, 105–106, 112–116; village mentality of, 109–110. *See also* receiving communities; Texas

Hurricane Betsy, 204

Hurricane Camille, 204

Hurricane Ivan, 203, 205

Hurricane Katrina, 1; as microcosm, 240, 251–252; as ongoing disaster, 100; as political opportunity, 233, 237, 242; race, class, and gender inequalities revealed by, 11–12, 164; racial framing of, 127–128

"Hurricane Katrina: The Black Nation's 9/11!" (Muhammad), 237

Hurricane Mitch, 199, 202, 204, 207, 212, 217n9

Hurricane Rita, 183, 214, 222

IHP (Individuals and Households Program), 64, *65*, 65, 70, 74

INCITE! Women of Color Against Violence, 236

Individuals and Households Program. *See* IHP

informal assistance, non-network, 158–161, 166n11

informal networks, 10, 146–148, 150–151. *See also* networks of care; social networks

Interim Coordinating Committee (ICC), 236

Jackson, MS, 5, *6–7*, 8–9. *See also* receiving communities
Jenkins, Pamela, 22, 148, 257–258; research site of, *4*

Katrina. *See* Hurricane Katrina
Katrina Disaster Housing Assistance Program. *See* KDHAP
Katrina fatigue, 27, 32, 33, 34–35, 44–45; defined, 32, 33, 44–45
Katrina Research Network, 21–24, 24n1
"Katrina's Latinos" (Trujillo-Pagán), 212
KDHAP (Katrina Disaster Housing Assistance Program): assistance offered by, 64, *65*, 65, 66; incorrect implementation of, 73, 74; and landlord discrimination, 71; property inspection requirement, 72
Khan, Mafruza, 20n27

Lafayette, LA, 5, *6–7*, 8–9. *See also* receiving communities
Latinos: in Columbia and West Columbia, SC, 28, 81, 96, 98; discrimination against, post-Katrina, 212–214; invisibility of, in New Orleans, 200, 212, 216; portrayed by the media, post-Katrina, 215
Lein, Laura, 22, 27, 258; research site of, *5*
levees, 1, 2, 130
Liebenthal, Mayaba, 236
Litt, Jacquelyn, *5*, 22, 23–24, 146–147, 258
looting, 15, 124
Louisiana, 18n5, 79, 119, 120, *120*
Louisiana Family Recovery Corps (FRC), 183, 189
Louisiana Technical College-West Bank (LTC), 146, 152
LTC. *See* Louisiana Technical College-West Bank
Luft, Rachel E., 21–22, 231, 259; research site of, *5*

Lumumba, Chokwe, 234, 236, 238, 253
Lutheran Family Services, 33, 97

MacArthur Foundation, 164
macro economic policies, defined, 28
Malcolm X Grassroots Movement, 236
Manpower Demonstration Research Corporation, 152
martial law, 18n5
Martin, Gina, 249–251; gendered analysis of PHRF given by, 249; mentioned, 234, 236, 244, 252, 253; needs of, met through political activism, 250–251; and political activism and social service, 241, 246, 247–248
Martinas, Sharon, 254
Mason, Beverly J., 22, 146, 147, 259; research, 4; research site of, *5*
McRae, Mary B., 224
media: in Denver, CO, 34; discrimination against survivors by, 124; and images of chaos and desperation, 149, 167; informal assistance among survivors ignored by, 181; and Katrina fatigue, 33, 44; and the Park, 189; portrayal of New Orleans Latinos and African Americans, 15, 215; rhetoric about evacuees recovering, 55; and West Columbia's opposition to Somali Bantu resettlement, 97
mental health, 13, 37, 45, 55, 61
Miller, Lee M., 22, 27, 28–29, 259; research site of, *5*
Mississippi, 18n5, 79, 119, 120, *120*
Motes, Patricia Stone, 228
Muhammad, Curtis, 236
Muhammad, Saladin, 237, 238

Nagin, Ray, 130
National Association of Home Builders, 88
National Basketball Association, 190
National Football League, 190
National Guard, 18n5
National Science Foundation (NSF), 48, 62n8
needs, basic. *See* basic needs

networks of care: and dispersal after evacuation, 177–180; and emergency situations, 175; and evacuation, 171–177, 180, 182n6; and identity, 167, 169, 184; ignored by formal networks, 181; and necessity, 169–170; prior to Katrina, 167, 169–170, 175, 182n7; and race and class, 180–181; and reciprocity, 167, 175; and success of recovery, 167

New Orleans, 1; characteristics of, 6–7, 81, 82, 108; compared to receiving communities, 5, 6–7, 8–9, 25; congregations in, 219; as a disaster prior to Katrina, 196; increase in crime in, 136; population change data, 16, 81, 82; poverty in, 151; racial and ethnic composition, 4, 5, 6–7, 16, 20n21, 20n27, 31, 51, 108; racial division and community destruction in, post-Katrina, 198; reasons people remained in, 2, 16; rebuilding, 17; returning to, 28, 119, 134–138; social networks in, 151, 167, 169–170; unique culture and traditions of, 26, 27

NSF. See National Science Foundation

Obama, Barack, 87
Opening Doors Demonstration Study, 152
Operation Safe Haven, 33–34
Oyo, Miss., 248, 249, 252

Pardee, Jessica W., 4, 22, 27–28, 259–260; research site of, 5
Park, The: conditions in, 187, 188–189, 190, 196, 197n3; and the decision to return to New Orleans, 195; depression and stress experienced by residents of, 191–193; donations to, 190; FEMA policies in, 190–191; occupations of residents of, 184, 191; reinvention of residents of, 194–195, 196; research on women in, 183–184, 197n1
Paxson, Christina A., 152
Peek, Lori, 4, 22, 26, 27, 29, 117, 197, 254, 254n8, 260; research site of, 5
People's Hurricane Relief Fund, 10, 233;

constituency of, 234; formation of, 236; motivation for evacuees to participate in, 243–245; political principles, 236–238, 240, 242, 251; Reconstruction Work Groups, 237; research on, 231, 234–235; senior leadership, 236; social service viewed by, 238–240, 247, 249, 251, 252, 253; Survivor Councils, 237, 240, 243–244, 245–246, 248

People's Organizing Committee, 236
permanent temporariness, 121, 131–134, 138, 139–140; defined, 121, 138–140
pets, 125
PHRF. See People's Hurricane Relief Fund
physical health, 13, 37
Portes, Alejandro, 107, 108
poverty basement. See basement of poverty
poverty programs, 47–48, 49
prayer, 222
Prescod, Margaret, 236
public assistance. See social services
public transportation: and disabilities, 91, 92–93, 94–95; and employment, 51, 93; and future disaster planning, 29; lack of, in receiving communities, 12, 26; and Section 8 housing, 57; in South Carolina, 87; in West Columbia, SC, 90–93

Quarantelli, Enrico L., 110

race, 79, 198; and activism, 231; and post-disaster planning, 17, 20n27; and research, 23–24
racism, 32, 36–37; children's encounters with, 41–44, 126; in Colorado, 40, 41–44; covert, 40; more overt in Louisiana, 40; in public settings, 36–37; in schools, 41–44. See also discrimination; harassment; stereotypes
receiving communities, 2, 15, 25–26, 27–30; character of, and reception of the displaced, 27, 28, 105; and local economic factors, 109; and migrants prior to Katrina's displaced, 95–96; and pre-disaster social organization,

110, 118n16; and the therapeutic community, 112

refugees. *See* displaced persons

Renaissance Village. *See* Park, The

repetitive displacement, defined, 28

Republic of New Africa, 241

research, 2; on African American women in the Park, 183–184, 197n1; in Colorado, 32; in Columbia and West Columbia, SC, 84–86, 101–102n11, 101n10, 168, 182n5; on displaced children, 32, 121–122, 141n16, 141–142n17, 142nn18–21; on the Garifuna community, 198–199, 200–201, 217n7; on Huntsville, TX response to displaced persons, 105, 106–107; jobs held by subjects of, 149n1, 184; locations of interviewees, 3, 4; locations of network members, 4; on low-income women in housing programs, 66–68; on low-income women's social networks, 152–154; methods, 3, 4, 23; network, 21–24, 24n1; on Orleans Parish congregants in Baton Rouge, 220, 228n4, 229n7; on the PHRF, 234–235; on satellite congregations, 220, 228n4; socioeconomic status of interviewees, 4–5

resettlement, 12, *12*, 26, 34

Rhodes, Jean, 152

Rockefeller Foundation, 254

Rosey's Kids, 190

Rouse, Cecilia, 152

Rumbaut, Ruben G., 107, 108

Russians, 28, 96

"Saddest Days, The," 200

Safe Return, 248

Sams-Abiodun, Petrice, 152, 165

Sanford, Mark, 87

schools, 41–44, 60, 126, 128, 131–133; bullying in, 41–42, 43, 44, 126–128, 138; in New Orleans, 135–136

Section 8: assistance offered by, *65*, 65, 66; and Columbia, SC displaced, 83; and landlord discrimination, 70; mentioned, 64, 74, 89; property inspection requirement, 72; and voucher values, 75, 88

shelters, 13, 118, 125, 131, 138; observations in, 121, 122; workers in, 141n16

social movements, 231, 233, 251, 253

social networks, 26; and assistance from strangers, 158–161, 166n11; capacities of, 150, 151, 154–158; developing new, 193–194; and emotional support, 151, 161; and evacuation, 52, 157, 163–164, 185, 196; and family and friends, 154–158; and gender, 148; and a home church, 148–149; and homophily, 146, 150; and identity, 184; importance of familial, 185–186; and initial warnings of Katrina, 154; limits of, 146, 147–148, 150, 154–158, 157–158; in New Orleans, 151, 167, 169–170, 184; and the norms of reciprocity, 147; and outside networks, 151; and poverty, 48, 61, 151; prior to Katrina, 175, 182n7; and recovery, 167, 182nn7–8; remaking, 145; strategy of, 146; and systems of inequality, 145; weaknesses of, revealed by Katrina, 15–16, 154–158, 161–164; and women, 15–16, 147. *See also* formal networks; informal networks; networks of care

Social Science Research Council (SSRC): Research Network on Persons Displaced by Hurricane Katrina, 24n1, 45, 254; Task Force on Katrina, 22

social services: and attitudes of personnel in, 95; for displaced women, 27; and future disaster planning, 30; and obstacles obtaining, 12–13; privatized in Texas, 52; and rhetoric about recovery, 55; in South Carolina, 93–94, 99; strained by local demand, 25, 26; and traumatic dislocation, 61. *See also* poverty programs

Sojourners of the Caribbean (Gonzalez), 200

Somali refugees, 28, 97

Soros Foundation, 190

South Carolina: compared to New Orleans, 93–95; economic and social policies in, 80, 93, 98, 100; multinational, multicultural complex competing for resources in, 98; poverty and quality-of-life indicators in, 80; public assistance in, 93–94, 98, 99; public transportation in, 87; resentment of displaced persons in, 94; unemployment in, 86–87

South Carolina Cares, 83–84, 100, 101–102n11

South Carolina Emergency Management, 88

Southern political economy, 79–80, 98

Standard and United Fruit Companies, 198, 200

stereotypes, 15, 36, 37, 38–39, 43, 45. *See also* discrimination; harassment; racism

stimulus bill, 87

Suber, Malcolm, 234, 236, 253

Superdome, 2, 11, 104, 123, 124; conditions in, 124; and government assistance, 173; media depictions of, 149

survivors. *See* displaced persons

Taylor, Wilma, 234, 236, 252, 254; gendered analysis of PHRF given by, 249; and political activism, 241, 246–247; and social service, 247

Texas, 52, 108

Thompson, Delores A., 224

transportation, public. *See* public transportation

trauma, 161–164; collective, 163–164

Truehill, Reverend Marshall, 228, 228n4

Trujillo-Pagán, Nicole, 212

Unified New Orleans Plan (UNOP), 20n27

United Nations: Guiding Principles on Internal Displacement, 237; Human Rights Committee, 64

United States: characteristics of, 81, *82*; population change data, 81, *82*

UNOP. *See* Unified New Orleans Plan

Urban League of Houston, 200, 211

victims. *See* displaced persons

volunteers, 15, 32–34, 131, 141n16; burnout among, 33, 44

Volunteers of America (Denver), 33

Waters, Mary C., 152, 165

Weber, Lynn, 22, 25, 28, 254, 260; research site of, *5*

West Columbia, SC: characteristics of, 80–81, *82*; compared to New Orleans, 86, 87; displaced persons in, 83–84, 96, 97–100; housing crisis in, 87–90, 98; migrants to, prior to Katrina, 96–98; and the needs of the local poor, 98–99; political climate in, 86–87; population change data, 81, *82*, 83, 101n7; public transportation in, 90–93, 98; transition in racial and ethnic composition, 95. *See also* South Carolina

women, African American: economic and social vulnerability of, 150–151, 181n2, 181–182n3; New Orleans as a disaster for, prior to Katrina, 196; and resource exchange, 181–182n3

women, displaced, 145, 149n1; and affordable housing, 27; African American, 27, 167, 172, 180; jobs held by research subjects, 149n1; low income, 63, 66–68, 68–69, 151; resourcefulness of, 2; and social networks, 15–16; and social services, 27

Women of Katrina (Litt), 182n5

women's movement, 251

Wylie, TX, 159–160

Zapatistas, 252